SHAKESPEARE'S FEMININE ENDINGS

In this elegant and provocative book, Philippa Berry rewrites critical perceptions of death in Shakespeare's tragedies from a feminist perspective.

Drawing on feminist theory, postmodern thought and queer theory, Berry shows how, through a network of images clustered around female or feminized characters, these plays 'disfigure' death as a bodily end.

Through her close reading of the main tragedies, Berry discovers a sensuous and meditative Shakespearean discourse of materialism. The scope of these tragic speculations was radical in Shakespeare's day, yet they also have a surprising relevance to current debates about gender and sexuality, as well as to contemporary discussions of time and matter.

Philippa Berry is Fellow and Director of Studies in English at King's College, Cambridge.

D0162412

FEMINIST READINGS OF SHAKESPEARE

Literary studies have been transformed in the last 20 years by a number of new approaches which have challenged traditional assumptions and traditional ways of reading. Critics of Shakespeare and English Renaissance literature have been at the forefront of these developments, and feminist criticism has proved to be one of the most important areas of productivity and change.

'Feminist Readings of Shakespeare' is a series of five generically based books by leading feminist critics from Britain, continental Europe and North America. Each book outlines and engages with the current positions and debates within the field of feminist criticism and in addition provides an original feminist reading of the texts in question. While the authors share a commitment to feminist values, the books are not uniform in their approach but rather exemplify the richness and diversity of feminist criticism today.

ENGENDERING A NATION: A FEMINIST ACCOUNT OF SHAKESPEARE'S ENGLISH HISTORIES
Jean E. Howard and Phyllis Rackin

ROMAN SHAKESPEARE: WARRIORS, WOUNDS, AND WOMEN
Coppélia Kahn

SHAKESPEARE'S FEMININE ENDINGS: DISFIGURING DEATH IN THE TRAGEDIES
Philippa Berry

SHAKESPEARE'S FEMININE ENDINGS

Disfiguring death in the tragedies

Philippa Berry

London and New York

First published 1999
by Routledge
11 New Fetter Lane, London EC4P 4EE

Simultaneously published in the USA and Canada
by Routledge
29 West 35th Street, New York, NY 10001

Routledge is an imprint of the Taylor & Francis Group

Typeset in Baskerville by Keystroke, Jacaranda Lodge, Wolverhampton
Printed and bound in Great Britain by TJ International Ltd., Padstow, Cornwall

British Library Cataloguing in Publication Data
A catalogue record for this book is available from the British Library

Library of Congress Cataloging in Publication Data
Berry, Philippa, 1955–
Shakespeare's feminine endings: disfiguring death in the tragedies /
Philippa Berry.
p.   cm. — (Feminist readings of Shakespeare)
Includes bibliographical references and index.
1. Shakespeare, William, 1564–1616—Tragedies. 2. Feminism and
literature—England—History—16th century. 3. Feminism and
literature—England—History—17th century. 4. Women and
literature—England—History—16th century. 5. Women and
literature—England—History—17th century. 6. Shakespeare,
William, 1564–1616—Characters—Women. 7. Sex role in literature.
8. Death in literature. 9. Closure (Rhetoric) I. Title.
II. Series.
PR2983.B47 1999
822.3′3—dc21   99–19812
CIP
ISBN 0–415–06894–0 (hbk)
ISBN 0–415–06895–9 (pbk)

IN MEMORY OF PEGGY ANN HOWARD
1945–1994

I cannot thinke *Nature* is so spent, and decay'd, that she can bring forth nothing worth her former yeares. She is alwaies the same, like her selfe. And when she collects her strength, is abler still. Men are decay'd, and *studies*: Shee is not.

(Ben Jonson, *Timber*)

CONTENTS

PLATES

SERIES EDITOR'S PREFACE

As I write this towards the end of 1996, feminist criticism of Shakespeare has just come of age. While we will no doubt continue to rediscover and celebrate notable pre-feminist and proto-feminist precursors, it is usually acknowledged that the genre as we know it began 'officially' just 21 years ago with Juliet Dusinberre's *Shakespeare and the Nature of Women* (London: Macmillan, 1975), a book taken as the obvious starting-point by Philip C. Kolin in his *Shakespeare and Feminist Criticism: An Annotated Bibliography and Commentary* (New York and London: Garland, 1991) which lists 439 items from 1975 to its cut-off date in 1988. A glance at any publisher's catalogue will reveal that the rate of publication has certainly not slowed down during the eight years since then; it is clear in fact that feminist criticism continues to be one of the most lively, productive and influential of the current approaches to Shakespeare.

Shakespeare and the Nature of Women has just been reissued (London: Macmillan, 1996) with a substantial new Preface by Dusinberre entitled 'Beyond the Battle?'. The interrogative mode seems appropriate both in relation to the state of feminist scholarship itself – *is* the battle lost or won? – and to the extent to which the whole enterprise has been about asking questions: asking *different* questions about the Shakespearean texts themselves and using those texts to interrogate 'women's place in culture, history, religion, society, the family'. It seems to me that these questions are now inescapably on the agenda of academic enquiry, and that they have moved from the margin to the centre. The growth and variety of feminist approaches in Shakespeare studies has been complemented and supported by work in feminist theory, women's history, the study of women's relationship to language and the study of women's writing. A summary of the achievements of feminist criticism of Shakespeare in its first 21 years would for me include the following:

1 Since *Shakespeare and the Nature of Women* looked at Shakespeare's works in the context of the history of contemporary ideas about women, drawing on non-literary texts to do so, feminist studies have contributed to the now widely accepted view that works of art can and should be treated within a social frame of reference.

2 While sharing some features of their work with new historicist critics, feminist critics have also provided a critique of new historicism, notably by objecting to its neglect of gender issues and its concentration on male power relationships, and by resisting the conservative idea that subversion is a calculated form of license, always in the end contained.

3 Feminist critics have changed what scholars and students read: there are many more texts by women of the Renaissance period available now, and more studies of women as writers, readers, performers, patrons and audiences. Publishers are responding to the demands of feminist critics and their students for more and different texts from those traditionally taught.

4 Feminist critics have changed how we read: women readers no longer have to pretend to be men. Reading is seen as a complex interaction between the writer, the text and the reader in which the gender of the reader is not necessarily irrelevant.

5 The performance tradition has been affected, with feminist approaches making new stage and screen interpretations possible. Supportive relationships exist between feminist scholars, directors and performers, and a female-centred study of Shakespeare in performance is burgeoning.

6 Our perceptions of dramatic texts have been changed by work on women's access to language and women's use of language. We are opening up the discussion of the gendering of rhetoric, public and private voices, the stereotypes of the 'bad' vocal shrew and the 'good' silent woman.

I believe of course that the five books in this series will help to consolidate these achievements and further the aims of feminist criticism of Shakespeare in a number of ways. The books are generically-based studies by authors who would define themselves as feminist critics but who would not see this as an exclusive or narrow label, preventing them from being, at the same time, traditional scholars, psychoanalytic critics, textual critics, new historicist critics, materialist critics and so forth.

When I first proposed the series in 1990 I wanted to commission books which would on the one hand outline the current positions and debates within the field and on the other hand advance original feminist readings of the texts in question. I wanted the books to demonstrate the full range of possibilities offered by feminist criticism and to challenge the standard over-simplifications voiced by hostile critics, namely that feminist criticism is limited to the study of female characters and that it is driven by a desire to co-opt Shakespeare on behalf of the feminist movement.

Certainly the authors of the books in this series are not uninterested in female characters, but they are also interested in male characters. The first two books to appear are on the History plays and the Roman Tragedies – not on the whole noted for their wealth of substantial female roles. The authors are not asking 'Is this woman a good or bad role-model for women today?' as nineteenth-century writers did, or 'Is Shakespeare capable of creating strong females?' as some early feminist critics did, but 'How has theatrical and critical tradition re-presented and re-read these texts in relation to the issue of gender difference?' They accept that systems of gender differentiation are historically specific and they seek to relate the practices of Shakespeare's theatre to their contemporary context as well as to the range of literary and historical materials from which the narratives are derived. They feel no obligation to claim that Shakespeare was a feminist, or to berate him for not being one, but they are interested in exploring ways in which his work can at times seem feminist – or can be appropriated for feminist purposes – while still being totally consistent with Renaissance conceptions of patriarchy.

The study of Shakespeare in the late 1990s is a vigorous and exciting field to which feminism is making a major contribution. In just 21 years it has become quite difficult for anyone to perform, read, teach or study Shakespeare without an awareness of gender issues and I am confident that this will prove to be a permanent and positive change in our attitude to the plays and their extraordinarily rich afterlife in international culture.

Ann Thompson

ACKNOWLEDGEMENTS

This book has had a long gestation period, and I am very sensible of the tactful restraint as well as kindness shown to me both by the series editor, Ann Thompson, and by my Routledge editor, Talia Rodgers, during the protracted process of composition. The unpalatable discovery, after a period of illness, that I would have to pace my speed of literary production gave me a vivid insight into a Renaissance commonplace which now seems of especial relevance to our hyperactive age: that intellectual digestion is a sometimes mysterious procedure, and one which does not always follow our preferred timetable. This required change of tempo also impressed upon me, in a most timely fashion, that the complexities of the Shakespearean corpus are not easily deciphered in a hurry – at least not by me!

In the course of writing, I have been assisted and encouraged by many friends and colleagues, all of whom have helped in specific as well as subtle ways to give the book its final shape. Dympna Callaghan and Margaret Tudeau-Clayton have read most of the chapters, and have given me both detailed and general advice as well as their consistent, very energetic support and friendship – gifts which no amount of thanks can adequately repay. Jayne Archer has been another generous friend both to myself and the project, who not only provided me with much practical assistance by researching numerous obscure points, but also, as the book neared completion, dialogued with me inspiringly and most productively on the feminist critical issues raised in Chapter 1. Ann Lecercle, Patricia Parker, François Laroque, Susie Hamilton, John Kerrigan, Ian Donaldson, J. Leeds Barroll, Juliet Fleming, Willy Maley, Richard Wilson and Marie-Dominique Garnier all took the time to read individual chapters, offering me numerous critical insights which have enriched my argument. And the final manuscript has benefited significantly from the incisive comments of Ann Thompson. But many details of this book's argument also developed through dialogue with several generations of students at King's College and the University of Cambridge, in the context of courses on Western tragedy and Shakespeare; my thanks to Tansy Troy, Bibi Jacob, Susanna Parry, Leo Mellor, Patrick Sheil and David Jay, in particular, for some wonderful conversations.

I am grateful to the Provost and Fellows of King's College Cambridge for generously providing me with two periods of leave in which to research and write *Shakespeare's Feminine Endings*. For help with photographs, my thanks to Anthony Wells-Cole of Temple Newsam House, Leeds; to Elizabeth McGrath and Paul Taylor, of the Warburg Institute, London; and to Alessandra Corti, of Fratelli Alinari, Florence. I am also grateful to the staff of the following libraries for their friendly and prompt assistance: King's College Library; Cambridge University Library; the English Faculty Library, University of Cambridge; the British Library; the library of the Shakespeare Institute, University of Birmingham, at Stratford-upon-Avon.

Outside the academic sphere, I have been sustained and re-energized by Barbara Harding's vigorous tuition in astanga yoga, by the herbal tinctures of Peter Jackson Main, and by the practical wit and inspired wisdom of Jean Churchman, Ann Walton, and Rhea Quien. My mother, Celia Berry, has been a constant source of encouragement and strength, as well as a superb example of ageless vitality. And above all, Frank Payne has given me endless emotional and psychological nourishment – besides acting as an uncomplaining trouble-shooter in numerous cases of computer crisis!

But several of those close to me died during the period in which I was pondering Shakespeare's creative disfigurement of dying. The death of my father, Tom Berry, had first prompted me to begin research into representations of death and mourning in Renaissance literature: a project that later metamorphosed into a book on Shakespearean tragedy. His death was followed, a few years later, by those of my aunt Monica Pateman, my uncle David Berry, and my godmother Irene Cooper. In different ways, this book has been touched by each of them. It is dedicated, however, to a dear friend whose warmth and ever profound insights are sorely missed, since it was she who warned me, with unnerving prescience, that this book might take rather longer to complete than I expected.

A section of Chapter 3, 'Hamlet's Ear', was presented at the International Shakespeare Conference at Stratford-upon-Avon in August 1996, and subsequently at the TIMEE seminar in Renaissance Studies held at the Ecole Normale Supériéure, Paris, in June 1997. This essay was published in *Shakespeare Survey*, 50 (1997) and is reproduced, in revised form, courtesy of Cambridge University Press. An early version of Chapter 5 was published in the *European Journal of English Studies*, 1(3) (1997), as 'Reversing History: time, fortune and the doubling of sovereignty in *Macbeth*', and is reproduced, also revised, courtesy of Swets and Zeitlinger Publishers.

A note on citations of Shakespearean texts

All citations from the plays of Shakespeare are from the most recent Arden editions of these works; thus citations from *Antony and Cleopatra, Henry 5, Julius Caesar, King Lear, Othello*, and *Titus Andronicus* are taken from the new editions published as part of Arden 3. Citations from *The Sonnets* use the edition by Stephen Booth (New Haven: University of Yale Press, 1977).

1

DISFIGURED ENDINGS: SEXUAL MATTERS AND SHAKESPEARE'S *ARS MORIENDI*

What is then woven does not play the game of tight succession. Rather, it plays on succession. Do not forget that to weave (*tramer, trameare*) is first to make holes, to traverse, to work one-side-and-the-other of the warp.

(Derrida, *Margins of Philosophy*)[1]

[Y]ou'll be rotten ere you be half ripe, and that's the right virtue of the medlar.

(*As You Like It*, 3.2.117–18)

In one of Shakespeare's most evocative anticipations of tragedy in and through a female character, Richard II's queen laments her husband's recent departure for Ireland. And she tells one of Richard's favourites, Bushy, that she has a vivid premonition of disaster:

> I know no cause
> Why I should welcome such a guest as grief,
> Save bidding farewell to so sweet a guest
> As my sweet Richard. Yet again methinks
> Some unborn sorrow ripe in Fortune's womb
> Is coming towards me, and my inward soul
> With nothing trembles; at some thing it grieves,
> More than with parting from my lord the king.
> (2.2.10–13)

The queen's words – from a play described on the title page of its first Quarto as a tragedy – provide us with a proleptic insight into the topic which this book addresses: the ambiguous function, not simply of women, but of feminized figures of speech in a Shakespearean interrogation of the meanings of tragedy. For the tropes of her speech create a strikingly contradictory representation of the queen's state of grief. The inexplicable amplification of her emotion is evidently allied to the impending tragedy; at the same time, however, conventional notions of tragic suffering are unsettled by the troping of grief's arrival in terms not just of hospitality but of a quasi-sexual penetration and a highly physical 'ripening'.

The future sorrow which Richard's queen uncannily anticipates is a state she imagines receiving as 'a guest' that is both like and unlike the 'sweet' or sexually intimate guest who is her departed husband. Indeed, this other 'guest', who uncannily arrives just as Richard departs, is figured as a mysterious addition to her present grief, since 'at some thing it grieves / *More* than with parting from my lord the king' (my emphasis). What the queen so fearfully anticipates, it seems, is some future experience of nullification or 'nothing' – the image ultimately invoked by Richard himself to trope his tragic fate – that will paradoxically involve both a coming to fruition and a very different 'parting': a birth from 'Fortune's womb'. This half-buried layer of sexual imagery performs a suggestive doubling of ends, as anticipation of the climactic closure of Richard's tragedy – with his death – becomes peculiarly conflated with an oxymoronic as well as interlingual conception of grief: as the bearing of a burden (in French, *grevé*) which compels the opening or 'parting' (and here a cognate French word is *crevé*) of a 'ripe' bodily end.[2]

This book argues that Shakespearean tragedy performs a comparable, albeit infinitely more extensive interrogation of tragic sensibility, as countless puns and other tropes that emphasize the open bodily 'ends' of women (and sometimes, those of men) enunciate a subtle differing – a *disfiguring* – both of tragic discourse and of concepts of death as bodily extinction. The Shakespearean 'shapes of grief' that are refracted through a feminine figural lens have an intricate cultural specificity. Moreover, they remind us of some of the complexity, indeed the inherent strangeness, of Renaissance thought, as quasi-philosophical as well as political speculations are perplexingly interwoven, not only with mythic or emblematic motifs, but also with a partially abjected vein of grossly material imagery, drawn from popular culture. Commenting on the often remarkable difficulty of Shakespeare's tropes, Ann and John O. Thompson point out that this Shakespearean drive towards figurative difficulty is inseparable from 'a sense of the groundedness of these elaborations in . . . everyday metaphor'.[3] My contention here is that, if we examine these textual nodes from a critical perspective that aims to reassess the complex materiality of the Shakespearean text, we can hopefully decipher what might be described, *pace* Bakhtin, as an impacted lower stratum of this textual archaeology, and begin to examine its complex relationship to other strata of tragic signification.[4] For while this multilayered, 'earthy', and primitive sediment of meaning unsettles some of the seeming *gravitas* of tragedy, it has an obscure, philosophical and political 'weight' of its own, as it challenges dominant cultural notions of what is 'fundamental' and 'final' both to tragedy and to human identity.

A major study of the 'issues of death' in English Renaissance tragedy, by Michael Neill, has recently restated some of the key assumptions which typically inform critical responses to tragedy, by describing tragedy as 'a profoundly teleological form whose full meaning will be uncovered in *the revelation of its end*' (my emphasis).[5] Neill's book is richly innovative in many respects, and he is certainly right in his observation that the formal structure, or the narrative design, of tragedy is 'fiercely end-driven' in its movement towards a seemingly unambiguous *telos*, or end, in and through which a heroic masculine identity will paradoxically be confirmed. But in a deliberate departure from this teleological and structural perspective, my reading of the tragedies uses a heightened attention to textual detail in order to question the presumed finality and fixity of these cultural versions of ending, along with the diachronic, linear versions of both identity and temporality that appear to inform them. The centrality to the Shakespearean literary corpus of what Patricia Parker describes as 'preposterous' or 'arsy-versy' figures and tropes that question the aesthetic, as well as political and sexual, drive to containment and the certainty of endings has been brilliantly demonstrated in her book, *Shakespeare from the Margins*.[6] This seminal re-evaluation of Shakespeare's wordplay signals a new climate in Shakespeare studies, in which critics can at last begin to interrogate in detail these previously neglected aspects of the most 'canonical' of texts, and consequently, to elucidate the multifaceted, fluid model of sexuality which Shakespeare's puns delineate. In an attempt to draw out some of the wider philosophical implications of this complex figurative dimension within the tragedies, my book aims to show how a repetitive pattern of feminine or femininized tropes performs an allusive reweaving both of tragic teleology and of orthodox conceptions of death. Within this mobile textual process, as in the account of 'Fortune's womb' given by Richard's queen, endings are repeatedly unravelled, like those of Penelope's forever unfinished tapestry in the *Odyssey* (in fact, in a suggestive textual detail that is often overlooked, this famous textile was actually a shroud). And as the 'end' of tragedy is refigured not as a closure, but rather as an opening of meaning, Judaeo-Christian notions of history as a singular and successive movement towards 'a promised end' or *eschaton* are similarly undermined. Gesturing beyond death as a *fin* or end to a grossly sensuous as well as numinous version of the *infini* or unfinished, this Shakespearean (dis-)figuration of tragic endings, not as a limit or boundary, but rather as a resonant surfeit of signification, may plausibly be compared to the 'feminine endings' found in much Shakespearean blank verse.

Feminine endings

The feminine endings of verse (which I distinguish here from the rather different device of 'feminine rhyme') are metrical supplements to an iambic pentameter in the form of an eleventh syllable, usually unstressed, that assists the transference of poetic sense from one line to the next. In *Shakespeare's Metrical Art*, George T. Wright observes of this device:

> Whether the choice of *feminine* as a term to describe this ending was accidental or fitted contemporary notions of gender, iambic verse that regularly ends with an unstressed syllable takes on a quality which, in different lines, may variously be described as soft, haunting, yearning, pliant, seductive. In verse that is enjambed, it helps to threaten our sense of the line as a line, as pentameter; in endstopped verse, it subtly undermines the line's iambic (or masculine) character.[7]

In the queen's speech quoted on p. 1, two words extend beyond the structural limit conventionally imposed by the ten-syllable line of the iambic pentameter: 'soul' at the end of line 11, and the last syllable of 'grieves' at the end of line 12. Both words imply a surplus of meaning, and also of affect, that issues beyond the expected poetic limit. Indeed, the selection of these particular words for metrical marginality hints at the connection of the feminine ending's semiotic surplus both with the experience of grief *as a process* (in 'grieves'), and with what, for the late Renaissance, was the increasingly problematic status of that ghostly supplement to visible human identity: *soul*, that 'with nothing trembles'. The tragedies' figurative insinuation of an abjected and feminized supplement to versions of death as an end is marked by a similar emphasis on the uncanny mobility, even vitality, which informs tragic experience.

In an elaboration and interrogation of Freud's theory of the death drive, Julia Kristeva has commented on the ways in which 'the unrepresentable nature of death [i]s linked with that other unrepresentable – original abode but also last resting place for dead souls in the beyond

– which, for mythical thought, is constituted by the female body'.[8] In her work on abjection, Kristeva has shown how this liminal condition of the female body evokes a cultural response in which not only fascination and horror, but also motifs of sacredness and pollution, are peculiarly combined.[9] But what has been described as 'the figure that crosses femininity with death' can be interpreted in diverse ways. Elizabeth Bronfen's elegant study of that distinctively modern aestheticization of death which is accomplished, as she convincingly demonstrates, by constant repetition of this figure, concludes that 'over her dead body, cultural norms are reconfirmed or secured'.[10] My contention here, however, is that Shakespearean tragedy uses a similar figure precisely to unsettle cultural norms, since it tropes not only female characters, but also tragic protagonists whose masculinity is figuratively unsettled by their encounter with tragedy, not as stable signifiers of any singularity of either gender or meaning, but rather as sites of maximum undecidability or uncanniness. By redefining dying as a state that is open rather than closed, these tragedies both problematize and amplify orthodox religious knowledge of and around death, disrupting the orderliness of such established significations in a complex layering of figurative detail that is often emblematically embodied, near the end of the play, by a dead or dying woman.

Whether literally enacted or presented solely in tropical guise, Shakespeare's feminine dyings figure death repeatedly, not as an ending, but as a process: an *interitus* or passing between.[11] The motif is common to most religions; but – drawing on pagan currents of thought as well as the obscene imagery of popular culture – the tragedies reinflect it as a highly material, bodily process that is mysteriously productive. So the body of the living Juliet (who by her marriage is no longer a Capulet) proves to be an uncannily disruptive force in her own family vault, while the 'maimed rites' of Ophelia's corpse generate social and political disturbances on a comparable scale in the Elsinore graveyard. As they hover disturbingly upon the borders of death and life, Cordelia and Desdemona likewise have peculiarly equivocal 'ends'.

Gisèle Mathieu-Castellani has observed that Renaissance culture had a pervasive sense of the 'strange reversibility' of death and life, or *le jouir de mourir* – the pleasure in dying.[12] This interrelationship could be variously inflected, however. In the religious literature of the period, the motif of death-as-life typically produced the grotesque conception of men and women as walking cadavers: a perception that is echoed at key points in Shakespearean tragedy, and most notably by Hamlet. At first glance, the dead or dying women of the tragedies are represented as effecting what was culturally a quite familiar conjunction of sexuality or physical attraction with death (in the case of Cordelia, this imagery of desire is implicit rather than explicit, and focused in a single emblematic device, the mirror which is held to her dead lips – a familiar attribute of the medieval Venus luxuria). But whereas this well-worn trope was commonly used in the Middle Ages and the Renaissance to reinforce the traditional Christian equation of sin (here in the form of female sexuality) with death, the tragedies accord it a notably heterodox significance, by using these feminine endings to explore the strangely erotic vitality of death and putrefaction, as 'kissing carrion'. So Cleopatra's dying words, as she suckles the asp that kills her, perform an ironic unsettling of biblical chronology, in a figurative conjunction of the fall of man (through the temptation of Eve by the serpent) with images of the Virgin and Christ child – the newborn 'Prince of Peace': 'Peace, peace! / Dost thou not see my baby at my breast / That sucks the nurse asleep?' (5.2.307–9). The dying pagan queen is momentarily both the first and the second Eve, while Eve's serpentine tempter is problematically fused with the saviour of mankind. Several lines later, in a reference whose palimpsest-like layering of allusions assimilates both Protestant and Catholic imagery into a highly erotic spectacle of death which exceeds the doctrines of each faith, we are told by Caesar that: 'she looks like sleep, / As she would catch another Antony / In her strong toil of grace' (5.2.345–7). These words evoke another contradictory medley of Christian images: the 'dormition' of the Virgin Mary – a final falling asleep whose difference from normal death was doctrinally reasserted at the Counter-Reformation; the first Christian disciples fishing for men's souls; and the Calvinist emphasis on the role of divine grace in the process of salvation. Yet elided with these different versions of Christian salvation is the image of a female body whose sexuality is seemingly active even after death: Shakespeare and his contemporaries frequently punned on the homophonic association of 'grace' with the 'greasiness' of carnival pleasures (as in Mardi Gras or Shrove Tuesday), and the 'greasy' end of the genitalia in particular. In this late Renaissance 'gallimaufry' – which involved a riddling juxtaposition of diverse images – contemporary religious concerns for the fate of the soul are differed and dilated by a bawdy emphasis upon the seemingly inextinguishable vitality concealed within the dead or dying female body.

Reading tragedy awry

The Freudian definition of the *Unheimlichkeit*, or uncanny, encompasses any moment when meaning has proceeded so far in the direction of ambivalence that it effectively coincides with its opposite, in a disturbing collapse of semantic differences.[13] In their exploration of death through a series of feminine, or what might best be described as *feminized* figures (since they invariably problematize the boundaries of both gender and desire), the tragedies privilege similarly uncanny moments of semantic ambiguity, in what seems a deliberate exploitation of the contemporary uncertainty as to death's meaning that was felt by many at this liminal moment of religious and intellectual crisis. The result is a quasi-alchemical transmutation of tragic discourse, in which the etymological connection of the Greek *tropos* or trope, with ideas of turning away from a particular course (*trope* was the word used by Greek astronomers to refer to the turning path of the sun at key points in the solar year), is performed in a recurrent turning aside or disfiguring of meaning.

In the same scene from *Richard II* which I took for my starting point, the king's favourite Bushy offers a response to the queen's speech whose pragmatism is designed to allay her fears; it is a reply, however, that indirectly provides us with further insights into the type of critical perspective which might be best suited to analysis of the supplementary meanings of Shakespearean tragedy. For he tells her that:

> . . . Sorrow's eye glazed with blinding tears,
> Divides one thing entire to many objects,
> Like perspectives, which rightly gazed upon
> Show nothing but confusion; eyed awry,
> Distinguish form: so your sweet majesty,
> Looking awry upon your lord's departure,
> Finds shapes of grief more than himself to wail,
> Which looked on as it is, is nought but shadows
> Of what it is not . . .
>
> (2.2.16–24)

The favourite's argument, founded in an unemotional empiricism which anticipates a post-Renaissance or modern sensibility, is that 'Sorrows eye' finds a meaning in suffering which is erroneous. This 'eyeing awry' of what Bushy sees as the fundamentally meaningless shapes of grief by the mournful queen gives them a 'form' that he believes is a dangerous figural excess, producing 'shapes of grief more than himself [the departed Richard] to wail'. The sceptical favourite allies his rejection of her premonitory sadness with a brief dismissal of the new mannerist device of anamorphosis, whose 'perspectives' aimed uncannily to unsettle the viewer by inviting a 'looking awry' that revealed a formerly concealed dimension of the artistic work. But just as the 'more' that Bushy dismisses, yet which is positioned so emphatically at the caesura of its line, actually creates a homophonic anticipation of Richard's death as *mort* or *mors*, so ensuing events will prove the sentiments of Richard's queen to have been prophetic. And in the unfolding of Richard's tragedy, Bushy's matter-of-fact rejection, along with the queen's intuition, of the innovative artistic technique of anamorphosis appears also to be called into question, in a subtle reminder that an angled or oblique – a genuinely *tropical* – point of view may actually be required if we are to comprehend tragedy's double or multilayered significance.

This book performs a partial mimesis of the 'eyeing awry' of grief performed by Richard's French queen, in a 'reading awry' in which individual chapters (although finally focused on a single play) also construct diverse 'perspectives' from which to view the tragedies as a generic group. Yet whereas many of the anamorphic perspectives of the Renaissance revealed the skull beneath the skin (the presence of death in the midst of life), this feminist version of anamorphosis performs a contrasting reversal of perspective, by showing how – equally uncannily – a polymorphous and heterodox version of material vitality is concealed behind the cultural façades of death. The bodily difference revealed by this reading awry of Shakespeare's art of dying is best described as *obscene*, in that what is shown to be adjacent to the *scena* of formal tragic representation is a grotesque material and bodily excess which transgresses the generic purity conventionally expected of élite cultural productions.[14] Writing of the implicit threat posed to classical forms of art by the figural excess of the female body, Lynda Nead has argued that:

> If the female body is defined as lacking containment and issuing filth and pollution from its faltering outlines and broken surface, then the classical forms of art [in the shape of the female nude] perform a kind of magical regulation of the female body, containing it and momentarily repairing the orifices and tears. This, however, can only be a fleeting success; the margins are dangerous, and will need to be subjected to the discipline of art again.[15]

I read Shakespearean tragedy, however, as deliberately affording us a dual perspective: one which is *both* classical *and* obscene. Yet it performs this doubling, not at the level of visual representation, but rather through a use of wordplay or paronomasia whose frequent obscenity is only now beginning to be accepted by modern editors of the plays.[16] Indeed, while anamorphosis demands a reordering of our visual response, I will show

how the tragedies incorporate a disturbing figurative excess which unsettles all of the sensory responses that comprise bodily knowledge.[17] While each tragedy gives varied attention to most or all of the senses, my excavation of this particular stratum of figurative detail traces an erratic trajectory: from the devouring mouths of the 'star-crossed' lovers in *Romeo and Juliet*; through the ambivalent attentiveness (to secreted meanings) of Hamlet's ear; across the monstrously dilated eyes of Othello (with their suggestive bodily ambiguity) and the uncannily tactile 'hairiness' of 'the Scottish play'; to a consideration of the stinking tragic refuse whose stench ultimately reaches the nose of King Lear. As each sense – taste or eating, hearing, smelling, touching, as well as seeing – is reconfigured with an obscene difference, what is implicitly produced is an experiential knowledge of the secrets of matter. In this highly material mode of tragic 'knowing', a familiar humanist metaphor of knowledge as digestion is ironically extended – to encompass the refuse, waste or 'trash' normally expelled or excluded from elite cultural production.[18] What these figures of tragic digestion (and its eventual, grossly material product) perform is a chiastic inversion of the 'no' of tragic negation, as they reposition a bodily site of negation and waste as a paradoxical place of beginning, rather than a certain end.

My reading 'awry' is informed both explicitly and implicitly by the 'postmodern' critical perspectives whose oblique relationship to both knowledge and textuality has sometimes been compared to the technique of anamorphosis: deconstruction and French feminist theory.[19] But it also has a multilayered historical specificity. For while Shakespeare is perceived increasingly as an 'early modern' writer, the tragedies are interpreted here as products of an essentially liminal cultural and historical moment, whose *interstitial* position between medieval and modern attitudes is currently in need of re-emphasis and re-evaluation.[20] By disentangling some of the extraordinarily diverse levels of cultural and historical detail that are enfolded around their feminine and feminized figures, I aim to demonstrate how the tragedies' oblique reordering of human knowing implies an amplification and differing, not only of conventional Christian views of death, but also of the emergent 'modern' model of knowledge and identity, which aimed to master or 'discover' death along with the rest of material existence.

In their tropical interrelationship of woman and death, the tragedies trace repeated deviations from both narrative and bodily conceptions of sequence and succession; a comparable reversal of ends, as Parker has shown, is performed by many other tropical interconnections elsewhere in the Shakespearean corpus.[21] Just as the figures associated with them repeatedly divert tragic discourse from its ostensible *telos*, deferring a communicative as well as a performative end in their synchronic emphasis upon a fleeting rhetorical insight, so at the level of plot the tragedies' female characters frequently disrupt the stability and continuity of masculine identity. Yet the changing relationship which the tragedies subtly delineate – between, on the one hand, an 'heroic' masculinity whose identity is ostensibly defined both by a teleological system of meaning and by a patrilineal system of inheritance, and, on the other, an uncannily mutable, open-ended femininity – is never one of simple opposition, if only because the physical bodies of women were absent from the English Renaissance stage. Indeed, the female characters who most frequently emblematize this paradoxical state of absence-as-presence, of boy as woman, occupy an exceptionally labile position at the level of performance. Shakespearean tragedy converts this physical insubstantiality of its female characters into an immense figurative resource, in its recurring focus upon a sexuality whose definition in terms of lack or negation – producing punning speculations upon woman's devouring (genital) 'eye', and her equivalence with 'nothing' – often appears to call its gendered specificity into question. Through such tropes, the peculiar doubleness or hybridity of these women who are not women is reinforced, as they delineate ghostly traces of the 'more' that is mysteriously inherent in absence and loss, and hence in the tragic protagonist's experience of death.

For as the disturbing natural as well as aesthetic excess that is embedded within these textual 'moors' of the human spirit grows tropically 'to seed' – assisted by the grotesque fecundity of woman's especially intimate conjunction with death, as 'my Lady Worm' – its tropical turning aside of conventional notions of linear succession performs a scatological metamorphosis of masculine identity. By relating its eventual encounter with death to the production of bodily waste, Hamlet figuratively decomposes royal power, as he meditates upon the possibility of a dead king's 'progress through the guts of a beggar' and of the noble dust of Alexander 'stopping a bunghole'. A similar sense of the relationship of death's 'rottenness' to a natural organic cycle, within which the activity of an obscure feminine principle of generation ensures that nothing is ultimately wasted, can be found in diverse other texts of this epoch. Thus in Pierre de Ronsard's 'Hymne de la mort' the poet declares that 'with the help of Venus, Nature finds means to reanimate, by long and divers changes, any remaining matter – all that which you eat' (Ainsi, avec Venus la Nature trouva / Moyen de r'animer par longs et divers changes, / La matière restant, tout cela que tu manges). This gross, but simultaneously philosophical, interest in nature's recycling of the 'waste' or surplus that remains after death is intimately related to a newly expansive sense of the richly fecund 'matter' of the vernacular tongues, as they established new semantic relationships with one another as well as with the classical languages. As wordplay which exploits the multiple affinities between English words is interwoven with more oblique, 'second-meaning' puns that are often interlingual – such as the unspoken connection between 'grief' as 'parting', and the French word *grevé* – what is produced is a supplementary yet also sedimentary layering of 'earthy' figurative meanings.[22] From this geophysical perspective, as Marie-Dominique Garnier has recently observed, we can begin to read Shakespearean tropes as a series of complex 'telluric folds'.[23]

Yet as is vividly suggested in the excremental imagery used by both Hamlet and Ronsard, the divided yet productive end to tragic suffering that is repeatedly emblematized by the body's 'nether' regions is of indeterminate gender. It may signify either the female genitals, or the backside, or both; in observing that, by the end of the sixteenth century, 'arse' carried vaginal overtones, Gordon Williams reminds us of the period's frequent elision of one sexual opening with another, and of heterosexual with homoerotic – and sometimes, sodomitical – desire.[24] The medlar, or 'open-arse' tree to which Romeo's 'mistress' is compared by Mercutio affords an apt emblem of this figurative equivocation in relation to an ending both 'rotten' and 'ripe' – an equivocation evidently influenced by the bodily ambiguity of the boy actor. In *Macbeth*, however, it is the open, or 'breached' bodies, not of boys, but of a king and an ancestor of kings – Duncan and Banquo – that are represented, not only as distinctive tropes of tragic horror (in which the shedding of royal blood is momentarily configured as an act of sodomitical abuse), but also as contradictory conjunctions of waste with fruitfulness. A less sexualized version of this 'breaching' of the king is performed by the imagery of *Lear*, where the tragic hero is figuratively metamorphosed into an ass / arse. Once deceived by Iago, Othello too is 'tenderly . . . led by th'nose / As asses are' (2.1.400–1), just as Romeo's cratylic or nominal connection with the 'R' of 'arse' is stressed in *Romeo and Juliet*; the imagery of both tragedies interweaves a heterosexual, with what appears to be a more transgressive, and possibly sodomitical, desire.[25] In these recurring figurations of a tragic masculinity as asinine, we can decipher a Shakespearean *ars moriendi* whose chiastic crossing of intense suffering with obscene physicality – of the *ars* of dying with the *arse* – combines tragic horror with a grotesque scatology that restructures a bodily as well as an aesthetic hierarchy of values.

Since, as I have already observed, the perspective that is produced by this obscene reordering of aesthetic values is not singular, but double, it seems plausible that it may also hint at a riddling synthesis of the seeming antitheses of body and spirit. The emblematic and esoteric complexity of the bestial ass in both ancient and Renaissance thought has recently received detailed attention in two studies of the heterodox and ultimately heretical late Renaissance philosopher, Giordano Bruno, for whom *asinità* or 'asininity' had a status comparable to Erasmus's paradoxical folly. According to Karen Silvia de Leon-Jones, Bruno's ass represents 'a sort of ineffable negativity of the divine'.[26] In Shakespeare, however, what we find is a version of 'asininity' whose materiality merely hints at the possibility of a hidden spiritual import. This scatological perspective has most obvious affinity to the thought of Rabelais – a writer who made riddling allusions to the passage of soul through the *cul* or arse – but it also appears indebted to a new philosophical discourse of materialism.[27]

Shakespearean materialism reconsidered

In the tragedies' accretion of intricate tropical details whose covert or explicit wordplay combines learned humanist insights with the obscene imagery of popular culture, we can discern the faint, yet palpable, trace of a brief period of freewheeling intellectual speculation that was arguably unparalleled until the late nineteenth century. Different permutations of this loosely articulated and highly syncretic intellectual nexus can be discerned in diverse works of late Renaissance literature, by Pierre de Ronsard, François Rabelais, Michel de Montaigne, and, in England, by figures as diverse as Samuel Daniel, Christopher Marlowe, Ben Jonson and John Milton, as well as in the texts of philosophers and natural philosophers such as Bernardino Telesio, Francesco Patrizi, Girolamo Cardano, and Giordano Bruno.[28] In an emphasis upon the freedom of morals putatively associated with it, this palimpsest of heterodox ideas has sometimes been described as 'libertinism'; but while its concerns extend across a range of important topics – encompassing speculations on the nature of identity, desire and death, the character of time, and the peculiar materiality of the state – its central philosophical motif is what Michel Jeanneret has described as an animist or vitalist conception of matter.[29] This animist or vitalist materialism differs funda-mentally from conventional philosophical emphases, inherited from the thought of Aristotle in particular, upon the opposition and inferiority of matter to form or spirit. The previously dominant Aristotelian conception of *materia* – as a formless and receptive sphere which requires both shaping and ruling – had not only informed many branches of thought, including grammar and rhetoric, but had also determined ideas of women, since the female sex was conventionally associated with this formerly degraded sphere.[30] Since the implicit or explicit rejection of

Aristotelian physics by many late Renaissance thinkers was influenced by a very different, vitalist, conception of matter, it has important implications for our understanding of both subjectivity and gender in this period.

When Lear, entering in Act 5 scene 3 of *King Lear* with the dead Cordelia in his arms, declares that 'She's dead as earth', his view of earth as 'dead' anticipates modern views of matter as intrinsically inert or 'dead', as a *natura naturata*. Yet Lear's perspective is strikingly at odds with the overall context of the play, which depicts nature instead as a dynamic sphere of perpetual becoming, as a *natura naturans*. Like Cordelia's 'nothing' (which is significantly positioned at the beginning rather than the end of the play) this intrinsically mobile and unruly force is shown to be far more powerful than Lear's own royal will, with a healing as well as destructive potency that performs a highly material refiguration of the Aristotelian concept of tragic *catharsis*: a term which Aristotle may have borrowed from Greek medical conceptions of bodily purgation. Indeed, what is articulated in Shakespeare's repeated emphasis, throughout his work, upon nature's thaumaturgic vitality is a late Renaissance materialism that is also emphatically premodern, since it views matter not (as in both Christian and modern perspectives) as separable from the sphere of spirit, but rather as an all-encompassing reality, such as that described as early as 1582, in *Batman upon Bartholome his Booke*:

> As for the Earth, it is the Bace, and Foundation of all the Elementes . . . It contayneth in it the seedes, and seminall vertues of all things . . . Of it selfe, it is receyver of all fruitefulnesse, and as it were also, the first springing Parent of all things, the Center, Foundation, and Mother of all things.[31]

In this humanist reinflection of the idea of a spiritualized nature, all seeming opposites, including the categories of death and birth, ultimately coincide. Although its central concerns would be displaced over the course of the seventeenth century by the new mechanistic philosophy (which typically conceived of nature not as an organic unity but as a machine), this widely disseminated concept of a dynamic yet purposeful nature was arguably the closer philosophical complement to the Copernican hypothesis – not yet proven by Galileo – of a mobile rather than static earth.

While this late Renaissance materialism echoes and amplifies themes which are found in several medieval texts, only some of the ideas which it explores were directly available to medieval culture. This vitalist or animist conception of matter owes its specific contemporaneity to the humanist re-engagement with a wide assortment of classical texts, including Ovid's *Metamorphoses*, Plato's *Timaeus*, Lucretius' *De rerum natura*, the *Orphic Hymns*, the *Hermetica*, some fragments of the thought of Empedocles and other pre-Socratic philosophers, and the texts of Cicero and Plutarch. Some of the connections between this 'new' conception of matter and the tragedies' implicit paradoxicality have been explored in Thomas McAlindon's very perceptive account of the plays' debt to Empedoclean theories of the strife between the elements, which was chiefly responsible for the popularity in Renaissance thought of ideas of *discordia concors* or the harmony of contraries.[32] Yet probably the most accessible and acceptable of the various doctrines associated with this new materialism was Stoicism, which had accommodated or borrowed from the ideas of many earlier thinkers such as Pythagoras and Empedocles.

The extensive influence of Stoicism upon Renaissance culture was due in large part to the resemblance of its austere ethics (especially its emphasis upon endurance in the face of misfortune and death) to Christian teaching, as well as to its influence upon the texts of venerated classical and early Renaissance writers such as Cicero and Petrarch. Stoic attitudes to death and suffering were also very widely disseminated through Renaissance enthusiasm for the writings of Seneca: an aspect of Stoic influence upon Shakespearean tragedy that has been very widely discussed. What has been virtually ignored, however, is the relevance to the tragedies of a more belated Renaissance interest in the monism of Stoic physics, which perceived the cosmos as a single living being animated by an active principle usually described as a fiery breath or *pneuma*, and variously called God, nature, necessity or the world soul.[33] In *On the Nature of the Gods* (De natura deorum), Cicero echoes Stoic doctrine in explicitly equating Nature with the supreme being:

> That which we call Nature is therefore the power which permeates and preserves the whole universe, and this power is not devoid of sense and reason. . . . It follows that the being in which is found the organizing principle for the whole of nature must be the supreme being, worthy of power and dominion over all. . . . So the universe must be a rational being and the Nature which permeates and embraces all things must be one, and all the life of the world must be contained within the being of God.[34]

Hence while the exemplary ethics of Stoicism attracted many Renaissance thinkers because of its apparent parallels to Christian morality, its physics revealed a disturbing pantheism underlying this philosophical system, in which, moreover, the 'world-mind', or God, was identified with a principle traditionally personified as female: Nature.

It is not to Stoicism, however, but to the other late classical philosophy with which it was most frequently compared and contrasted in the Renaissance – that of Epicureanism – that the affinities of this new materialism with a certain worldly and even bodily pleasure can most plausibly be traced. Lucretius' *De rerum natura*, a vivid poetic account of the perpetual motion of 'the nature of things' according to Epicurean thought, had been rediscovered at the beginning of the Renaissance, and inspired a number of Italian humanists, including Marsilio Ficino and Lorenzo Valla, to reassess the importance of worldly pleasure or *voluptas*. While they declared that matter could never perish, but only be changed, Epicureans also emphasized the lack of causality in nature, which they described in terms of chance collisions between atoms moving through empty space. Moreover, they held that the soul as well as the body was involved in death. Its deliberate liberation of man from the fear of divine judgement in an afterlife was used by Epicureanism to recommend the value of *voluptas*. In view of this emphasis upon the body and the senses, it seems apt that the only deity directly involved in the perpetual flux of Lucretius' 'wonder-working earth' (*daedala tellus*) is Venus:

> Mother of Aeneas and his race, darling of men and gods [*hominum divumque voluptas*], nurturing Venus, who beneath the smooth-moving heavenly signs fill with yourself the sea full-laden with ships, the earth that bears the crops, since through you every kind of living thing is conceived and rising up looks on the light of the sun . . . as soon as the vernal force of day is made manifest, and the breeze of the teeming west wind blows fresh and free, first the fowls of the air proclaim you, divine one, and your advent, pierced to the heart by your might . . . you alone govern the nature of things, since without you nothing comes forth into the shining borders of light, nothing joyous and lovely is made.[35]

Although Roman Venus is usually remembered as a goddess of love, she was once an archaic deity of nature's fertility. Commenting on what is now thought to be the influence (together with that of Florentine Neo-platonism) of Lucretius' goddess of natural generation upon Botticelli's

Primavera (a painting in which, as in Lucretius' opening lines, the power of nature is first signalled by the fertilizing breath of the west wind, Zephyr), Charles Dempsey has noted that: 'In Lucretius's Venus Genetrix there appears the full nature goddess that Venus once was, the true Venus Physica of the ancient Romans'.[36]

While the extraordinary poetry of *De rerum natura* – which combines scientific and philosophical speculation with a pervasive paronomastic wit – made it an admired stylistic model throughout the sixteenth century, historians of ideas have typically assumed that its intellectual influence does not begin in earnest until the seventeenth century, with the Christian rehabilitation of Lucretius by Gassendi, and a contrasting 'libertine' appropriation of Epicurean ideas in sceptical intellectual circles.[37] Yet it is clear from explicit and implicit references to Lucretius, in texts as diverse as those of Rabelais, Spenser, and Montaigne, that elements of Epicurean thought were frequently assimilated into a late sixteenth-century syncretism which, while often 'libertine' in its exploration of unorthodox ideas of matter as well as of worldly pleasure, was not necessarily atheist. Similarly, Brian Copenhaver and Charles Schmitt describe most of the new natural philosophers of the late sixteenth century as combining 'a volatile blend of animist naturalism with religious temerity'; opposing to the idea of spirit's pre-existence and transcendence an immanentist and monist emphasis upon the material interdependence of body and soul, almost all of them perceived the world of universal nature as 'charged with organic sympathies and antipathies'.[38] This syncretic philosophy commonly entwined distinctively Epicurean themes, such as atomism and hedonism, with motifs from other classical sources. While a purely Epicurean naturalism saw the metamorphic mobility of an eternal nature as ultimately aimless, the even more extensive influence upon late Renaissance natural philosophy of Stoic physics caused most exponents of the new naturalism to assert an underlying form or purpose within it. Thus while a thinker such as Giordano Bruno came to see matter, like Lucretius, as composed of atomic particles, Bruno drew on both these classical systems, as well as on other, pre-Socratic ideas, in extending the Lucretian principle of nature's constant renewal to encompass human experience:

> But when we consider more profoundly the being and substance of that in which we are immutable, we will find there is no death, not for us, nor for any substance; for nothing substantially diminishes, but everything, moving through infinite space, changes its aspect.[39]

This new, metamorphic naturalism consequently seems best described, as recently by Michel Jeanneret, as a distinctively Renaissance version of classical pantheism, in which matter is as it were spiritualized and spirit is materialized; Jeanneret interprets it as 'a philosophy of birthing [*naître*] which is opposed to that of being [*être*]: to be born and to be born again, is to exist in the precariousness of perpetual oscillation, is not to be [*n'être*]'.[40]

Like other exponents of this new materialism, Bruno also affirmed matter's eternal existence. He could have acquired this heretical position directly from Lucretius, but also from several other sources, such as Ovid's *Metamorphoses*, whose opening account of a pre-existent matter or Chaos reveals the influence of both Lucretius and Empedocles:

> Before the Sea and land were made, and Heaven that all doth
> hyde,
> In all the worlde one onely face of Nature did abyde,
> Which Chaos hight: a huge rude heape, and nothing else but even
> A heavie lump and clottred clod of seedes together driven
> Of things at strife among themselves for want of order due . . .
> No kinde of thing had proper shape, but ech confounded other . . . [41]

This idea of prime matter was heretical because it contradicted the Christian doctrine of creation from nothing (*ex nihilo*). Yet prime matter was held by the Stoics to be coeternal with their material and corporeal godhead. Cicero had declared that:

> the infinite Nature of the universe as a whole is the original
> source of all freedom and all movements . . . Such is the nature
> of the moving spirit of the universe, so that it may properly be
> called the divine wisdom or providence (*pronoia*), which has
> formed the world to endure and lack for nothing . . . [42]

It is this ambivalently creative and destructive originary matter, of course, as a 'dungy earth' that 'alike / Feeds beast as man' (1.1.36–7), which provides the quasi-alchemical, but also Lucretian setting for Shakespeare's most explicit exploration of late Renaissance vitalism, *Antony and Cleopatra*. As a perplexing embodiment of Lucretius's Venus Genetrix, Cleopatra has seemingly metamorphosed her heroic Roman lover into an 'Epicurean' or 'libertine', who is 'tie[d] up . . . in a field of feasts' (2.1.23). Yet in the 'trail' left by the 'pretty worm of Nilus' who has fatally consumed Cleopatra – a trail of obscure semiotic traces suggesting the nature of her death – 'slime' is peculiarly juxtaposed with a philosophically suggestive mixture of blood and air, for the dead queen's body is troped as mysteriously 'vent[ed]' or 'blown' by the bites of the asp:

Dolabella: Here on her breast
                    There is a vent of blood, and something blown,
                    The like is on her arm.
1 Guard: This is an aspic's trail, and these fig-leaves
                    Have slime upon them such as th'aspic leaves
                    Upon the caves of Nile.

                                                            (5.2.347–52)

These clues hint at the possibility that, like the Stoic cosmos, the lovers' full-blooded 'voluptuousness' – together with their geographical implication in the 'slime and ooze' of Egypt – was mysteriously informed by that vital breath (as *pneuma* or *spiritus*) thought to be carried within the human body, by blood, and whose 'vent', passage or passing can only partially be distinguished after death, as a slight bodily *disfigure-ment*.[43] This suggests that Cleopatra's announcement of her dying metamorphosis into 'fire and air' – an elemental combination which echoes Stoic descriptions of the *pneuma* that informs the entire cosmos – is ultimately central to her enigmatic personification of the perpetual transmutation of matter, as one in whom 'vilest things / Become them-selves' (2.2.248–9).

Thus while a syncretic assembly of vitalist ideas was expounded explicitly in the work of late sixteenth-century natural philosophers, Shakespeare speculates upon the human implications of vitalism as – like other Renaissance writers exploring these ideas, and notably Rabelais – he compounds them with motifs borrowed from more popular discourses. In this elision of new ideas of material flux with an abjected or obscene sphere of bodily pleasure, Shakespeare, like Rabelais, owes a complex debt to the symbolism of carnival and festivity, as François Laroque has shown.[44] But his recurring figuration of bodily putrefaction and decay as a process rather than an end is also implicitly indebted to the quasi-popular discourse of alchemy, which in the late classical period had been closely interwoven with anti-Aristotelian speculations on the nature of matter. Alchemy perceived matter as containing a spiritual principle that – in a process at once self-devouring and self-generating – ultimately perfects it, through repeated reversions to the state of prime matter.[45] Alchemists frequently observe that 'the place or earth in which they [the wise] are putrified is the Female'; yet they also describe 'Our Mercury', the hidden spirit within matter, as a *rebis*, or double-sexed.[46]

In Shakespeare's disfiguration of tragic endings in relation to a grossly material, feminized, but not unequivocally female origin – a tropical location that is both consuming and regenerative – classical philosophy is distinctively conflated with the carnivalesque and alchemical imagery of more popular cultural tradition.

Given the darkness and obscurity of both classical and alchemical versions of originary matter, it is not surprising that so many of these tragedies are set in a legendary or early historical context, or that several of the plays explore a racialized version of origins whose apparent barbarism is explicitly disturbing. By this means, the interrogation of individual tragic endings – which often involves a figurative 'decom-position' of kings in relation to an emblematic yet abjected 'seat' – is repeatedly interwoven with a parallel examination of what seems to have been a similarly abjected 'ground' of national and cultural identities. Thus in *Macbeth* and *King Lear*, Shakespeare's dramatic investigations of the origins of a distinctively British sovereignty, the obscure materiality of the state is represented as an uncanny and implicitly feminine potency which is implied to have a peculiarly paradoxical and unsettling relationship to the new 'British' kingship of James I.

This suggestive association of Shakespearean tragedy with a distinctive historical reversion or turning backwards is entirely consistent with its many tropical deviations from ideas of linearity and strict succession. An increased critical awareness of this pattern, related by Parker to the trope of the 'preposterous', suggests that a critical reassessment of the temporality of both Shakespearean tragedy and history is now due, since the tropical patterns of these plays supplement the diachronic or linear process of tragic narrative with a repetitive and circular model of timing, in which a bodily end or tail becomes the instrument of a temporal reversion that is both spiritual and material. Here, as in the motto of Marie de Guise, later adopted by her unfortunate daughter Mary Queen of Scots, *En Ma Fin Git Mon Commencement*: in my end lies my beginning. The *impresa* which both women used with this motto was the bird of temporal repetition, the phoenix (a device also used by Mary Stuart's cousin Elizabeth Tudor); but in *Minerva Britannia*, a collection of emblems presented to Mary's son James I, Henry Peacham provides an implicitly sexualized emblem of a feminine end that is also a beginning (Plate 1). This is a female personification of Eternity, whose bodily association with temporal recurrence is depicted by the emergence of an *ouroboros*-like circle from 'nether partes' that Peacham describes as 'twin'd'. Yet it is apparent from the device that this feminine end which is not an end is not simply 'twin'd'; it is also *twinned* or doubled.

A VIRGIN faire, purtraicted as you fee,
　With haire difpred, in comelie wife behind:
Within whofe handes, two golden balls there be:
But from the breft, the nether partes are twin'd
　Within a ftarrie circle, do expreffe,
　Eternitie, or *Everlaftingnes*.

ETERNITIE is young, and never old:
The circle wantes * beginning and the end:
And vncorrupt for ever lies the gold:
The heaven her lightes for evermore did lend,
　The Heathen thought, though heauen & earth muft paffe,
　And all in time decay that ever was.

Fuit quædam ab infinito tempore æternitas, quam nulla circumfcriptio temporum metiebatur, fpatio tamen qualis ea fuerit intelligi non poteft.

Plate 1 'Eternitas'. Henry Peacham, *Minerva Britannia* (London: 1612). By
permission of the British Library.

2

DOUBLE DYING AND OTHER TRAGIC INVERSIONS

Romeo and Juliet (c.1596)

> The newly dead are conceived of as double, simultaneously present in the tomb and in some spiritual realm. In this liminal position they are regarded as dangerous and polluted.
>
> (Elizabeth Bronfen, *Over Her Dead Body*)[1]

> Puns deceive because people generally expect language, and indeed nature, not to confront them with doubles.
>
> (Frederick Ahl, *Metaformations*)[2]

When she is troped as a 'breeder of sinners', the sexuality of a female character may represent a uniquely disturbing image for the protagonist of Shakespearean tragedy: a grotesque bodily emblem of death-in-life. Yet Renaissance writers loved to demonstrate, above all through their delight in wordplay, that every paradox can be inflected in diverse ways, and a familiar tropical association between death and sexuality is both amplified and complicated in the tragedies, through their elaboration of a figurative nexus which stresses the uncanny liminality of erotic desire: its mysterious Janus-aspect as a portal of both life and death. By using diverse rhetorical figures, and puns in particular, to suggest the affinity of a penetrable body *both* with the here and now of bodily experience, *and also* with an invisible and undefined beyond, the tragedies effect a peculiar doubling of their imagery of death; this doubling is echoed, moreover, by a curious detail of their plots, the figuratively dual or multiple dyings of female tragic protagonists, which anticipate romance versions of a similar device, in *Pericles* and *The Winter's Tale*. In this tropical and performative duplication of tragic 'ends', a chiastic reversal or inversion of death's meaning is persistently implied, whereby death is momentarily reconfigured as the mirror image, the differed double, of its presumed opposite: of comedy, pleasure, vitality and festivity. In the deaths of Ophelia, Desdemona and Juliet in particular, different

21

versions of death as festival connect their 'feminine endings' with specific moments in the seasonal calendar of holidays. As it is figuratively crossed by the cyclical, repetitive time of the festive calendar, the temporal singularity of tragic dying is subtly called into question.

In their focus upon the sexualized female body as the site of a chiastic 'crossing' or inversion of death with life, these plays often appear to privilege the female genitalia or womb as the locus of life's renewal; yet Shakespeare's troping of the deaths of several of his male characters in terms of a fertilizing sexual penetration (notably those of Old Hamlet, Duncan and Banquo) serves to remind us, not only that the gendering of this chiastic process is ultimately indeterminate, but also that there are other bodily gateways of death and life, including the ear and the anus. Indeed, Porphyry had observed that:

> Since nature arose out of diversity, the ancients everywhere made that which has a twofold entrance her symbol. . . . Plato says that there are two orifices, one through which souls ascend to the heavens, the other through which they descend to earth.[3]

It is important to remember in this connection that the sexuality represented by the female protagonist of tragedy is neither simple nor singular, but implicitly double – not just because the part is played by a boy, but also because of the frequent figurative association of a desirable woman with the arse or backside.[4] In an important reading of *Romeo and Juliet* from the perspective of queer theory, Jonathan Goldberg has argued that:

> Juliet's living-dead status could be taken to prevaricate in bodily terms between the generative and ungenerative desires whose paths cross each other in the play; much as she has and has not been deflowered by death, her union with Romeo is, from the end of the second act of the play, legitimated by marriage and continues to summon its allure from the unspeakable terrain of sodomy.[5]

Goldberg points out that 'this move across gender . . . allows a subject position for women that is not confined within patriarchal boundaries'.[6]

As their wordplay elides this double bodily 'end' of woman – which allows both genital and anal penetration – with the enigmatic duality of her tragic 'endings', the tragedies perform a Rabelaisian amplification of ancient Platonic lore with carnival scatology, in oblique echoes of Hotspur's reference in *I Henry IV* to 'the very bottom and the soul of hope' (4.2.50). In *Romeo and Juliet*, this association is most explicitly stressed by the bawdy language of Mercutio, first in his association of Romeo's mistress with the medlar or 'open-arse' tree, and later by his extended wordplay with Romeo on 'soul' and 'sole', which extends to 'the whole depth of my tale' (2.4.59–99). The shared jest hints at that contemporary uncertainty as to the precise bodily location of the 'seate' of the soul which has been noted by Jeffrey Masten in his exploration of the foundational properties of the 'fundament' or anus.[7]

The conceit of the duality of death had philosophical as well as literary antecedents; just as Platonic philosophers frequently differentiated between two stages of deaths, in terms of the gradual separation of the soul from the body, so Christianity distinguished individual bodily dying from an eventual last judgement of souls.[8] However, David Armitage has noted that a rather different, amatory conceit of 'double dying', or *gemina nece*, is encoded in Ovid's narrative of the myth of Orpheus and Eurydice, where it is Orpheus' loving look as he leads her out of Hades that kills his wife over again.[9] Armitage points out that in Arthur Golding's 1567 rendering of this episode into English, his turn of phrase gives especial emphasis to the peculiar character of Orpheus' misfortune: 'This double dying of his wife set *Orphye* in a stound'. In Shakespearean tragedy, it is likewise through the figuration of a literal death in sexual terms that the dying female body becomes an oxymoronic image of life-in-death, whose simultaneous 'deflowering' and 'devouring' by death (like that of the mechanicals' Thisbe in *A Midsummer Night's Dream*) juxtaposes the prospect of death as an individualized end to a finite existence with the possibility of a virtual infinity or endlessness of erotic 'deaths'. This is of course the mode of dying preferred by Cleopatra, of whom Enobarbus declares: 'I do think there is mettle in death which commits some loving act upon her, she hath such a celerity in dying' (1.2.149–51).

This Shakespearean differing of death through its 'crossing' with the enactment of desire seems, in an important sense, to be a deferral of bodily endings, since by this device the sexualized body is mysteriously privileged rather than overcome. Given what we now know of his family's Catholic sympathies, of the extent of recusancy in Elizabethan Warwickshire, and also of Shakespeare's probable association with a recusant aristocratic family in the early years of his dramatic career, it seems that we may need to reconsider, not only the plays' possible debt to Counter-Reformation motifs, but also the residual, if markedly ambiguous, traces in these texts of medieval popular piety, especially the 'idolatrous' cults of the saints.[10] The tragedies' 'love-deaths' often suggestively parallel the ecstatic deaths of Catholic saints, especially those images of the Dormition and Ascension of the Virgin Mary favoured by baroque culture; like the deaths of saints and martyrs, these tragic dyings often have a distinctly sacrificial quality. In the tragedies, however, the erotic imagery associated with death alludes to the real performance of sexual desire, rather than to its religious sublimation; at the same time, Catholic motifs are often interwoven both with pagan motifs derived from classical culture and with the grotesque, pantheistic imagery of popular festivity. Indeed, it is primarily the metaphoric or metonymic affinity that is created in the plays between the dead or dying female body, and what is implied to be a thaumaturgic principle hidden within nature that tempers the tragic conception of death as terminus.

The divine riddle

Since their tropical affinity seems to be, not with nature *per se*, but rather with a hidden principle which uncannily, and sometimes grotesquely, informs it, the double deaths of Shakespeare's female characters appear to emblematize the ambiguous duality of the feminine-gendered soul. Plotinus had described soul as 'the divine riddle'; as a mediator between what were conventionally seen as the contrasting spheres of matter and spirit, the concept had possessed a distinct ambivalence from the beginning of its history. This was because both individual soul and the category which much classical philosophy posited as its macrocosmic equivalent, the *anima mundi* or soul of the world, were supposed not only to inform and animate nature but also to connect it with Universal Mind or spirit.[11] In the late sixteenth century, among natural philosophers, Paracelsans, and alchemists who shared a monist, rather than dualist view of nature, the *anima mundi* became the emblem of the new, heterodox conviction of spirit's intrinsic unity with matter which is asserted in these animist philosophies of nature. These thinkers sometimes image it as a kind of world-sap: a principle of quickening and endless vitality which animates and preserves the world.[12] At this liminal intellectual moment, just before more mechanistic views of nature become dominant, it is possible even for a leading scientist such as William Gilbert, the author of an influential account of the magnetic activity of the earth (*De magnete*, published in England in 1600), to regard the world as a living organism: 'we deem the whole world animate, and all globes, all stars, and the glorious earth too, we hold to be from the beginning by their own destinate souls governed'.[13]

The revival of classical ideas of the world soul in late sixteenth-century speculations on nature is attested to in Montaigne's *Apologie of Raymond Sebond*, where he quotes from Virgil's *Eclogue IV* to show the currency of the concept in classical literature. It is notable, moreover, that the Virgilian text which Montaigne cites explicitly allies the activity of this 'generall soule' with the non-existence of death:

> Some have saide, that there was a generall soule, like unto a great body, from which all particular soules were extracted, and returned thither, alwaies reconjoyning and entermingling themselves unto that Universall matter:
>
> *– Deum namque ire per omnes*
> *Terrasque tractusque maris coelumque profundum:*
> *Hinc pecudes; armenta, viros, genus omne ferarum,*
> *Quemque sibi tenues nascentem arcessere vitas,*
> *Scilicet huc reddi deinde, ac resoluta referri*
> *Omnia: nec morti esse locum.*
>
> For God through all the earth to passe is found,
> Through all sea-currents, through the heav'n profound,
> Heere hence men, heardes and all wylde beasts that are,
> Short life in birth each to themselves doe share.
> And all things resolved to this poynt restor'd,
> Returne, nor any place to death affoord.[14]

This description of the participation of soul in an unending process or 'reconjoyning and entermingling' that is also a 'resolving' is paralleled in the philosophical speculations of Giordano Bruno. Following the pre-Socratic thinker Empedocles, Bruno contended that one 'who would know the greatest secrets of nature [must] observe and contemplate the minimums and the maximums of opposites and contraries',[15] and he emphasized the capacity of the soul to contain and reconcile these differences or opposites within matter:

> If then the spirit, the soul, the life, is found in all things, and it, according to certain gradations, fills all matter, it certainly becomes the true act and the true form of all things. The soul of the world, then, is the formal and constitutive principle of the universe and of that which is contained in it. I say that if life is found in all things, the soul becomes the form of all things. She presides throughout matter and *is dominant in mixtures, effectuates the composition and constituency of the parts.* [my emphasis][16]

A comparable conception of the world soul is articulated by the pagan Queen Cecropia in Sidney's *Arcadia*, to whom is attributed the view that 'one universall Nature, which hath been for ever, is the knitting together of these many partes to such an excellent unity'.[17] But while Sidney frames this opinion as misguided heresy, Shakespeare's figurations of his tragic women imply a persistent interest in just such a universal solvent, able to resolve, if only at the level of tropes, the painful divisions and partitions of bodily, as well as of tragic experience.

The death of Ophelia, as narrated by Gertrude, affords a striking instance of the tragedies' figurative entwining of the complex duality of woman's erotic dying, both with popular festivity, and also with an animating principle within nature which appears to parallel ideas of the world soul. For as nature itself becomes her lover, the deranged young woman's 'muddy death' is troped as a strangely pleasurable, but also implicitly fruitful, surrender to the dirtiness and ambiguity of bodily desire in her watery river-bed. The reversal inherent in an uncanny doubling or mirroring of lovers (of the willow tree in the stream) is central to this paradoxical death-as-conception:

> There is a willow grows askant the brook
> That shows his hoary leaves in the glassy stream.
> Therewith fantastic garlands did she make
> Of crow-flowers, nettles, daisies, and long purples,
> That liberal shepherds give a grosser name,
> But our cold maids do dead men's fingers call them.
> There on the pendent boughs her crownet weeds
> Clamb'ring to hang, an envious sliver broke,
> When down her weedy trophies and herself
> Fell in the weeping brook. Her clothes spread wide,
> And mermaid-like awhile they bore her up,
> Which time she chanted snatches of old lauds,
> As one incapable of her own distress,
> Or like a creature native and indued
> Unto that element. But long it could not be
> Till that her garments, heavy with their drink,
> Pull'd the poor wretch from her melodious lay
> To muddy death.
>
> (4.7.165–82)

In this scene, as commentators have often pointed out, the various plants and flowers afford specific natural images both of Ophelia's sexuality and of her unhappiness in love. But they also trope her as a demented flower-goddess, a May queen who, even in tragedy, displays the attributes of popular festivity. Earlier in her madness, Ophelia has sung of 'sweet Robin', traditionally the King of the May, and her fatal attempt to garland the willow recalls the 'pagan' decorations and garlands associated with the maypole and Mayday festivities which so disgusted the Puritans.[18] The willow was a conventional emblem of disappointment in love, later to be associated with Desdemona in the 'willow song' and also linked by Shakespeare, in *The Merchant of Venice*, with Dido deserted by Aeneas. Yet the masculine and highly eroticized personification of this tree in the *Hamlet* passage also functions to confirm Joel Fineman's emphasis upon its figurative association with masculine 'will' or desire, for as Ophelia goes to 'hang' her circular garland of weeds on its 'hoary leaves', which are mirrored or 'shown' in the stream, the 'pendent' posture of these leaves echoes the hanging of the male genitals.[19]

The contradictory associations of the willow tree encapsulate the perplexing duality of Ophelia's death, as a process of natural decay which is nonetheless 'indued' with the sexual vitality of the May games. The hoariness of the willow's leaves denote its great age, but also hint at the antiquity of the festive and sexual practices associated with it; similarly, while the mould or 'hoar' frost upon these leaves associates it with a wintry process of natural decay, 'hoary' also punningly evokes desire of, and for the sexual woman or 'whore', whose bodily encircling of the male member Shakespeare plays upon repeatedly in his corpus. In slipping into the river, Ophelia's loss of her 'crownet' of flowers functions as a metaphorical defloration; indeed, she appears to fall into the brook backwards, as the Nurse's husband told the infant Juliet that she would do, when 'thou comest to age'. It is now that, as her clothes 'spread' wide, and she sings songs *either* of religious praise *or* of festive joy (in the second Quarto, Ophelia sings 'lauds', but in the first Quarto and Folio, she sings 'tunes'), the inherent ambiguity of Ophelia's death is stressed: she is *either* 'one incapable of her own distress'; *or* 'like a creature native and indued / Unto that element', who is compared by the Queen to a mermaid. 'Mermaid' was a bawdy epithet for a prostitute at this time, which associated sexual activity with submersion in water, as well as with a siren-like song. But while the willow tree is personified as a figure of heterosexual desire, its doubling in the stream implies that there is another lover hidden in this watery mirror, who embraces Ophelia from behind as she falls backwards: this is 'muddy death', whose affinity is seemingly both with the bottom of the river and with the fecal muddiness of the backside.

The bawdy iconography of Ophelia's death suggestively amplifies the play's other representations of death, preceding, yet supplementing Hamlet's morbid – and more conventionally Christian – graveyard meditations upon a skull with a startlingly different mode of dying. At the same time, the metamorphic character of this reported death differs strikingly from Hamlet's own end, which is troped, not in terms of nature and the body, and certainly not as pleasure, but rather as a compulsory submission to a strict masculine force of law and judgement – 'this fell sergeant, Death, / Is strict in his arrest' (5.2.341–2) – that is associated with a more absolute or final 'rest': 'And flights of angels sing thee to thy rest' (5.2.365). In contrast to this Christianized version of death as judgement and ending (arrest/rest), the sexualized *process* of Ophelia's watery dying encompasses imagery of birth or conception (in the reference to her garments as 'heavy with their drink') which has an implicit pagan subtext, recalling the birth of Venus, goddess of love, from the water. In her emblematic dissolution into a muddy 'dew', therefore, Ophelia differs Hamlet's original desire for disembodiment, through resolution 'into a dew', by obliquely personifying the fertilising *return* of this dew, into the muddiness of matter. In *De antro nympharum*, a late classical text whose imagery is echoed in several aspects of Shakespearean 'double dying', Porphyry had observed that, like water nymphs or naiads, incarnating souls settle by water, and that it is therefore 'a delight, not death, for souls to become moist'.[20]

The death of Desdemona performs a more airy version of 'double dying', which focuses upon the equally ambiguous associations of soul with air or wind. Yet this dying likewise combines emphasis upon the strangely porous character of the boundary between life and death with a suggestive doubling of lovers or 'Lords'. As if to dispute Othello's view of death as an absolute and impermeable border, Desdemona comes and goes between life and death for several lines after she has been smothered, 'stirring' even after her murderer has declared her 'still as the grave'; several commentators on Shakespeare's bawdy have noted the use of 'stir' as a pun for copulation. Hence, tragically, but also uncannily, Desdemona does appear to die more than once. Yet the vital result of this ghostly 'stirring' is that Emilia discovers her murder, and performs her mistress's last instruction to 'commend me to my kind lord', by clearing her name. The end of the play leaves uncertain, however, the precise nature of Desdemona's 'lord', as she is effectively wedded to Death by Othello – the Moor who is also the grim representative of *mors*. In the first Quarto of the play, Desdemona exclaims: 'O Lord! Lord! Lord!' as she is smothered (5.2.83). What seems an explicitly religious reference, to the Christian 'lord' whom she expects to meet in the next world, is rendered both ambiguous and more intimate by the next words in the text, as Emilia calls Othello through the chamber door: 'My lord, my lord! what ho, my lord, my lord!' (5.2.84). Emilia's echo of her mistress's words is one of several ways in which Desdemona's voice appears to linger after her presumed death; it further complicates the boundary between death and life, moreover, by leaving us uncertain as to who in fact is 'lord' at this point in the play: in particular, who is 'lord' in relation to death and the other world. It is at precisely this juncture, of course, that Othello's martial authority – his power in relation to life and death – begins to melt away from him.

A long-standing association of the soul with breath, air or wind was derived from the Greek and Latin words *pneuma* and *spiritus*, and Desdemona's Eurydice-like recrossing of the boundary between life and death is imaged as an uncanny survival of that 'balmy' breath which Othello has attempted to extinguish. Indeed, Emilia finally promises to 'be in speaking, liberal as the air' in the second Quarto and Folio, 'north' is substituted for the first Quarto's 'ayre' (5.2.218), presumably a reference to the north wind. Yet this reference by the bawdy Emilia to air's liberality also echoes a chain of carnivalesque and scatological imagery in the play which has been very interestingly elucidated by François Laroque. Commenting on the Shrovetide carnival practice of consuming flatulent foods and then breaking wind, which suggested a correlation between the microcosm of the human body and cosmic forces as a whole, Laroque notes that:

> The importance popularly attached to wind and the circulation of blasts of air at carnival time was also connected with a number of supernatural beliefs, for *gusts of wind were associated with the return of dead souls*, who were thought to roam around freely during the period of the new moon that ushered in the cycle of movable feasts. [my emphasis][21]

He points out that the wind imagery that runs through *Othello* draws on this carnivalesque tradition of fertilising bodily winds. The play initially configures desire as a promiscuous movement of wind which promises to 'swell' Othello's sail, so that he can 'Make love's quick pants in Desdemona's arms' (2.1.78–80); with the advent of his jealousy, however, this is transformed by Othello's imagination into 'The bawdy wind that kisses all it meets', now 'hushed within the hollow mine of earth' (4.2.79–80). Laroque plausibly allies this theme of an airy promiscuity or *ventositas* with the play's carnivalesque interest in the motions of bodily wind or flatulence, evoked both in Iago's scatological-medical figuration of the kiss between Cassio and Desdemona in terms of 'clyster-pipes' (2.1.176), and in the Clown's jesting depiction of the human body as a 'wind instrument' with 'a tail' (3.1.6–10). Amid the festive over-eating which traditionally characterized the carnival days preceding Lent, the strange scatological connection between the windy movements of the soul and farting was often grotesquely imaged by the applications of a bellows to the backside of an ass.[22] In this context, Emilia's final release of breath, after her iteration of "Twill out, 'twill out', probably has carnivalesque, as well as tragic connotations, especially since it prompts her to label Othello as himself a figure of folly, a coxcomb: 'O murderous coxcomb, what should such a fool / Do with so good a wife?' (5.2.231–2).

Through the emphasis upon breath, speech and song in the deaths of Ophelia and Desdemona, there is a significant doubling of the mouth or throat with the sexual genitalia; this particular duplication of 'ends' also assumes figurative importance in *Romeo and Juliet*'s earlier version of 'double dying'. Yet in contrast to the imagery of water and air which informs the deaths of Ophelia and Desdemona, Juliet's double dying is implicated in a network of fiery, solar imagery that is specifically allied with the over-heated season of late summer. Thereby, the play appears to allude to the putative fieriness of soul, and its implicit relationship with the repeated deaths and rebirths of *sol* or sun. Mentioned in Book VI of Virgil's *Aeneid*, the fiery character both of individual souls and of the *anima mundi* was often reiterated by classical commentators; Cicero cited the opinion of the Stoics that a 'creative fire' pervades the world, and Marsilio Ficino wrote that:

> The sun of the world, the substance of natural life, completely possesses and bears that which the rest of the world has parts of. Therefore some have placed the soul of the world in it, on account of its rays being everywhere diffused.[23]

The implication here is that soul is a mediator of the traditional fieriness of spirit; in this respect the world soul paralleled the Christian conception of the Holy Spirit (although the comparison was held by the Church to be heretical), whose first Pentecostal advent was signalled by a rushing wind, but which was described as descending upon the disciples in cloven tongues of flame.[24]

'All things change them to the contrary'

The imagery of carrying or bearing a fire/burden, as an experience that is sometimes analogous to love, at other times to the function of the soul, is a central element in *Romeo and Juliet*'s representation of death's strange duality, as the site of a mysterious chiasmus or reversal of meanings and perceptions. While the clichéd use of oxymoron and paradox as part of the Petrarchan conceit is parodied in Romeo's initial rhetoric about Rosaline, the play implies that his subsequent love for Juliet informs these airy abstractions with a subtle substance, by allying them with an effectively dual view of reality, as highly material yet also simultaneously informed by uncanny or supernatural principles. In Romeo's affected use of the Petrarchan poetic style, love is a 'heavy lightness, serious vanity, . . . / Feather of lead' (1.1.176–8); he tells his friends: 'Under love's heavy burden do I sink' (1.4.22), and speaks at the end of the play of shaking off 'the yoke of inauspicious stars'. The play amplifies Romeo's conceit of light heaviness in diverse ways. In Juliet's 'Gallop apace' speech, the paradox is obliquely evoked in connection with the putative global catastrophe of *ekpyrosis*, or destruction by fire, which was discussed in some ancient philosophy. A particular instance of *ekpyrosis* was attributed by mythographers to the ambitious Phaeton, who had foolishly asked to drive the chariot of his father the Sun; in a needle-work representation of this myth, on a cushion cover owned by Bess of Hardwick, the positioning of the astrological signs in the sky above Phaeton associates his fall with the sign of Leo (Plate 2). Juliet explicitly compares the passionate hastiness of the lovers to that of Phaeton, as she waits for her wedding night: 'Gallop apace, ye fiery footed steeds, / Towards Phoebus' lodging. / Such a waggoner as Phaeton would whip you to the west, / And bring in cloudy night immediately' (3.2.1–4). It was because 'his weight was light' (*leve pondus erat*), according to Ovid, that Phaeton could not control his father's horses:

> The burthen was so light as that the Genets felt it not.
> The wonted weight was from the Waine, the which they well did
> wot.
> For like as ships amids the Seas that scant of ballace have,
> Even so the Waine for want of weight it erst was wont to beare,
> Did hoyse aloft and scayle and reele, as though it empty were.[25]

Although the lovers first meet at a dance, they do not dance together. Yet after this encounter, as Mercutio's punning exchange with Romeo about souls and feet implies, the soles/souls of both Romeo and Juliet appear to acquire an aerial or leaping gait which imitates the levity of Romeo's wordplay with Mercutio, eliciting Friar Lawrence's observation that 'A lover may bestride the gossamers / That idles in the wanton summer air / And yet not fall; so light is vanity', together with his admonition that 'Too swift arrives as tardy as too slow' (2.6.15–20).

Indeed, *Romeo and Juliet* also frames this erotic 'lightness' as a heavy and tragic burden. The play begins with a Capulet servant evoking

Plate 2 The Fall of Phaeton. Cushion cover from Hardwick Hall, Derbyshire, late sixteenth century.

through negation the act of carrying 'coals'; this apparently insignificant image, which introduces the tragedy's imagery of fire, light, and weight, allies it to another mythological transgression – the theft of fire from the gods by Prometheus. The same myth may be alluded to in the reference of Quartos 2 to 4 and the First Folio to the young women at the Capulet ball as 'fresh fennel buds' (1.2.29); according to Hesiod, it was in a hollow fennel stalk that Prometheus hid the glowing coal he stole from Zeus, and Zeus punished man by giving him woman, in the form of Pandora.[26] This motif of fire stolen from heaven in the form of women as 'earth-treading stars' recurs in the lovers' allusions to their love as a 'lightning'. In spite of the implication that the lovers are repeating mythological acts of transgression, their recurrent images of fire, as well as of birds, suggest that the heaviness of both physical desire and of fate confers a peculiar lightness and blessing. Jonathan Bate has argued that through their golden statues Romeo and Juliet 'are granted the sort of metamorphic release which Ovid usually gives his characters but, exceptionally, denies to Phaethon'.[27] Yet in its use of wordplay, the play performs an ongoing work of metamorphosis before death. Mercutio tells Romeo that 'when maids lie on their backs', it is the gossamer-light Queen Mab 'that presses them, / And learns them first to bear, / Making them women of good carriage' (1.5.92–4): in other words, to bear men sexually, and also to give birth.[28] Here the lovers' eroticized 'sinking' under the burden of worldly flesh is at the same time configured as an act of fertilization and engendering, and this reversal is echoed in Romeo's 'lightning before death' in Mantua and in the Capulet tomb. But it is primarily through its representation of Juliet as a 'living corse' that *Romeo and Juliet* invites us to see the body, not only as heaviness – a gross physicality leading to death – but also as light – in its uncanny illumination by an otherworldly presence.

Birthdays, saints' days, and idolatry

The play's figurative reversal of heaviness into lightness is reminiscent of the ritualized inversions of popular festivity or holiday, and indeed the delight in wordplay which is so prominent in the first half of the play is closely related to its interweaving of tragedy with the 'arsy-versy' holiday pleasures and cyclical temporality of comedy.[29] Specifically, the play's imagery of late summer heat allies the implicit duality of a fire-bearing soul-principle with a highly specific calendrical structure of festive play and worship. While festive imagery derived from May Day and Shrove-tide subtly informs the double dyings of Ophelia and Desdemona, *Romeo and Juliet* embeds this peculiar motif (which in this case Shakespeare derived from his primary sources) much more explicitly in a festive context: here, that of late July and Lammastide. Through this device, as the ostensible singularity of tragic time is framed by a seasonal structure of temporal repetition, the exemplary death of Juliet in particular (which significantly occurs just a few days before the anniversary of her birth) is implicitly reconstructed as the site or occasion for a perpetual doubling or repetition, through its quasi-festive memorialization: 'That whiles Verona by that name is known, / There shall no figure at such rate be set / As that of true and faithful Juliet' (5.3.300–2).

In Arthur Brooke's *Romeus and Juliet*, the lovers first meet at a Christmas feast, and their tragedy does not escalate until Easter. In contrast, Shakespeare sets his version of the tragedy in late summer: specifically, just before Juliet's fourteenth birthday, which the Nurse tells us she is to celebrate 'a fortnight and odd days' after the Capulet ball, on 31 July or Lammas Eve. Yet this late summer dating of the tragedy is also intermittently inverted, in calendrical terms, by fleeting references to the season of the year which directly opposed it in the calendar: this was the carnival context of Shrovetide, which heralded the beginning of Lent.[30] Through these fluctuations in its temporal allusions, the play explicitly embeds both Juliet herself, as a 'dear saint' for whom Romeo is 'the god of my idolatry', and also the lovers' brief tragedy in a curiously palimpsestic calendrical structure. Late July was intimately allied with some important forms of popular festivity, most notably pageants and fairs, and also with some important saints' days; yet it also had enormous importance in the astrological time-reckonings of antiquity. In consequence, Shakespeare's setting of the story of his 'star-crossed' lovers at this time has some very complex resonances, which enable him to weave an intricate network of associations between festivity, temporality and the doubling of tragic ends.

In *Shakespeare's Almanac*, David Wiles stresses the complexity of calendrical measurement in Elizabethan England, as a result of the interlocking of what he identifies as five different, and sometimes dissonant time schemes:

1   the Protestant/urban rhythm of the six-day working week in relation to Sunday;
2   the rural/elemental cycle of seasonal change, as well as the oscillation between day and night;
3   the clerical/liturgical rhythm, constituted by the regime of the Prayer Book;
4   the pagan/festive calendar;
5   the astrological calendar, which Wiles argues was more important in the Tudor period than modern scholarship has realized.[31]

What Wiles omits from this catalogue, however, is the Catholic calendar of the saints, which although officially abolished by Protestantism, continued to exert a strong imaginative influence on calendrical observation, as was attested by its reinstatement under James I. In accounts of the Christian liturgical calendar, the month of July is sometimes characterized as marking the beginning of the half-year of 'secular time', but Eamon Duffy has recently re-emphasized its importance in the context of pre-Reformation popular piety in England:

> A major feast of England's most important saint, Thomas Becket, the translation of his relics, fell on 7 July . . . In the same month there were . . . the feasts of St Mary Magdalene [22], St Margaret [20], St James the Apostle [25], and St Anne [26] . . . all were immensely popular and very widely kept.[32]

Duffy notes too that before the Reformation the great civic festivities of the year were often observed at the end of July or on the first day of August (Lammas):

> At Lincoln, the greatest convergence of civic and sacred ceremonial came on Saint Anne's day, at the end of July, when the city gilds organized an elaborate series of pageants. Even at York, where the most famous Corpus Christi cycle in England was normally played on the feast day itself, the Creed play and

the Paternoster plays which sometimes replaced the Corpus Christi plays were performed in Lammastide.[33]

Many of the most popular saints' days of this period were excised from the liturgical calendar in 1536 at the Reformation, partly to increase the time available for agricultural labour: 'all feast days falling in harvest, from 1 July to 29 September . . . were abolished, excepting only feasts of the Apostles, the Blessed Virgin, and St George'. This left only the feast day of St James the Apostle, on 25 July, which had enjoyed increased significance before the Reformation, because it was then shared by St James with the gigantic Christ-bearer, St Christopher. Not until a decade later, however, between 1547 and 1548, were the images of saints ordered to be removed from churches or defaced.[34] Both the slowness and the uncertainty of this process of reform was attested to on the accession of Elizabeth I in 1559: on the one hand, there was another wave of image destruction; on the other, many saints' days were reintroduced. A 1563 convocation voiced the dissatisfaction of many clergy at the continued existence of saints' days, but it seems that 'purging the calendar was easier to proclaim than enforce'. David Cressy points out that law terms were still marked by the ancient religious festival days, as were the legal calendars of all courts operating by civil rather than common law, while popular almanacs likewise kept in mind memories of holy days that the reformers would rather have seen suppressed. In areas with a developed culture of recusancy, however, amongst which the counties of Lancashire and Warwickshire were foremost, this memorial survival would presumably have been far more complete.[35] Amidst this uneven process of cultic extirpation, the end of July and beginning of August seem to have retained a symbolic significance, primarily as marking the official end of summer, the first fruits of the harvest and (specifically at Lammas), the time of a quarterly payment of rents and the opening of common lands for pastures. A catalogue of fairs in 1661 showed that 58 towns had fairs on St James's Day, 28 on Lammas; it was probably no coincidence, also, that James I and his queen, Anna, were crowned on 25 July, the date of St James's Day and the eve of St Anne's Day.[36]

Shakespeare's decision to accord a specific temporality to his tragedy of *Romeo and Juliet* draws upon this residual Catholic culture of holy days. Not only would he have been especially aware of this festive calendar as a young man growing up in Warwickshire (where there were two churches of St James the Great in his immediate vicinity: one in Stratford-on-Avon itself, and another in his grandfather's village of Snitterfield); the memorial importance of this period of holy days would have been augmented for the son of a probably recusant father, most of whose mother's family, the Ardens, also retained their Catholic faith. Shakespeare's father was reputedly given a copy of *The Spiritual Testament of St Charles Borromeo* by the Jesuit priest and martyr Edmund Campion, and it now seems highly plausible, as Ernst Honigmann and Richard Wilson have argued, that the young Shakespeare spent part of the 1580s in the Catholic household of the Hoghtons of Lancashire: a family whom we now know to have had very close links with Edmund Campion during his English mission.[37] It is perhaps not wholly coincidental, in this connection, that the 'fearful date' of the lovers' first meeting, and the beginning of their tragedy, seems to be the eve or day of 16 July. This was the date of an event which sent shock waves through the entire recusant community in the Midlands and North of England, for it was on that day in 1581, some fourteen years before Shakespeare's presumed composition of his play, that Campion was finally arrested, while saying mass at a house outside Oxford. An additional coincidence is that the date chosen by Shakespeare for Juliet's anticipated fourteenth birthday, 'a fortnight and odd days' later, was 31 July; this was the day on which Campion was first put to the rack.[38] (31 July was also the date of death in 1556 of the founder of the Jesuits, Ignatius Loyola; when Loyola was canonized in the seventeenth century, it became his feast day.)

Not only is the language of idolatry integral to the lovers' courtship, their tragedy ends with the families' election of the striking memorial device of two golden statues, in what seems a final idolatrous echo of the cults of the saints; *The Second Tome of Homelyes*, published in 1563, inveighs against 'the glorious gylte images and ydolles [of the saints], all shynynge and glytterying with metall and stone, and covered with precious vestures'.[39] Only the saints Francis and Peter are specifically mentioned in the play; St Peter, to whose church Juliet is to be dragged by Capulet in order to marry Paris, 'on a hurdle', like a condemned traitor or recusant priest going to his death, had 1 August or Lammas as one of his feast days, when his miraculous liberation from prison was commemorated by the feast of St Peter-in-Chains. St Peter's name, with its inevitable 'Roman' connotations, is echoed in that of the Capulet serving man, Peter, while the name of another Capulet servant, Samson, as well as that of the 'holy' Friar Lawrence, evoke two other saints associated with this calendrical period – St Samson, 28 July and St Lawrence, 10 August. At the same time, the name of the other Capulet servant, Gregory, was not only a familiar saint's name, but also that of numerous Popes, including St Gregory the Great (sometimes called the apostle of the English), who had famously affirmed the legitimate use of icons, and Pope Gregory XIII, who in 1582 had reformed the calendar. Yet there is also an implied and seemingly very significant allusion to a still more notable saint of this late summer period, in the decision of Romeo, on his way to the Capulet ball, to be a light-bearer: 'Give me a torch, I am not for this ambling; / Being but heavy, I will bear the light' (1.4.11–12). St Christopher, who shared his holy day of 25 July with St James, owed his name to the story of his carrying the Christ-child (the light of the world) over a river. St Christopher's association with travel linked him, like St James, with pilgrimage to the shrines of saints, and it is as a 'pilgrim' and 'palmer' that Romeo subsequently presents himself at Juliet's 'shrine'.

'The moneth of out-rage' (5.3.216, Q4)

Yet the putative traces within the play, both of pre-Reformation festivities, and of a residual Catholic 'idolatry' which may have had an additional layer of tragic topicality for those associated with recusancy, are juxtaposed with prominent allusions to the stars. The lovers are 'star-crossed' by a 'consequence yet hanging in the stars', and while Romeo sees 'Two of the fairest stars in all the heaven' in Juliet's eyes, she asks Night 'when I shall die' to 'Take him and cut him out in little stars'. These allusions hint at the influence upon the text of another, astrological calendar, which had been influential in antiquity, and was still acknowledged in popular almanacs. In this stellar calendar, the latter part of July and most of August was described as the 'canicular', or dog days, since this was the time of the heliacal rising of the brightest star in the sky, Sirius, chief star of the constellation Canis Major, when it was once more visible on the horizon just before dawn (Plates 3a and 3b).[40] In its extended use of imagery related to the dog days, *Romeo and Juliet* affords a suggestive parallel to a group of French texts whose interest in this season of the year has been pointed out by Claude Gaignebet: this is François Rabelais' narrative of his grotesque family of giants, in his comic romances of Gargantua and Pantagruel.[41] Like *Romeo and Juliet*, Rabelais' *Pantagruel* and *Tiers Livre* combine focus upon the complex calendrical significance of the month of July with exploration of mankind's relationship to extreme heat and fiery passions; at the same time, in their emphasis on the pleasures of feasting, these books also associate eating with a descent into the jaws, or mouth, of death.

Associated visually with the 'enormous gaping jaws' of Leo, Sirius was positioned in the mouth of the greater dog constellation, like a fiery torch: 'The tip of his [Canis Major's] terrible jaw is marked by a star that keenest of all blazes with a searing flame and him men call Serius'.[42] The dog-days were traditionally a time of dramatic climactic extremes,

.LIBER III,   93

A   Lælaps.   ♋

Canis maior habet unam in capite primæ magni-
tudinis, nomine Alhabor, splendidissimam stellam, Ve
neri ferè similem. Habet deinde quoq; tertiæ magnitu
dinis unam in pede dextro, alteram in coxa sinistra,
tertiam inter duas coxas, quartam in extremitate cau
dæ, et quintam in extremitate pedis dextri. reliquæ in
auribus, collo, pectore & genibus sunt quartæ et quin
tæ magnitudinis.

Canis leporem fugientem con-
sequēs, posterioribus pedibus
diuiditur ab hyemali circulo, pedem
dextrū Orionis penè suo capite con
iungēs, capite ad occasum spectans,
sed caput ad æquinoctialem circulum tendit. occidens oriente sagittario, ex-
oriens autem cum cancro, habet in lingua stellam unam quę Canis appellatur.
in capite autem alteram, quam nonnulli Sirion appellāt, de quo prius diximus.
Praeterea habet in utrisque auribus obscuras singulas. In pectore dyas, in pede
priore tres, inter scapulas tres, in sinistro lumbo unā, in pede posteriore unam,
In pede dextro unam, in cauda quatuor. omnino sunt decem & nouem.

Plate 3a 'Laelaps' or Canis Major. *Hyginus fabularum liber* (Basel: 1549). By
permission of the Syndics of Cambridge University Library.

graphically figured by the ancients as a fiery devouring mouth which,
by *doubling* 'the burning heat of the sun', initiates an annual experience of
ekpyrosis:

> When the lion of Nemea [the constellation of Leo] lifts into view
> his enormous gaping jaws, the brilliant constellation of the Dog
> appears: it barks forth flame, raves with its fire, and doubles the
> burning heat of the sun. When it puts its torch to the earth and
> discharges its rays, the earth foresees its conflagration, and
> tastes its ultimate fate . . . the world looks for another world to
> repair it.[43]

The Roman astronomers Aratus and Manilius stressed the perplexing
duality of Sirius' effects:

> When he rises with the sun, no longer do the trees deceive him
> by the feeble freshness of their leaves. For easily with his keen
> glance he pierces their ranks, and to some he gives strength but
> of others he blights the bark utterly.[44]

> No star comes on mankind more violently or causes more
> trouble when it departs. Now it rises shivering with cold, now it

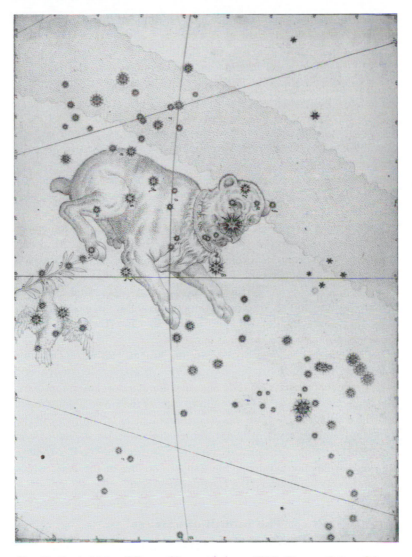

Plate 3b Canis Major. J Bayer, *Uranometria* (n.p.: 1603). By permission of the Syndics of Cambridge University Library.

leaves a radiant world open to the heat of the Sun: thus it moves the world to either extreme and brings opposite effects. Those who . . . observe it ascending when it returns at its first rising learn of the various outcomes of harvest and seasons, what state of health lies in store, and what measure of harmony. It stirs up war and restores peace, and returning in different guise affects the world with the glance it gives it and governs with its mien. Sure proof that the star has this power are its colour and the quivering of the fire that sparkles in its face. Hardly is it inferior to the Sun . . . In splendour it surpasses all other constellations.[45]

The association of Sirius with a seasonal extreme that could be fatal to crops extended to both humans and animals; in his discussion of the agricultural associations of this period in antiquity, Marcel Detienne concludes that the appearance of the Dog Star was thought to inaugurate a period of exaggerated imbalance in humans, animals and plants, which involved a switching between opposite extremes.[46] The dog days were seen as a time of erotic madness, when, according to Hesiod, 'women are most wanton, but men are feeblest, because Sirius parches head and knees, and the skin is dry through heat', at the same time, the star was thought to cause outbreaks of rabies (in French, *la rage*) which engendered madness in dogs.[47] Some versions of these ancient superstitions survived in Europe until the seventeenth century; incredibly, it seems to have been quite widely believed that to have sexual intercourse or to take medicine during the dog days was dangerous.[48]

Yet it was also because of the extreme heat of this time, Detienne points out, that the most precious spices – frankincense, myrrh and balsam – could be harvested. The ancient commentators knew, therefore, that while the canicular days brought to most of the world a doubling of solar heat which could have *disastrous* consequences (connoting injuries resulting from the stars), it could also confer exceptional blessings; in Egyptian antiquity, the heliacal rising of Sirius had marked a time of renewed fertility by heralding the annual flooding of the Nile, which simultaneously inaugurated the Egyptian new year.

'The mouth of outrage'

When the nurse tells Romeo that the letter which begins his name is 'the dog's name, R is for the –' (2.5.205), she is connecting the growling 'ar' of the dog with the arse. And in its exploration of both the disastrous and the beneficial aspects of this 'moneth of out-rage', which in Quartos 2 and 3 as well as the Folio text is 'the mouth of outrage', the play's interweaving of festivity and death with a calendrical specificity identifies this fiery devouring month/mouth with a familiar aspect of time – as devouring time – but also with the sexual heat of the genitals or back-side.[49] The apparently trivial wordplay between the two Capulet servants in the opening scene of the play inaugurates this fiery imagery, which is immediately suggested by the name of the first servant, whose biblical namesake, Samson, was allegorically interpreted as a type of the sun, and whose most famous exploits involve a very curious, and seemingly symbolic focus, upon death's relationship to fruitfulness, to fiery ends and devouring mouths: tying firebrands to the tails of three hundred foxes and setting them among his enemies' corn, killing a thousand Philistines with the jawbone of an ass, slaying a lion with his bare hands and subsequently discovering bees and honey in its decomposing carcase.[50] Sampson and Gregory perform a comic parody both of Samson's exemplary biblical heroism and of his mystical riddling, but their quibbles on *coal–collar–choler* and *maidenhead* anticipate some of the play's recurring motifs, in figurative oppositions of darkness to light/heat and mouths/necks/throats to the genitals:

Sampson: Gregory, on my word, we'll not carry coals.
Gregory: No, for then we should be colliers.
Samp: I mean, and we be in choler, we'll draw.
Greg: Ay, while you live, draw your neck out of collar. . . .
Samp: I will show myself a tyrant, when I have fought with the men, I will be civil with the maids; I will cut off their heads.
Greg: The heads of the maids?
Samp: Ay, the heads of the maids, or their maidenheads, take it in what sense thou wilt.
Greg: They must take it in sense that feel it.

                                                                (1.1.1–24)

To 'carry coals' was a colloquialism for accepting an insult; however, the additional sense here is of a material blackness which can become inflamed, through a 'choler' or rage that may lead either to literal death (the 'collar' of the hangman's noose) or to a sexual dying (the lost maid-enheads).[51] The seasonal, or canicular, character of this rage is implied not just in Sampson's implied association (through his biblical namesake) with the lion, but also in his attribution of choler to 'a dog of the house of Montague'. At the same time, the servants' riddling exchanges introduce the crucial question of what 'sense' to make of such jests; the physical sense is clear enough, and may encompass an unspoken play on 'coal' and *cul*, French for the backside or arse (thereby evoking the biblical Samson's additional connection with foxes' tails and with an ass). Yet in their biblical and religious associations, the servants' names appear to hint at another level of meaning, and a possible allusion to that iconoclastic repetition of martyrdom which typically involved cutting off

41

the heads of saints' statues, in order to extirpate their cults (from the Latin *colere*, to venerate).

Later in the first act, this ambivalent throat/mouth imagery is associated with Juliet herself, whose weaning 'aleven years' ago the Nurse remembers though its metonymic association with the earthquake, in a troubling anticipation of that subterranean opening or 'maw' in which the lovers will literally die. In this connection, her charge's nickname echoes suggestively within the Nurse's tediously repetitive narrative: while the Nurse's juxtaposition of 'Jule' with 'Ay' echoes the month's own name, Lammas was sometimes called the Gule of August in the middle ages (a word whose probable derivation is from Celtic words for feast) and 'Jule' has a homonymic affinity with *gula* and *gueule*, the Latin and French words for mouth.[52]

Both the nurturing and the devouring associations of the mouth are implied in the lovers' first meetings; at the feast, Romeo tropes Juliet's mouth as 'saint's lips', while in Act 5 he reports a dream in which, as he imagines himself to be dead, she 'breath'd such life with kisses in my lips / That I reviv'd, and was an emperor' (5.1.8–9). In the balcony scene, however, their love is imaged in terms of the predatory avian mouths of hawks: the 'tassel-gentle' and the 'niesse'. In falconry, the hawk's hunting instinct to fly upwards with its prey, towards the sun which it was said to represent for the ancient Egyptians, has to be trained and redirected though the hooding of their eyes, and as she waits for her wedding night, Juliet asks Night to 'Hood my unmanned blood, bating in my cheeks, / With thy black mantle' (3.2.14–15).[53] Through these avian tropes, as the idea of sexual dying is expanded to encompass physical death as a mutual feasting, the Platonic figuring of the second death as a *mors osculi*, or kiss of death, is given a highly material application. According to Pico della Mirandola, in this second death the lover unites with the 'heavenly' aspect of his beloved in 'an indissoluble embrace':

> Each transfers its own soul into the other with kisses; it is not so much that they exchange souls, as that they are so perfectly joined together that each of them can be called two souls, and both can be called a single soul.[54]

Yet it is consistent with her natal association with the Lammas festival of the first fruits of the harvest that the feast which is focused upon at the end of the play is chiefly provided by 'the feasting presence' of Juliet's body, as that 'dearest morsel of the earth' upon which death's 'detestable maw' has 'gorg'd' itself. Juliet's status as food, implicit in the lovers' meeting at the Capulet feast, is reiterated by the hurried culinary preparations for her wedding to Paris which immediately precede the discovery of her 'death', and is confirmed by the 'sticking' of rosemary on her 'fair corse': while it was strewn at both weddings and funerals, the verb 'to stick' relates to the herb's culinary usage, as an aid to both taste and digestion, whereby it was 'stuck' in an incision made by a knife in a joint of meat. Juliet's 'sticking' with the rosemary whose affinity with Romeo has already been stressed by the Nurse therefore identifies her lover both with a culinary-erotic act of incision which is repeated in her death-wound, and also with her body's herbal garnish, itself doubled with his death on her 'corse'.

This representation of death as a quasi-sexual feasting is reminiscent of the medlar image identified with Romeo's mistress by Mercutio, for the fruit of this 'open-arse' tree can only be consumed when it is rotten. Grotesque horror, but also a sense of the seasonal significance of this feast, is evoked in the Prince's command to 'Seale up the mouth / month of outrage for a while'; at the same time, his words echo the Prologue's reference to 'their parents' rage, / Which, but their children's end, nought could remove' (10–11). In Rabelais' *Pantagruel*, enormous medlars or *mesles* grow from the blood shed by Cain in his murder of Abel his brother, an image of the paradoxical harvest of familial or civil strife. As another unexpected 'fruit' of civil strife, the lovers' rotten ends may 'seal up', if only for a time, the potential for 'out-rage' or tragedy; yet the anticipated duplication of the lovers' decaying bodies by less mutable golden statues reminds us of the wider preoccupation of the play, with a calendrical process of seasonal repetition and cultural memorialization in which endings are endlessly duplicated, along with their peculiar conversion into fruitfulness and festivity. Certainly the play's cumulative network of imagery leaves us with the distinct impression that the double dying(s) of Romeo and Juliet – whether as a textual or as a bodily *and* spiritual matter – remains open rather than closed.

3

ECHOIC LANGUAGE AND TRAGIC IDENTITY

Hamlet (1600)

What needs / This iterance, woman?

(Othello, 5.2.145–6)

Rethinking and liberating that which has been relegated to Greek *physis* [nature] – allowing it to speak, perhaps making it speak differently, in new spaces, within entirely new structural configurations . . . this project has everything to do with woman and thus with women.[1]

This observation by Alice Jardine defines the task of feminist theory as an undoing of those intellectual bonds which have constrained our ideas of nature in the modern era. But how could nature 'speak'? What would be the distinguishing marks of such a discourse or, more plausibly, of such a resonance? Would a resonance of or in nature effect a differing of previous conceptions of nature, or *physis*, in the performance of what Jacques Derrida has described as '*physis* in *différance*'? And would this communicative 'difference' have a close affinity with the degraded category of woman, to whom nature has so often been compared, or would it precisely work to undo the perceived binary opposition between the sexes? This chapter argues that an obscure elemental vocality reverberates throughout Shakespearean tragedy: a tragic resonance in or through nature and the body which some of the recent concerns of deconstruction and feminist theory can usefully elucidate.

Along with its apparent privileging of writing or *écriture*, postmodern literary theory has also heightened our sensitivity to those rifts or gaps within literary, and especially poetic, language which are created by effects of voice or rhythm. Martin Heidegger saw sound and rhythm (which he distinguished from metre) as the key to the alternating play, within poetry, of what he termed 'revealing' and 'concealing', or presence and absence. In the work of Jacques Derrida, it is likewise tonality, in its appeal not to the eye but to the ear, which creates those *double entendres* that mark the uncanny materiality of textual language. He prefaces *Margins of Philosophy* with a suggestive disquisition on the relationship between textuality and the potential dislocation of meaning produced in the *tympan* or tympanum of the ear. The ear serves here as the figure for 'the timbered time between writing and speech', since 'this thing, a tympanum, punctures or grafts itself'.[2] In this trope of grafting, together with its play on 'timbre' and 'timber' (used as a synonym in the English Renaissance for unformed matter, or *silva*), Derrida's meta-phorization of the ear reminds us that the phon(em)ic resonances within the literary text have a specific materiality. But they are also frequently personified as female: Maurice Blanchot, for example, comments of the narrative voice that she [*la voix*] is a 'spectral, phantom-like effect', 'always different from that which proffers it, she is the indifferent difference that alters the personal voice'.[3] In remapping the subtle intersections within Shakespearean tragedy of gender, poetic language and philosophical concepts of nature, Julia Kristeva's specifically feminist analysis of this resonant polysemy of poetic language is of especial relevance.[4]

In *The Revolution of Poetic Language*, Kristeva borrows the philosophical concept of *chora* from Platonic cosmology in order to explore the con-tinuing influence, within language, of a pre-oedipal stage of psychic development in which the child is still dependent upon the mother and the mother's body. In Plato's *Timaeus*, *chora* signifies that primal matter which is the stuff of creation, as an obscure 'receptacle of becoming' whose maternal attributes are explicitly noted.[5] Plato's *chora* is marked by a perplexing formlessness, by a constant mobility and flux, and, according to Kristeva, it is the rhythmic fluctuations of *chora*, or of language as process (*la signifiance*), that unsettle the relationship of the 'I', or ego, both to its objects of knowledge and to the symbols of authority which it internalizes on its entry into language and the symbolic order. The dynamic properties of language associated with the semiotic *chora* are manifested most notably in moments when sound takes precedence over sense: for example, in a poetic recombining of language with musicality, or in that homophonic play upon words which is funda-mental to paronomasia or punning. In this unsettling or reordering of linguistic meanings through sound, Kristeva suggests, there is a return of the hidden materiality of language which exists as a musical tonality before it becomes meaningful utterance. The affinity between this disruption and physical desire is suggested in the sexual and bodily import of many puns and 'paragrams'. And the association of *chora* with a multiple, rather than a singular, individualized mode of communication is also suggested by Kristeva's stress on the production, through the collision between semiotic and symbolic operations, of a 'polylogic' discourse; her subsequent comparision of *chora* to the *chorus* of Greek drama, as a 'dancing receptacle', also hints at its connection with bodily expression and gesture.[6]

The Kristevan *chora* is a paradoxical place, as well as process, allied with both generation and destruction. Its constant undermining of the stability of the 'I' within signification confirms the affinity of this originary and maternal receptacle with those death drives which Freud had allied to the *id*: 'The place of the subject's creation, the semiotic *chora* is also the place of its negation, where its unity gives way before the process of charges and stases producing that unity'.[7] In this association with the uncanny realm of death or unbeing, together with a musicality, or resonance, within language that evokes the memory of a body that, while inhabiting a broadly feminine sphere dominated by the mother and 'natural' forces (the drives), is as yet unmarked by gender, Kristeva's *chora* affords a suggestive parallel to the classical mythology of the nymph Echo.[8]

Tragic resonance

In early versions of her myth, such as that of Longus, Echo was accorded a musical skill by the Muses which was envied by Pan himself, who also resented her chaste rejection of his advances. In revenge, the god caused Echo's death and dismemberment, but he could not eliminate her song. This was preserved within the earth, which had compassionately buried Echo's scattered limbs:

> The Earth in observance of the Nymphs buried them all [Echo's bones], preserving to them still their musick-property: and they by an everlasting Sentence and decree of the Muses breathe out a voice, and they imitate all things now, as she did when before a Maid, the Gods, Men, Organs, Beasts: Pan himself she imitates too, when he plays on the Pipe . . . [9]

The echoic voice is here allied with a feminine mimetic resonance which uncannily survives the loss of a body through dismemberment and death, through Echo's assimilation into nature. As the absent figure of a pure or disembodied voice, Echo is also the wind or *afflatus* that uses nature as its acoustic echo chamber (in *Twelfth Night*, Viola describes her as 'the babbling gossip of the air'), and was therefore often allegorized as the *spiritus* or breath of vocal inspiration. For this reason Renaissance writers often cited Macrobius' comparison of Echo to the world soul, as a hidden agent of (vocal) harmony within nature.[10] Sir Francis Bacon described Echo as an image of true 'discourse': 'which echoes most faithfully the voices of the world itself, and is written as it were at the world's dictation'.[11] But in *Metamorphoses* Book III, the Ovidian representation of this 'babling Nymph' (as Echo was called by Golding) also associates her with a dangerous excess in speech, in an account often moralized as a warning against a rhetorical *afflatus* that leads to inflation and error: the English mythographer Abraham Fraunce observed: '*Eccho* noteth bragging and vaunting, which being contemned and despised, turneth to a bare voyce, a winde, a blast, a thing of nothing'.[12]

In Ovid, although Echo has already been restricted by the punishment of Juno to the possession of a purely echoic voice, she is still embodied; it is her unrequited love for Narcissus which wastes the nymph's body away until finally she is nothing more than voice. Narcissus's fateful drowning and subsequent metamorphosis into a flower is his punishment for this solipsistic rejection of Echo as well as others, and his fate is proleptically evoked in Echo's plaintive iterations, which subtly unsettle the beautiful male's control of his words along with his self-absorption. Yet Jonathan Bate notes that Ovid's version of the myth also allies Echo's excess in speech with a transgressive and deceitful female sexuality:

> The point is that she blabs, she talks too much: her skill in speech was such that she succeeded in detaining Juno in conversation, giving her fellow nymphs the time to finish making love to Jove and then run away before the angry goddess could get to them. That is why her tongue is curbed. In the moralizing tradition, the figure thus becomes a type for the woman of active tongue who must be silenced – in short, the shrew who must be tamed.[13]

Echo could consequently serve as the figure for a surfeit of either feminine or masculine speech; similarly, while Kristeva defines her *chora* as a broadly feminine sphere, it crucially precedes the inauguration of sexual difference. Echo likewise denotes an inherently paradoxical conjunction of presence with absence, since she personifies an uncanny property within language which Renaissance allegorizations of her myths could interpret both as a divine or spiritual surplus to ordinary human speech (the *afflatus* of poetic inspiration), but also as a disturbing reminder of words' potential errancy. As the ghostly voice of one both dead and dismembered, Echo's mournful reverberations can mark the deficiency which forever haunts literary, rather than spoken language, as a site of bodily absence or loss. Yet Echo's resonant surfeit of signification may also be used to indicate the contradictory desire to use language to restore a pre-linguistic plenitude of meanings. This ambiguity is especially apparent in Echo's close connection with the homophone or the pun.

'Nothing' in excess

Abraham Fraunce equates Echo with 'nothing', and the most striking forms of echoic utterance in Shakespearean tragedy are associated with female characters who contribute similarly, both rhetorically and emblematically, to a reduction of tragic language to 'nothing'. This suggestive differing of a masculine tragic rhetoric by or in relation to female characters may appropriately be labelled 'feminine'; however, like the echoic effects of the 'babling Nymph' herself, the process is not restricted to a place of simple sexual opposition, since the boy actors who perform these parts occupy an ambiguous position of bodily, as well as vocal, difference (neither wholly male, nor female); so Banquo declares of the weird sisters: 'you should be women, / And yet your beards forbid me to interpret / That you are so' (1.3.45–7). In fact, I will argue below that the unique rhetorical status of Hamlet, as a tragic protagonist whom Joel Fineman has described as a figure 'placed between maternal presence and paternal absence', is closely allied to his brilliant manipulation of a notably echoic mode of language: the pun.[14]

The Italian humanist Francesco Piccolomini wrote that 'without a divine *afflatus* [rhetorical inspiration] man cannot be elevated to the divine'.[15] Yet Jonathan Goldberg points out that:

> Entrance into voice . . . although it may mean arrival on the scene of power, always bears its equivocations. When speech occurs, when the voice sounds, there is always another in the voice, an otherness that accompanies the utterer.[16]

And while the tragic soliloquy is conventionally regarded as the pinnacle of Shakespeare's dramatic achievement, it is in fact one of the recurring implications of these plays that, although a potent emblem of worldly power, the display of verbal skills is not necessarily a sign of profound insight or knowledge. Writing in Florence in 1485, Pico della Mirandola was already impatient of the humanist obsession with rhetoric or *oratio*; he argued in a letter to Ermolao Barbaro that this was by no means synonymous with what he termed *ratio*, the highest use of the intellect or reason (which he attributed rather to philosophy).[17] In England, in the second half of the sixteenth century, the elaboration of highly rhetorical and courtly styles of literary language coincided with a very different cultural emphasis, upon the limitations of an elaborate or courtly style of language, and an emphasis upon 'plain speech'. This trend was especially marked in texts influenced by an extreme and anti-courtly Protestantism; yet Michel de Montaigne expressed a similar distrust of 'words and language, a merchandise so vulgar and vile that the more a man has the less he is probably worth', while Ben Jonson, who (like Montaigne) was no Puritan, wrote in *Timber: or Discoveries*: 'A *wise tongue* should not be licentious, and wandring; but mov'd and (as it were) govern'd with certaine raines from the heart, and bottome of the brest'.[18]

This fear of a rhetorical copiousness running out of control may be attributed in part to that disturbing polyvalency in the words of the vernacular tongues which the Renaissance delight in punning was making so apparent (although to this extent the Renaissance was only rediscovering a pleasure which had been well-known to the writers of classical antiquity). Probably the most common referent of the bawdy pun was the sexualized or figuratively 'open' female body, and Patricia Parker has shown how Renaissance anxieties about rhetorical excess or *dilatio* often compare this performative surplus to the 'dilated' body of the whore or harlot.[19] In their persistent implication that the body is the ultimate referent of all language, as not only its origin but also its end, in the final speechlessness of death, the multiple puns that are embedded within Shakespeare's tragic language destabilize that authority which is typically enacted in the rhetorical excesses of his male protagonists. The plays' much discussed puns on 'nothing' are especially suggestive in this connection, by implicitly eliding the concept of extinction with two orifices, the vagina with the mouth (the word appears to have connoted, not only genital sexuality, but also, as 'O', the mouth shaped to produce speech).[20] 'O' is frequently used by the male protagonist as an exclamatory utterance in his final tragic catastrophe: 'O Desdemon!, dead, Desdemon. Dead! O, O!' (*Othello*, 5.2.279); 'O thou'lt come no more, / Never, never, never, never, never. / Pray you undo this button. Thank you, sir, / O, o, o, o' (*Lear* 5.3.306–8); 'The rest is silence, O, o, o, o' (*Hamlet*, F, 5.2.363). In these elisions of the inexpressible shock of tragic *anagnorisis* with an implied return to a maternal origin through echoes of an infantile babble, language is reduced to one bare, but potent – because potentially generative – vowel-sound: or to what Maurice Charney has called a series of 'O-groans'.[21]

Several of Shakespeare's tragic catastrophes focus the audience's as well as other characters' attention upon that 'O' which is the mouth of the female corpse. This orifice is suggested to be an enigmatic and inherently contradictory emblem, wherein to be 'dead as earth', as Lear exclaims of Cordelia, is simultaneously figured as a possible opening of breath or spirit: an *afflatus* whose meaning may oscillate, as in Desdemona's double dying, between the supernatural and the scatological. Shakespeare's use of the female mouth to signify something which is undecidable or uncanny begins with the grotesque streams of blood which flow from the mouth of the raped and mutilated Lavinia in *Titus Andronicus*. Different versions of this motif reappear in the 'niesse' Juliet's affinity with the predatory mouth of death as she lies in the 'maw' of the Capulet tomb; in the riddling songs of Ophelia; in the imperfectly stifled Desdemona; and in the unfinished death speech of Cleopatra. This recurring focus upon the lips of a dead or suffering woman implies that her mouth may provide a bodily opening or gateway to the other world, one which both resembles and differs from that afforded by the female pudendum. The lips were often referred to as the gateway of the soul, and a figurative (and O-sounding) connection between mouth, gateway, and death was certainly familiar to speakers of Latin, where *os* could signify gate or portal, bone, as well as mouth.

Insincere echoes

Central to the tragedies' exploration of that vivid equation made by the furiously self-loathing, compulsively rhetorical Hamlet, between a surplus of 'words' and 'whores', is a cluster of disturbingly eloquent as well as powerful women, often depicted as punitive mother-figures, who briefly mimic and exploit for their own ends the superabundant discursive activity of a patriarchal culture: Tamora, Lady Macbeth, Volumnia, the Player Queen in *Hamlet*, Goneril and Regan. And several of these female characters additionally personify the grotesque horror encoded in Shakespeare's tragic 'O's, as they elide the dilations of a corrupt political rhetoric with bodily openings or dilations that are similarly amoral. This gynaphobic strand of Shakespearean tragedy is also explicitly 'reginaphobic', since by associating the misuse of a courtly language of compliment with whoring, these plays repeatedly depict the tragedy queen as a 'quean' or harlot. Surprisingly, given its dangerous topicality, this queen-as-quean motif is already explicit in Shakespeare's Elizabethan drama, notably *Henry VI* and *Titus Andronicus*. In *Titus*, the connection of a feminine rhetorical performance that is explicitly figured as echoic with both female sexuality and the violence of physical extinction (imaged as consumption by the 'O' of genital pit or mouth) is graphically staged.[22] It seems hardly accidental that in the play's pivotal forest scene, Tamora – the captured Queen of the Goths who has become Empress of Rome – is portrayed both as a parodic version of Diana, the goddess of wild nature, hunting and chastity to whom Elizabeth was most frequently compared, and also as another Dido, the Carthaginian queen of Virgil's *Aeneid*, whose other title of Elissa encouraged her comparison to Eliza or Elizabeth.

In her woodland meeting with her black lover Aaron, Tamora displays a manly or 'mannerly' language of great poetic fluency, with overt Virgilian overtones; however, her reference to a 'babbling echo' which 'mockingly' confuses the sounds of nature and culture marks this performance as dangerously different from other forms of cultural mimesis. And indeed, this lyrical episode occurs just before she is discovered by Titus' daughter Lavinia and her husband Bassianus, whereupon, just as Diana punished Actaeon, Tamora wreaks a terrible vengeance for her exposure *in flagrante*:

> The birds chant melody on every bush,
> The snake lies rolléd in the cheerful sun,
> The green leaves quiver with the cooling wind,
> And make a chequered shadow on the ground:
> Under their sweet shade, Aaron, let us sit,
> And whilst the babbling echo mocks the hounds,
> Replying shrilly to the well-tuned horns,
> As if a double hunt were heard at once,
> Let us sit down and mark their yellowing noise:
> And after conflict such as was supposed
> The wandering prince and Dido once enjoyed,
> When with a happy storm they were surprised,
> And curtained with a counsel-keeping cave,
> We may, each wreathed in each other's arms,
> (Our pastimes done) possess a golden slumber,
> Whiles hounds and horns and sweet melodious birds
> Be unto us as is a nurse's song
> Of lullaby to bring her babe asleep.
>
> (2.3.12–29)

In its overt Virgilian resonances, Tamora's speech appears to interweave an epic and heroic strain with a refined courtly pastoralism. But as Virgilian commentators often pointed out, the setting of a forest (*silva* in Latin) allegorically evokes the disorderliness of primal matter (as *silva, hyle* or *chora*), and Tamora's echoic deployment of this courtly poetic idiom redirects attention to sound rather than sense, as the prelude to her surrender to bodily sense in the arms of Aaron. Since Tamora's speech attributes an echo of the Dido–Aeneas episode from Virgil's epic poem to an Empress of Rome, its emphasis upon the gratification rather than the curbing of desire suggests a disturbing inversion of the morality of Virgil's hero Aeneas, whose repeated attribute of 'pius' is now Titus' surname, and who had sacrificed Dido and desire to the needs of empire. Moreover, the poetry's textual echoes are undercut by its more acoustic reverberations, in its emphasis upon the 'babbling' echo within the grove which 'mocks' the hounds and, by implication, the culture that directs them. The speech ends, in its assimilation of these different resonances into an originary and quasi-maternal utterance – the nurse's song – with a final elision of nature and nurture whose intrinsic barbarism is soon to be demonstrated by the Empress's grotesque revenge. In this alliance of poetic language with a return both to wild nature and to a maternal origin which threatens rather than affirms social controls, Tamora's echo-like speech parallels the activity of those psychic drives associated with the semiotic *chora* and the *id*.

Yet Tamora's feigning of a 'mannerly' courtly language is punctured by another mode of echoic iteration with the arrival of Lavinia and Bassianus, whose bawdy remarks draw out the sexual implications in the Empress's elegant tropes of hunting. In reply to Bassianus' ironic comparison of her to Diana, Tamora retorts that:

> Had I the power some say Dian had,
> Thy temples should be planted presently
> With horns, as was Actaeon's, and the hounds
> Should drive upon thy new-transformed limbs,
> Unmannerly intruder as thou art.
>
> (2.3.61–5)

In her response, it is now Lavinia – the woman who had been chosen as Rome's Empress before Tamora – who occupies the uncanny place of the 'babbling echo' which has doubled the sounds of this imagery of 'hounds' and 'horns', as she quibbles on the sexual meanings of Tamora's words:

> Under your patience, gentle empress,
> 'Tis thought you have a goodly gift in horning,
> And to be doubted that your Moor and you
> Are singled forth to try experiments.
> Jove shield your husband from his hounds to-day:
> 'Tis pity they should take him for a stag.
>
> (2.3.66–71)

By this play on 'horning' (as copulation and cuckoldry, as well as the sound of the hunters' horns), Lavinia displays a knowing wit whose ill-advisedness is made apparent by the terrible ensuing events, which result in the death of Bassianus and her own complete silencing by rape and mutilation. As in the myth of Echo and Pan, echoic forms of utterance are here shown to have a disturbingly close connection not only with a female sexual knowing, but also with violence, dismemberment and death.

The mastery of a compellingly persuasive rhetorical style is also of central importance in the furthering of the devices and ambitions of both Lady Macbeth, on the one hand, and Goneril and Regan on the other. Once again, while the assertive rhetoric wielded by these women initially masquerades as 'mannerly', as synonymous with civility, love and service, it is quickly shown to serve a barbarous or wild human nature – what Lady Macbeth calls 'Nature's mischief'. Moreover, like the poetry of Tamora, as well as the rhetoric of Volumnia in *Coriolanus*, this female mimicry of masculine eloquence is intimately allied with – indeed, it promotes – an exaggerated and deadly version of man(ner)liness, which tends to tyranny.[23] Through its barbarism, brutality and tyranny, the masculine violence which is solicited by these women's fluency with language tends ultimately to its own destruction, but masculine authority is also subtly undermined by the frequent intrusion into these women's discourse of figures of the body and of sexuality.

When she receives his letter describing the meeting with the weird sisters, Lady Macbeth wishes that Macbeth will:

> Hie thee hither,
> That I may pour my spirits in thine ear,
> And chastise with the valour of my tongue
> All that impedes thee from the golden round,
> Which fate and metaphysical aid doth seem
> To have thee crown'd withal.
>
> (1.5.25–30)

This language allies a feminine mimicry of 'the valour of [the] tongue' with striking bodily metaphors – especially if we remember the association of vital spirits with generative force common at the time – with the result that the distinction between worldly power (the crown as 'golden round'), and those bodily pleasures afforded within the generative circle of woman's body, is rendered highly ambiguous. (At the same time, her references to 'spirits' and 'round' tropically allies Lady Macbeth's speech with the choric incantations and dances of the three weird sisters, in an oblique allusion to the association of a trangressive female sexuality with supernatural powers.) Subsequently, on Duncan's arrival at the castle, Lady Macbeth extends her manipulative use of language to the discourse of hospitality and feasting, which was closely allied to that of courtliness in English Renaissance culture, as she expresses her devoted service to the monarch: 'Your servants ever / Have theirs, themselves, and what is theirs, in compt, / To make their audit at your Highness' pleasure, / Still to return your own' (1.6.25–8). Yet as is implied by the use of 'compt' (a word frequently allied via homophony with 'cunt'),[24] her speedy abuse of the role of good hostess and housewife equates Lady Macbeth rather with the false c(o)unt of the 'huswife' who is a whore or brothel-keeper.

The 'audit' which the Macbeths are preparing is on one level to be Duncan's final 'compt', or account, in death. But as the hospitable castle which seems the epitome of civility is metamorphosed into an image of hell, the disturbing figurative links between a bloody usurpation of power masquerading as courtliness and the sexual entry of a feminized royal body are pressed home by the uncanny repetition of a relentless 'knocking'. In the scene that immediately follows Macbeth's grim comment, 'Wake Duncan with thy knocking: I would thy couldst!' (2.2.73), the Porter's puns connect this ghostly portent of tragedy both with the dead spirit's entry into hell or the otherworld, and also with the sexual opening of woman's body by a physical 'knocking'. This echoic device consequently stresses the connection between female sexuality and a resonance that is both bodily and ghostly, as the faithless hostess who keeps the infernal house becomes disturbingly entangled with an uncanny evocation of the butchered king.[25]

In order to win their dowries of land from their father, Goneril and Regan likewise display what for English Renaissance women would have been a quite exceptional mastery of a dissembling courtly rhetoric. The royal daughters' rhetorical contest is suggestively preceded and framed by a significant slippage of courtly language into bawdy wordplay in the play's opening scene, where Gloucester describes the extra-marital conception of his bastard son Edmund:

Gloucester: His breeding, sir, hath been at my charge. I have so often blushed to acknowledge him that now I am brazed to't.

Kent: I cannot conceive you.

Gloucester: Sir, this young fellow's mother could; whereupon she grew round-wombed, and had, indeed, sir, a son for her cradle ere she had a husband for her bed. Do you smell a fault?

(1.1.8–15)

Through Gloucester's pun upon 'conceive' (which echoes another bawdy exchange, between Hamlet and Polonius), we are alerted before Regan and Goneril even speak to an intimate affinity between the (mis-)interpretation of courtly speech and the sexualized female body as a site of transgression, of a 'fault' or *lapsus* in meanings as well as morals.

It is ostensibly in defence of a normative courtly ethos that the sisters subsequently refuse lodging to their father's retainers. Goneril tells her father:

> Here do you keep a hundred knights and squires,
> Men so disordered, so debauched and bold,
> That this our court, infected with their manners,
> Shows like a riotous inn. Epicurism and lust
> Makes it more like a tavern or a brothel
> Than a graced palace.
>
> (1.4.232–7)

As her feigned language of courtliness becomes disturbingly elided with the speech of the scolding housewife and mother-figure, Goneril remarks of her father: 'Now by my life, / Old fools are babes again and must be used / With checks as flatteries, when they are seen abused' (1.3.19–21). When Lear goes out into the storm, Regan observes that 'to wilful men, / The injuries that they themselves procure / Must be their school-masters' (2.2.492–4). Yet as the cryptic riddles and puns of the Fool predict, this emphasis upon a female defence of civilized order and restraint will soon be replaced by the complete breakdown of traditional codes of order and morality: the courtly mimicry of Goneril and Regan quickly makes explicit its own service of 'will' (or sexual desire as well as political self-interest), and their palaces or 'houses' are soon to be truly associated with housewifery as whoring.

Echoing otherwise

In the course of Lear's tragedy, he moves from revulsion at Cordelia's paradoxical and resonant 'Nothing' to a dying awareness of the breath, or *spiritus*, that informs speech. Ironically, it is through its absence from Cordelia's lips that this principle acquires its climactic significance in the play. Elsewhere in Shakespearean tragedy, a developed rhetorical self-consciousness is similarly opposed, not only by its grotesque feminine mimicry, but also by a vocal difference whose contrasting lack of individualization invites a more explicit comparison to Echo as 'breath' or wind. Juliet desires to emulate 'the airy tongue' of Echo in repetition of Romeo's name; in a dying that is 'as sweet as balm, as soft as air', Cleopatra's last speech is completed by Charmian; the 'weyard' sisters use their magical iterations not only to prophesy but also to control the winds, while they melt into the air 'as breath into wind' (1.3.82); and Desdemona's choric 'Willow' song, eerily punctuated by the sighing of the wind, sets up a haunting resonance that, like and yet unlike the knocking in *Macbeth*, will ultimately reverberate beyond the grave:

> *Desdemona* [*Sings*]:
> The poor soul sat sighing by a sycamore tree,
>> Sing all a green willow:
> Her hand on her bosom, her head on her knee,
>> Sing willow, willow, willow.
> The fresh streams ran by her and murmured her moans,
>> Sing willow, willow, willow:
> Her salt tears fell from her and softened the stones,
>> Sing willow, willow, willow.
> [*Speaks*] Lay by these:–
>> Willow, willow –
> [*Speaks*] Prithee hie thee: he'll come anon.
> Sing all a green willow must be my garland.
> Let nobody blame him, his scorn I approve–
> [*Speaks*] Nay, that's not next. Hark, who is't that knocks?
> *Emilia*: It's the wind.
> *Des.* [*Sings*]: I call'd my love false love: but what said he then?
>> Sing willow, willow, willow:
> If I court moe women, you'll couch with moe men.
> [*Speaks*] Now get thee gone; good night. Mine eyes do itch,
> Doth that bode weeping?
>> (4.3.39–59)

The 'Willow' song functions as an act both of remembrance and of pro-sopopoeia, in which not only are three female identities – the deserted woman of the song, the dead Barbary and Desdemona – curiously confused, but nature itself also appears to participate, as the willow and streams which 'sing', and the wind that interrupts or echoes the song with an uncanny and erotic 'knocking'. These interwoven voices of the living, the dead, and the non-human make the vocal reverberations which were especially characteristic of complaint (in which a mournful utterance is echoed by the natural environment) all the more eerie. The implicit association between the song and a chain of female deaths is confirmed two scenes later, in the murder of Desdemona, and also in its final echoing by yet another female voice: as Emilia addresses her dead mistress: 'What did thy song bode, lady? / Hark, canst thou hear me? I will play the swan / And die in music. [*Sings*] Willow, willow, willow' (5.2.244–6).

Hamlet's ear

The tragedies' tropical variations upon a feminine breath or air construct diverse variations upon a common interlingual pun, whereby *mollis aer* (Latin for soft air) was equated with *mulier* (Latin for woman). But while Shakespeare could apply this pun quite conventionally to female dramatic protagonists such as Imogen and Cleopatra, he also used it to trope the beloved youth of the *Sonnets*; while Imogen is compared to 'tender air' (5.5.234, 5.6.447–53) and Cleopatra, in her dying, is 'as soft as air' (5.2.310), the beautiful youth who is initially exhorted by the poet to 'bear' his father's memory through procreation is also a 'tender heir' (*Sonnets*, 1, 4). And this trope of air also has an important relationship to the motif of masculine inheritance in *Hamlet*, which is complicated by what most critics read as the elective character of the Danish monarchy. For just as this shadowy theme of monarchical election obliquely calls a patrilineal transmission of royal power into question, so the hero's airy and echoic utterances denote an implicit refusal to conform to traditional forms of masculine identity and sexuality; in particular, Hamlet rejects the figurative association which runs through the play, between kingship and 'earing' as copulation. Yet the play's subtle use of echoic forms of utterance encompasses not only Hamlet's own choric activity of punning, but also the suggestively different iterations of Ophelia.

An alienation from the hypocrisy of a courtly style or decorum in language afflicts young Hamlet from his first appearance in the play, even before the encounter with his father's ghost affords him a specific justification for his role as a courtly malcontent. The courtly airs or 'songs', the 'words of so sweet breath', the 'music vows', with which he wooed Ophelia are no longer part of his idiom, although he will briefly redeploy them to disguise his true state of mind. In Act 1 scene 2, we meet a Hamlet whose abrupt retreat from social intercourse is not only signalled by his mourning dress, but is also articulated through a satiric relationship to language. This scathing view of the world is articulated in all of Hamlet's language, in his soliloquies and monologues as well as in his dialogues with others; but it finds its most effective form of expression in his use of wordplay. Indeed, the centrality of the pun to the view of earthly mutability and death that Hamlet gradually elaborates in the course of the play is aptly illustrated by the fact that he puns not only on his own death ('The rest is silence'), but also as he finally accomplishes his task of revenge and kills Claudius, asking the king, 'Is thy union here?' as he forces him to drink from the poisoned cup.

In contrast to the use of wordplay as the supreme instance of a dialogic courtly wit which celebrates the shared values of an aristocratic group, an ironic use of iteration, and of the pun in particular, is deployed by Hamlet as a hostile weapon in order to expose the hypocrisy of the Danish court. This choric unsettling of courtly language reminds us constantly, in its figures, of Hamlet's familial displacement, as a son who occupies a complex and uncertain place in a monarchical system that, while seemingly elective, also affords a privileged status to heredity. Indeed, Hamlet's role as malcontent and revenger will succeed not so much by action as by his disordering, through wordplay, of social and political constructions of identity. While Hamlet's echoic discourse may seem mad, it is able to enunciate, albeit obliquely, the hidden meanings that are concealed within the polite language of the Danish court. Claudius tells Hamlet that 'You are the most immediate to our throne' (1.2.109). In his puns and related tropes, however, Hamlet delineates a very different version of his identity as a putative 'heir' of Denmark, one which ironically echoes and amplifies the politically sensitive motif of election, in that it radically redefines his association with the activity of the male monarch as one who both (h)ears and engenders: this imagery survives, of course, in a grotesquely distorted form, in Claudius' perceived political and sexual excesses, in the form of espionage and incest. One way in which this rejection, by Hamlet, of conventional masculine modes of (h)earing is imaged is in his abrupt refusal of any courtly playing upon him as a phallic pipe or recorder – the fault of which he accuses Rosencrantz and Guildenstern (3.2.327–54).[26] And in Hamlet's quibbles, as well as in the tropes which are applied to him by others, we find a curious refiguring of the heir – a word which, significantly, is evoked solely through homophony in this play – in relationship to 'th'incorporal air'.

In his magisterial study of *Shakespeare's Pronunciation*, where he aimed to recover many Elizabethan homonyms which are no longer pronounced alike, Helgë Kökeritz concluded that hair/heir/here/hare were four words often pronounced similarly in early modern English; in particular, he noted the likely pun on air/heir in *Hamlet*, together with related puns on hair/heir and heir/here from other Shakespearean plays.[27] The association of his 'air' imagery with a nexus of images related to hearing as well as to fertility serves to remind us that a disseminating, rather than inseminating, use of (h)earing is central to Hamlet's punning activity, which often appears to imply vocal play on 'ear' as well as 'air' in relation to an unspoken 'heir'. (Although Kökeritz did not mention 'ear' in his hair/heir/here/hear combination, elsewhere he noted homonymic play on ear/here, while he also observed that John Lyly puns on ear/hair in *Midas*.[28]) Through this hidden pun, Hamlet's airy and echoic utterances are implicitly related to his failure to conform to traditional forms of masculine identity.[29] Interwoven with this vocal play on ear/air in relation to an unspoken (or silent) heir, moreover, are other homophonic links which, also functioning through negation, differentiate Hamlet further from his environment at the same time as they illuminate a range of interrelated motifs which are fundamental to the dramatic plot, and closely related to its key tropes.

While there are certainly puns in Hamlet's soliloquies, punning requires a social context in order to be fully effective; it is therefore an apt instrument of the satirist. It is also one of the ways in which a rhetorical emphasis upon the singular fate of the tragic protagonist, as articulated through soliloquy or monologue, can be juxtaposed with a dialogic form of self-undoing, in a comic discourse which is less focused on the subjective 'I', and more on the exposure of an illusory social mask. At the same time, as Gregory Ulmer has observed, the pun can often function as a 'puncept', in its formation of new concepts which may hint at another order of knowledge.[30] Through multiple *entendres*, unobserved or hidden relationships can be demonstrated, as various homophones reverberate echoically throughout a text. It is above all through his relentless quibbling that Hamlet meditates upon the sexuality of, and within, families. Yet the oblique meanings of his wordplay also extend beyond this immediate sphere of familiarity. In ways which partly resemble the speech of, and about, the female protagonists of Shakespearean tragedy, Hamlet reintroduces nature, the body and death into the sphere of courtly discourse, reimaging courtly society in terms of an 'overgrowth' within nature, and thereby reassimilating culture into nature. Thus in a trope used several times in the play, 'rank' as the foul smell and abundant growth of weeds is substituted for social rank, while Claudius's kingship is troped as a sexual excess which is also a 'moor' or wilderness. In spite of his several misogynistic diatribes, which attribute this degenerative trend in nature to the female body and female sexuality in particular, his quibbling language tropes Hamlet himself as having an obscure figurative association with these processes of decay.

In his encounter with his father's ghost, the heir is informed of Claudius's twofold poisoning of the ear of Denmark. He has killed Old Hamlet with 'juice of cursèd hebenon', poured 'in the porches of my ears' (1.5.62–3); furthermore, he has deceived the court as to the nature of the king's death, 'the whole ear of Denmark / Is by a forgèd process of my death / Rankly abused' (1.5.36–8). But Hamlet, as the heir and other ear of Denmark, has already begun to hear Claudius's courtly discourse otherwise or satirically, and is now fully undeceived by his exchange with the airy spirit. Implicit in this imagery of ears may be a quibble upon 'earing' as copulation, since Claudius's assumed sexual appetite parallels what Hamlet sees as the disorderly disseminating power of nature – with the result that, in Hamlet's eyes, the state of Denmark 'grows to seed'. As a 'mildewed ear' of corn, Claudius is also distinguished from Hamlet – this 'usurper' is a chief tare or weed (in Latin, this could sometimes be *aera* as well as the more common *lolium*) in what Hamlet now sees as the 'unweeded garden' of the world – and of course, like Lucianus in 'The Murder of Gonzago', Claudius has literally used 'midnight weeds' to poison or 'blast' (like a strong wind) Hamlet's father's life, and poison will be used again by both him and Laertes in the tragic catastrophe. But while his uncle, as a 'mildewed ear', is associated by Hamlet with the paradox of a degenerative fertility within nature, Hamlet's own wit performs a more oblique and airy form of generation, inspired not so much by a commitment to the monarchy as the political (h)earing of the state as by a more feminine and aesthetically responsive form of hearing: one which is appropriate to the narration or the performance of tragedy, and which also interprets human suffering as inextricably interwoven with a tragedy within nature.

In Greek tragedy, the role of listener was an important function of the chorus, as the primary auditors and spectators of the tragic events. It is this feminine and choric mode of hearing which is implicitly required by the ghost of Old Hamlet when he describes his murder to his son: a hearing which is also comparable to that enacted by Dido when she asks Aeneas to tell her of the fall of Troy – for it is Dido's place that Hamlet effectively occupies when in Act 2 he asks the player to give an impromptu performance of Aeneas' tale. What is presented to him is an account of a political tragedy which, like the death of his father, is imaged in terms of a natural cataclysm: Pyrrhus' 'sable arms / Black as his purposes, did the night resemble', while his murder of Priam is compared to a storm:

> But as we often see, against some storm,
> A silence in the heavens, the rack stand still,
> The bold winds speechless, and the orb below
> As hush as death, anon the dreadful thunder
> Doth rend the region; so after Pyrrhus's pause,
> A rousèd vengeance sets him new a-work . . .
>
> (2.2.474–9)

When viewed in this context, the climax of the speech, in its account of the grieving Hecuba, presents a 'mobled queen' whose speechlessness, muffled face and 'all o'er-teemed loins' imply a close parallel to the violated and complaining Nature of literary tradition: a figure whose appearance was often muffled or veiled in medieval and Renaissance literature. It is perhaps in this metaphysical sense, as well as in the sense of being a theatrical illusion, that the Player's image of Hecuba is subsequently identified by Hamlet with 'nothing'. Certainly the more feminine faculty of hearing which motivates his interest in the drama appears to involve responsiveness to the mysterious resonance of nature within language, for he figures the more discerning members of the theatrical audiences of the times as 'the most fanned and winnowed opinions': they are like ears of corn which have been separated out from the chaff by the activity of the wind (this conception may derive from the winnowing of the soul by wind in *Aeneid* VI, 740). Indeed, through his ironic quibbling, Hamlet uses his different style of hearing to effect an airy and echoic reordering of the world around him, in a discursive equivalent to winnowing whose spiritual implications are apparent from the traditional affinity of air and wind with *spiritus*. A chief result of this reclassification through punning is a reinterpretation of those distorted relations between kin which are integral to the tragedy.

The theme of a kinship which is both rather less than affectionate and also excessive or incestuous is wittily introduced by Hamlet's first paronomastic play on 'kin' and 'kind'. Paronomasia or 'prosonomasia' depends on a slight change, lengthening or transposition of the letters in a word; Henry Peacham defines the trope as 'a certayne declyninge into a contrarye, by a lykelyhode of Letters, eyther added, chaunged, or taken awaye', while George Puttenham describes it as:

> a figure by which ye play with a couple of words or names much resembling, and because the one seems to answere th'other by manner of illusion, and doth, as it were, nick him, I call him the *Nicknamer* chaunged or taken awaye.[31]

In response to Claudius' greeting, 'But now, my cousin Hamlet, and my son—', Hamlet murmurs: 'A little more than kin, and less than kind' (1.2.64–5). The quibble aptly suggests the difficulty of finding words to represent Claudius's outrageous transgression of the conventional boundaries of kinship, which is also, Hamlet implies, a subversion of courtly conventions of *gentilité* or kindness. His subsequent homophonic quibble on 'son' is inspired by Claudius's indirect pun on son/sun in his query about Hamlet's mourning garb: 'How is it that the clouds still hang on you?'. Hamlet's reply, 'Not so, my lord, I am too much i' th' sun' (1.2.66–7), ironically suggests that whereas another homophone of kin and kind – king – does describe Claudius' situation through the traditional association of kingship with the imagery of the sun, it is also related to his own situation as a king's son who is also, from an elective, as well as hereditary perspective, an heir. Thus while this pun spells out more clearly the still unspoken pun on kin and king, allying an excess of *kinship* (since Hamlet is not Claudius's son, and Claudius has married his brother's wife) with an image of *kingship* (the sun) that is itself excessive (apparently because its brightness is incompatible with mourning), the quibble also reminds us that, as a son, Hamlet also has a homophonic affinity with the sun/kingship, in spite of his mourning attire, and that, like Claudius, he too may have an unexpected generative potential.

Yet the peculiar difference of Hamlet's disseminating activity is made clear in his retorts to Gertrude. Her description of dying as 'common' is allied by Hamlet's ironic iteration with the 'common' or vulgar usage of 'to die', evoking thereby the commonness of another, sexual, dying; similarly, her question, 'Why seems it so particular with thee?' is converted by Hamlet into a barbed criticism of the King and Queen's courtly semblance of mourning: 'Seems, madam? Nay, it is, I know not "seems".' This ironic differing of 'seems', which hints at the links between courtly seeming and the spilling of generative seed (Latin: *semen*), also anticipates the 'ensèamed bed' that he will later accuse the Queen of copulating in with Claudius. The rejection by Hamlet of sexual activity is also implied in his subsequent reference to a near-synonym for 'seems', when he tells Gertrude that 'I have that within which passeth show'; later, in his quibbling exchange with Ophelia during the play scene, the sexual meaning of 'show' will be stressed. None the less, it is Hamlet's mocking echoes of courtly language which turn the meaning of 'common' or ordinary words back towards the body and sexuality. He will warn Polonius, in a remark which appears to imply his own erotic intentions towards Ophelia: 'Let her not walk i' th' sun. Conception is a blessing, but as your daughter may conceive – friend, look to't' (2.2.184–6). This use of *antanaclasis*, in which the same word (conception) has two different meanings, clarifies the difference of Hamlet's disseminating powers from those of his uncle; the nephew's sun-like fertility seeds a legacy or inheritance that operates above all at the level of signs (Greek: *semeion*), and so in the realm of words and ideas. And while assisting conception, as understanding, in women in particular – for the 'conceits' which are attributed to both Gertrude and Ophelia (3.4.106, 4.5.44) are directly or indirectly inspired by Hamlet – this son also 'conceives' much himself. For him, morbid meditations or 'conceits' concerning natural and human corruption are themselves part of a (re)generative process. But if, through his quibble on 'conception', the gendered identity of the heir is effectively called into question, what kind of heir is he?

In Act II scene ii, at almost the exact mid-point of the play, as 'The Murder of Gonzago' is about to be performed, Claudius greets Hamlet with 'How fares our cousin Hamlet?'. Hamlet replies with a triple quibble. Redefining 'fares' in terms of sustenance, he simultaneously converts 'fare' to 'air' by paronomasia, and quibbles thereby on 'heir' also: 'Excellent, i'faith, of the chameleon's dish. I eat the air, promise-crammed. You cannot feed capons so' (3.2.86–8). The quibble makes explicit the obscure but important connection between this 'heir' and 'air' which runs through the play, at the same time as it presents us with the trope of the displaced heir as a chameleon or shape-shifter who is not, he warns Claudius, as stupid as a castrated cock or capon, that allows itself to be overfed for the table. Instead, it seems, Hamlet is mysteriously feeding on himself (as heir/air), in a way which is not only consistent with the mutable identity of the chameleon (which was nourished by air), but which also hints at his affinity with the mysterious singularity of the double-gendered phoenix. And the substance he feeds on is mysteriously full as well as empty; as 'promise-crammed', its fecundity is associated only with words. Thus while the empty flattery of Claudius to his 'son' is ironically dismissed by Hamlet, his quibble nonetheless suggests that the airy substance of speech does afford him a curious kind of nourishment, where none might be expected. This metamorphosis of the heir of Denmark through and in relation to air begins, of course, on the battlements of Elsinore, where, as Hamlet and his companions wait for the ghost to appear, he declares: 'The air bites shrewdly, it is very cold'. To this Horatio replies: 'It is a nipping and an eager air'. These words aptly convey the change that has already begun to affect Hamlet, in his assumption of a satiric demeanour, expressed through a mordant or biting wit which is eager or sour. In its later echo by the ghost's reference to the curdling of his blood by Claudius's poison, 'like eager droppings into milk' (1.5.69), this reference to the eager air or heir attributes to Hamlet a property of bitterness which parallels the corrupting effects of Claudius's fratricide. But these images in the first act also give a new, quasi-erotic dimension to Hamlet's satiric temper. For as he develops a new, biting relationship to the air as well as to the courtly language (or promises) which fill it, he is also consuming his identity as heir.

In feeding upon himself (as well as others) through his mordant quibbling, Hamlet plays the part of Narcissus as well as Echo. Like the addressee of Shakespeare's *Sonnets*, he can be accused of self-love, or of 'having traffic with thyself alone' (*Sonnets*, 4, 1.9). But in also assuming the implicitly feminine role of the 'tender heir' (as *mollis aer* or *mulier*) who will bear the father's memory (*Sonnets*, 1, 1.4), Hamlet is able to redefine both his father's and his own inheritance through his airy conceits. In this respect, his own legacy or inheritance will be twofold: while his 'story' (or history) is bequeathed directly to Horatio, who by telling it will preserve his name, it is Fortinbras who will be the ultimate recipient both of that story and of Hamlet's 'dying voice' – which favours him as king. Significantly, neither man is even a member of his kin-group, much less his child. Hamlet thereby refigures inheritance in terms of a phoenix-like, vocal, succession to other men which echoes and amplifies the practice of monarchical election, since not only does it circumvent the generative obligations of patriliny, it also transmits (different modes of) authority to two rather than to one. This formation of a different bonding between men – a bonding across rather than within families – is effected by the historical reverberations of Hamlet's echoing voice. However, this airy voice will reverberate rather differently in relation to women.

When Polonius refers to his replies as 'pregnant', he may be attributing a feminine or fecund character to Hamlet's quibbling, and certainly, the tropes and puns used by Claudius of Hamlet's melancholy or madness figure it as concealing an airy fecundity which is apparently feminine. The prince is twice imaged as a female bird on her nest in late spring or early summer: 'There's something in his soul / O'er which his melancholy sits on brood' (3.1.165–6); 'This is mere madness; / And thus a while the fit will work on him. / Anon, as patient as the female dove / When that her golden couplets are disclosed, / His silence will sit drooping' (5.1.274–8). But a more grotesque, and implicitly masculine, version of this differing of gendered models of generation is later offered by Hamlet when, in his remark to Polonius about the dangers of Ophelia walking 'i' th' sun' he defines the sun as a breeder of worms or maggots which eat the flesh, and so accelerate the decay of dead matter: 'For if the sun breed maggots in a dead dog, being good kissing carrion –' (2.2.181–2). Yet in the myth of the phoenix as reported by Pliny (an account which was often cited), we are told that such creatures play a central part in this creature's solitary work of regeneration through self-consumption: ' . . . from its bones and marrow is born first a sort of maggot, and this grows into a chicken'.[32]

In spite of Hamlet's apparent similarity to the figure of Narcissus, it is striking that several of the images which I have mentioned above were connected in Renaissance iconography with Hermes or Mercury, a classical deity whose identity was especially marked by paradox and doubleness. This god, whose emblematic creature was a cock, herald of the dawn, and who often held a pipe as well as his famous staff or caduceus encircled with serpents, combined his role as a divine messenger and god of eloquence with attributes of trickery, secrecy and concealment; according to Richard Linche in *The Fountaine of Ancient Fiction* (1599): 'Mercurie was often taken for that light of knowledge, & spirit of understanding, which guides men to the true conceavement of darke and enigmaticall sentences'.[33] This affinity between Mercury and obscure yet meaningful utterances makes it hardly surprising that in Ben Jonson's *Cynthia's Revels* it is Mercury who temporarily restores the speech of Echo, inviting her to 'strike music from the spheres, / And with thy golden raptures swell our ears' (1.2.63–4). (The play was acted at court on Twelfth Night 1601, as the first production of the 'little eyases' or young hawks whose 'aerie' was the Blackfriars playhouse, the Children of the Chapel.)

His identification by Macrobius with 'that power [of the sun] from which comes speech' hints at another aspect of Mercury's classical identity, whereby he was associated with the return of fertility to the earth in springtime (Plate 4).[34] Yet as Charles Dempsey has recently pointed out, in his reinterpretation of Botticelli's *Primavera*, it was Mercury as a wind-god (for example, in Virgil's *Aeneid*, IV, 223ff), able to calm harsh winds and storms and to disperse clouds by his magical direction of currents of air (Plate 5a), who was most explicitly regarded as a god of spring, or *Mercurius Ver*:

> Botticelli shows Mercury dispersing and softening clouds with his upraised caduceus in the *Primavera*, a representation of him that unequivocally identifies him as acting in his archaic persona as a springtime wind god. By this action he ends the season that began with the warming west wind blowing its regenerative breath over the bare earth, shown as Zephyr and Chloris, and that reaches its fullness in April, the month presided over by Venus.[35]

The springtime fertility associated with Mercury in classical literature and in Botticelli's painting is markedly different from the violent heterosexuality expressed by Zephyr in his rape of the nymph Chloris; in the *Primavera*, clusters of seeds swirl about Mercury's winged sandals, but no act of copulation is associated with this generative process (Plate 5b). Instead, Mercury's fertilizing role is implied to represent a mysterious supplement to that of Venus as a goddess of nature. Indeed, although the mythographers are understandably silent on the subject, their curious

Plate 4 Mercury. Detail from Botticelli's 'Primavera'. By permission of Archivi Alinari, Florence.

Plate 5a Detail of Mercury's wand, the 'Primavera'. By permission of Archivi Alinari, Florence.

debates about whether or not Mercury has a beard, together with the emphasis on his youthfulness (in other words, his difference from adult masculinity), create a distinct aura of ambiguity around his sexual identity which, in its association with Hamlet, serves to remind us also of the carnivalesque connection between a bodily wind or *flatus* and anality.[36]

The *Primavera* suggests that Mercury enjoys a different relationship with the feminine generative principle within nature from that attributed

Plate 5b Detail of Mercury's boots, the 'Primavera'. By permission of Archivi Alinari, Florence.

to figures of masculine generation. In alchemical texts, Mercury likewise emblematized the mysterious changes wrought within nature or matter by a principle of ambiguous gender, sometimes called *Mercurius duplex*; in this literature, 'our Mercury' was analogous to the *spiritus* which was the secret transforming substance within matter, and was variously described as 'divine rain', 'May dew', 'dew of heaven', 'our honey'. Such was its ambivalent character, however, that Mercury was also identified with that part of matter which, phoenix-like, fed upon itself in order to produce transmutation.[37]

Not only does this half-buried set of associations suggest that Hamlet's puns may indeed articulate a covert but coherent level of meaning, in a Renaissance alchemization of language; it also appears to confirm the strange affinity between punning and the primordial and disturbingly metamorphic activity of *chora* as emphasized by Kristeva. Like the *chora*, these mercurial messages function to disrupt the fixity of social identities – along with the embassies or utterances of aberrant father figures – while hinting at the existence of a different order, hidden behind the visible one. Douglas Brooks-Davies has pointed out that the imagery of Mercury was often appropriated by royalist panegyrics during the Renaissance;[38] yet in Mercury's oblique but, in my view, pervasive association with Hamlet, what appears to be figured is rather the enigmatic difference of a son and heir who is identified with air and movement, with verbal dexterity and with a grotesque form of verbal as well as vernal regeneration through worms or maggots (in French, worms are *vers*, which not only links spring – *le ver* – with the worm, but could also suggest an additional pun in Hamlet's discourse of worms: on the putrefying activity of *vers* as verse). This reminds us that Hamlet does not yet (and indeed, will never) occupy the solid place of the earthly father, but that instead he is distinguished by a mutability of identity which implicates him rather in the more sexually ambiguous spheres of nature and spirit, identifying him especially with the mobility of air or wind. It is noteworthy in this connection that it is the mercurial bird, the cock, to which Hamlet will allude in his ironic remark to Claudius about eating the air, whose sound dispels the apparition of the paternal ghost in the first scene of the play, eliciting allusions to the cock's connection with that other son/sun figure, Christ (with whom the Mercurius of the alchemists was indeed often equated).

Hamlet's satirical rejection of the generative activity which would make a son a father has often been dismissed as misogyny; by this move, however, he could be seen as commenting upon the uneasy relationship between the motif of election and ideas of patrilineal authority that is suggested by the plot of the play. Through his mercurial and quibbling language 'of darke and enigmaticall sentences', moreover, Hamlet accords the final inheritance of all costly or aristocratic breeding to nature and 'my Lady Worm's': 'Here's fine revolution, if we had the trick to see't. Did these bones cost no more the breeding but to play at loggats with 'em?' (5.1.86–8). In the grotesque metamorphosis of a corpse, gender differences are disfigured more or less completely, so that Hamlet can say to Yorick's skull: 'Now get you to my lady's chamber and tell her, let her paint an inch thick, to this favour she must come. Make her laugh at that' (5.1.183–6). But the apostrophe to Yorick also reminds us how many of Hamlet's grotesque conceivings are directly or indirectly addressed to women, whose proneness to 'conception' he has commented on to Polonius. It is almost immediately after his address to the skull, in fact, that the funeral procession of Ophelia enters, as if to provide the perfect exemplar of those processes of decay which he has just itemized.

'Her speech is nothing' (4.5.7)

Ophelia provides an apt example of Hamlet's alternative version of a feminine 'conception'. She does this, however, not only as a corpse who has already begun that 'breeding' of decomposition which Hamlet describes both to her father and, in the graveyard, to Horatio. For both the forms of her madness and the way in which her death is described by Gertrude ally her curiously metamorphic part in this tragedy to a cognitive mode of 'conception', in which like, and yet unlike Hamlet, she apparently sees the Danish court in a different light, and refigures it, by speaking 'things in doubt / That carry but half sense' (4.5.6–7), but which engender 'dangerous conjectures in ill-breeding-minds' (4.5.15). We are told that 'her speech is nothing'; yet like that of the 'mad' Hamlet, it combines the appearance of madness with acute social insights, albeit obscurely expressed, so that 'the unshaped use of it doth move / The hearers to collection' (4.5.8–9). It seems that Ophelia has indeed 'conceived' or understood the cryptic as well as bawdy utterances of her former suitor, after his 'words of so sweet breath' have been disturbingly replaced by a different vocal music, 'like sweet bells jangled out of tune and harsh' – a sounding of corruption and death. The metaphysical 'nothing' of which this new Hamlet speaks is also, of course, 'a fair thought to lie between maids' legs' (3.2.117). It seems, therefore, that an obscure form of cognitive insemination does occur.

But if Ophelia has indirectly inspired (or inhaled) the pungent breath of Hamlet's bitter words, it is her father's death that completes the interior crisis which results in her mimicry of Hamlet's mad and mournful demeanour – with an additional echoic difference. Indeed, by combining different types of lament – for a dead father-lover on the one hand, and for a lost physical innocence on the other – Ophelia's speech of 'nothing' reaffirms those links between sexuality and death which Hamlet has explored through his puns. This figurative interconnection is emphasized both by her address to the Queen in Act 4 scene 5 and by the fact that, like Hamlet as he leaves the Queen's closet with the body of Polonius, she exits from her first mad scene with a curious – and rather ominous – repetition of 'good night', which is addressed to 'sweet ladies', although Gertrude is the only woman who is present: 'Good night, ladies, good night. Sweet ladies, good night, good night' (4.5.72–3).

Ophelia's feminine echo of Hamlet's madness turns or angles our view of tragic grief and suffering, so that we see its shapes differently, as momentarily invested with an eerie beauty that is borrowed as much from nature as from art. Like Desdemona, her use of the collective idioms of song and ballad calls into question the status of an individualized tragic language of individuality, while her gifts of flowers and herbs oppose to the 'flowers' or tropes of rhetoric a speechless yet equally eloquent mode of communication. Hamlet's madness had dis-figured nature, in its quasi-alchemical reduction to decay and death. Yet in its evocation of the May Day revels which develops some of the themes of Ophelia's songs, the floral imagery of her madness and death imbues – or 'indues' – her figure with an extraordinary fecundity. Unlike Hamlet, it seems that Ophelia is able to make of earthly 'weeds' a garland or 'crownet'.

The first herb or flower which Ophelia bestows upon her astonished auditors is rosemary, 'for remembrance': this is a herb whose affinity with mourning is also coupled with a watery etymology, as *ros marinus* or dew of the sea; in consequence, it will gain added emblematic significance through the accident of her own death by drowning. Water, as the first clown puts it, 'is a sore decayer of your whoreson dead body'; he discusses with Hamlet the length of time which a corpse might be expected to 'keep out water'. But in her watery death, Ophelia's identity is dissolved into the element which was thought by some to be the fundamental constituent of primal matter: in the act of creation described in *Genesis*, the spirit of god breathed over 'the waters'. The concept of duration in historical time which will preoccupy the dying Hamlet is implied to be irrelevant to the temporality of this feminine metamorphosis. Yet while Hamlet's 'dying voice' or 'adewe' is assured of a kind of historical afterlife in its successful transmission, through Horatio, to Fortinbras, Ophelia's dying plangency also engenders a final echoic reverberation, which hints at an emotional rather than a political reparation. For both Gertrude's description of her death, and her strewing of flowers at Ophelia's grave, suggest that through Ophelia, rather than her son, this 'wretched Queen' to whom Hamlet addresses his last 'adieu' (5.2.338) may belatedly have come to see both death and mourning with a feminine difference.

4

DISCLOSING THE FEMININE EYE OF DEATH: TRAGEDY AND SEEING IN THE DARK

Othello (1602–3)

> In its fearful aspect, as a power of terror expressing the unspeakable and unthinkable – that which is radically 'other' – death is a feminine figure who takes on its horror: the monstrous face of Gorgo, whose unbearable gaze transforms men into stone.
>
> (Jean Pierre Vernant, *Mortals and Immortals*)[1]

> Nature loves to hide.
>
> (Heraclitus, *Fragments*, 123)

Through its elaboration of an aesthetically specific *ars moriendi*, or art of dying, Shakespearean tragedy unsettles the complacency of conventional conceptions of knowledge in a variety of ways. In particular, by dramatizing the crises in an ostensibly objective and implicitly masculine model of knowing, these plays often associate tragic experience with the discovery of the subtle difference of a sensory or bodily knowledge which is intimately allied to the enigmatic physicality of death. Given woman's close tropical affinity with death, it is no surprise that the female body is frequently invoked as an abjected emblem of this other knowing. For by using tragic suffering to problematize not only familiar assumptions about speech and hearing, but also other key aspects of human sensory perception, including smell, taste, and, perhaps most important of all, vision, these plays violently unsettle the authority of the masculine subject position along with the responses of their audiences. This chapter will consider how the masculine eye of its heroic protagonists – whose 'grim looks' are often emphasized – is dislocated in Shakespearean tragedy, along with the hero's 'I' or focused identity, as it is turned away from an implicitly limited, monocular point of view, and towards a more obscure, mutable, yet also implicitly enlarged or 'dilated' perspective.

This uncanny seeing in the dark has a close affinity both with woman's perceived bodily darkness and with paradoxical spectacles of lively death. By compelling the heroic protagonist to see with a difference, or to see 'nothing', tragedy's dark dilations of vision remind us that in its move from ignorance to knowledge, tragic *anagnorisis*, or recognition, often involves a complex, indeed highly contradictory, visual experience: a spectacle whose semiotic instability unsettles any confidence that what is seen can be intellectually deciphered and understood.[2]

In according an especial figurative importance to a female bodily reality in their shadowy process of *anagnorisis*, the tragedies ironically construct what is most notoriously excluded from the Shakespearean stage – the female body – as an absent presence which is intimately allied, not only to tragic vistas of death as 'nothing', but also to a subtle aesthetic awareness of nature as a site of mysterious self-concealment, in spite of contemporary scientific claims to disclose or unveil her secrets. The tragedies' uncanny imbrication of woman's bodily alterity with the *umbrae mortis* or shadows of death echoes the frequent elision, during the Renaissance, of the darkness of the tomb with the hidden bodily origin of all human life: the womb. In his last sermon, 'Death's Duell', John Donne would comment on this mysterious symmetry of our bodily ends with our beginnings:

> Our very *birth* and entrance into this life, is *exitus a morte*, an *issue from death*, for in our mothers *wombe* wee are *dead* . . . We have a winding sheete in our Mothers wombe, which growes with us from our conception, and we come into the world, wound up in that *winding sheet*, for we come to *seeke a grave*.[3]

In Shakespearean tragedy, however, an aesthetic entwining of the signs of death with an occluded feminine matrix is inflected in a less predictable way, for these paradoxical ciphers of an indecipherable 'end' are closely allied with the mysterious flux of nature, and are figured as concealing within themselves the traces or seeds of an ungraspable new beginning that is implicitly material as well as spiritual.

Obscuring the optics of knowledge

Greek philosophy had accorded sight an especially privileged position among the senses, and used it frequently as a metaphor for the highest forms of philosophical knowledge. While the Greek word for theory, *theoria*, means 'contemplation', Platonic philosophy emphasized the visual apprehension of beauty as a means to the acquisition of a knowledge of things invisible. Plato wrote in *The Republic*: 'He who has the capacity to see the whole is a philosopher, who does not is not'.[4] Commenting upon the continuing influence within Western thought of this philosophical definition of knowledge as direct visual apprehension, Martin Heidegger observed that 'In *theoria* transformed into *contemplatio* [by the Romans] there comes to the fore the impulse, already prepared in Greek thinking, of a looking-at that sunders and compartmentalizes'.[5] In the late Renaissance, this philosophical privileging of vision achieved a pervasive cultural dominance, as a crucial tool in early modern man's developing mastery of his environment. But certain other classical texts had bequeathed to Western culture a rather more paradoxical attitude to the visuality of truth; while this had previously informed some of the central motifs of Christian mysticism, the rediscovery of these ancient texts by the Renaissance inspired several less orthodox, aesthetic explorations of nature's mysterious self-concealment. In the *Orphic Hymns*, in Plutarch's *Moralia*, in Apuleius' *The Golden Ass*, and in diverse other texts, Renaissance writers could now find classical personifications of Nature as a mysteriously veiled figure, who is 'seen, yet unseen'; Edmund Spenser describes his veiled goddess Natura as 'Unseene of any, yet of all beheld'.[6]

In its iconoclastic rejection of the veneration of sacred images, its emphasis on the unrepresentable character of the divine, and its firm curtailment of the extravagance of medieval mourning (together with its attendant culture of tears), the Reformation was at one level inviting its adherents to practise a subtle form of 'dark seeing' comparable to that advocated by some medieval mystics; Luther described the soul which has been 'snatched' by the word of God as undergoing a metaphorical death that is also an entry into darkness: 'having entered into darkness and blackness I see nothing; I live by faith, hope and love alone'.[7] Yet ironically, the Reformers' censorship of the visual pleasures which had characterised popular religious culture in the middle ages (a move which had its effects even in Catholic countries) was to facilitate early modern redeployments of the powers of vision as instruments both of secular and of scientific authority. In the first place, as a substitute for the 'believer's vision' of the middle ages, the absolute monarchs of the Renaissance installed what Michel Foucault termed the 'sovereignty of the gaze' – 'the eye that governs' – manipulating elaborate and visually overwhelming spectacles in the service of political power.[8] But at the same time, the new scientific philosophy, which wielded both the telescope and the microscope among its chief instruments, claimed to be the purveyor of a newly objective and 'true' vision of reality. Descartes wrote that:

All the management of our lives depends on the senses, and since that of sight is the most comprehensive and the noblest of these, there is no doubt that the inventions which serve to augment its power are among the most useful that there can be.[9]

The role of this enlarged faculty of sight in the revelation of that which had formerly been hidden from human view was emphasized by several branches of the new science, as – in language which often suggestively echoed colonialist 'discoveries' of formerly uncharted geographical regions – their exponents claimed to lay knowledge newly open to view, by an 'anatomizing' or 'discovery' of that which had formerly been hidden within nature or the body.

Only in the course of the last century has our inheritance of this visual bias in the Western theory of knowledge begun to be explicitly questioned, by thinkers indebted to Heidegger's meditations upon the limitations inherent in the 'enframing' vision of modern culture.[10] The phenomenological critique of Western 'ocularcentrism' which was inaugurated by Heidegger questions the direct relationship that is assumed to exist in modern, post-Cartesian thought, between the eye and mind, and stresses the dangerous impersonality of the scientific gaze of knowledge, pointing not just to its disembodied character, but also to its dependence upon a fundamental separation between the subject and the object of the gaze. The philosopher David Levin has characterized Cartesian vision as follows:

Standing at the window to the modern world, Descartes looks out at men with a mechanical eye, withdrawn from the flesh of the world, immobile, unmoved by all fluctuations of sense and sensibility, functioning according to the laws of a strictly monocular rationality.[11]

For Levin, as for several other critics of ocularcentrism, Cartesian pers-pectivalism only confirms the emotional isolation of the one who looks, at the same time as it serves their subjective drive to power and intellectual mastery. Yet while this knowing scientific gaze, which has done so much to shape the modern world, is also implicitly masculine, the spectacle of woman – towards which the ocularcentric eye of the modern era is drawn as much as to nature – is inherently at odds with this drive to ocular dominance, since it is typically perceived as a site lacking bodily presence. As Luce Irigaray observes in *Speculum: Of the Other Woman*, woman functions instead as 'the representative–representation . . . of the death drives that cannot (or theoretically could not) be perceived without horror, that the eye (of) consciousness refuses to recognize'.[12] In the poetic logic of *Speculum*, the alternative to the masculine, monocular and implicitly disembodied gaze of Descartes is a dilated and inturned vision that is chiastically entwined with the darkness within matter, as well as within the 'empty' female body. This feminine seeing is aptly represented in Irigaray's text by the dark centre of the eye, the pupil, which expands or 'dilates' in darkness, and at whose centre is a physical hole or gap. In this account, the darkened eye becomes: 'A mirror untouched by any reflection . . . *a pupil – a kore –* dilated to encompass the whole field of vision, and *mirroring itself.* Reflecting nothing (but) its own void, that *hole* through which one looks'.[13] In Greek and Latin, as *kóre* and *pupilla*, the pupil was homonymically associated with a maiden or young girl, while the Greek word *kóre* also evokes the goddess of the underworld and death, Kóre or Persephone. Irigaray's dilated, feminine and bodily eye derives from that more open, primordial mode of seeing which phenomenology has explored as an alternative to the ocularcentric gaze, in which the subject of vision becomes chiastically identified with its object. In this altered seeing, the shadow points to 'something else, which it is denied to us of today to know', while vision is no longer used to distance us from an alterity which disturbs or perturbs us; instead, 'the perception of a thing opens me up to being'.[14]

In recent accounts of this contemporary philosophical rejection of ocularcentrism, its debt to an alternative, classical concept of visuality, whose traces are faintly perceptible throughout the history of Western culture, has been largely forgotten. But although the modern optics of knowledge were not explicitly critiqued until relatively recently, their increasing influence during the Renaissance was already being obliquely challenged on an aesthetic level, in works which drew upon the contemporary revival of interest in pagan philosophy, as well as on the Christian emphasis upon the hiddenness of God (somewhat ironically, this latter preoccupation informed both Protestant iconoclasm and the Counter-Reformation and baroque culture of tears, shadows and bedazzlement). For this reason, the tragedies' subtle dilation of the eye/I of their protagonists cannot be reduced to any single ideological or aesthetic influence. Instead, the English Renaissance stage, and Shakespeare in particular, uses the shadowy spectacles of tragedy to question any naivety of intellectual or spectatorial responses.

In Shakespeare's complex analysis of the relationship between death and seeing, not only female bodies but also bodies feminized by death assume an especial emblematic importance. Moreover, in the three tragedies of desire – *Romeo and Juliet, Othello,* and *Antony and Cleopatra* – the figurative entwining of the female body with death or fatality is explicitly troped as a luminous black eye; held to be a distinctive mark of feminine beauty in the Renaissance, this feature may have been artificially produced by the application of a distillation of belladonna or deadly nightshade to the eye, in order to dilate the pupils.[15] In the dilation of the pupil, whether because of a surrounding darkness or the application of belladonna, what is revealed is simultaneously obscure in its blackness. The same paradox, of a *discovery* which is at the same time a *covering*, characterizes Shakespeare's feminine spectacles of death. This early modern use of death as the focus of a resistance to perspectival thinking affords an interesting parallel to Heidegger's definition of truth in relation to an alternative, phenomenological visuality:

> Only what *aletheia* [Greek for truth] as opening grants is experienced and thought, not what it is as such. This remains concealed. Does this happen by chance? Does it happen as a consequence of the carelessness of human thinking? Or does it happen because self-concealing, concealment, *lethe*, belongs to *aletheia*, not just as an addition, not just as a shadow to light, but rather as the heart of *aletheia*?[16]

But early modern interest in the darkness of death also echoes pagan conceptions of Nature's veil as both mysterious and fraught with danger; according to Plutarch, the epigraph on the statue of the Egyptian goddess Isis stated that: 'I am all that is and that was and that shall be, and no *mortal* hath lifted my veil' [my emphasis].[17]

The Earl of Gloucester's blinding in *King Lear* is only the most obvious example of Shakespeare's persistent dramatic critique of the over-confident visuality of the early modern era. It occurs at the very centre of a play that is profoundly preoccupied by the interrelationship between sensory perception and tragic revelation, and whose royal protagonist dies exclaiming: 'Do you see this? Look on her: look, her lips, / Look there, look there!' (5.3.309–10). Neither we nor the other characters can see what Lear thinks he sees on Cordelia's lips, for what he is gazing at is a female corpse that is now, it seems, a dual spectacle of nothing, as both woman and death: 'She's dead as earth', he has just declared. The uncanny doubling effect of this conjunction between woman and the cold rigidity of death is visually emphasized by the mirror of 'stone' which Lear has asked to be placed by Cordelia's face. Gloucester's blinding (like that of Oedipus in Sophocles' Greek tragedy, which is performed on the dead body of his mother/wife Jocasta, and with her own brooches), similarly emphasizes tragedy's identification of 'seeing nothing' with the 'nothing to see' of the female genitals: a connection reinforced in the Renaissance by contemporary allusions to 'eyes' as slang for the genitals. Francis Bacon observed drily that: 'Much use of Venus doth dim the sight', and the sexual dimension of Gloucester's blinding is signified in dramatic terms by the cruel instigation of the act by Lear's highly sexualized elder daughters, Goneril and Regan.[18] But it is also reinforced by the metonymic association of Gloucester's treacherous bastard son, Edmund (who becomes the lover of both sisters), with the darkness and self-concealment of the female genitals; Edgar observes to Edmund of their father's suffering, 'The dark and vicious place where thee he got / Cost him his eyes' (5.3.170–1).

Any cursory examination of the imagery of Shakespeare's tragedies reveals that these plays are full of distracted looks, alluding again and again to eyes which seem to be ready to burst out of their sockets at the impossibility, the excessive horror, of that which they see – or think they see. So Gertrude tells Hamlet after the ghost has appeared to him for a second time, and in her closet, that 'Forth at your eyes your spirits wildly peep' (3.4.119); Desdemona, waking to find Othello in her bedchamber, exclaims 'And yet I fear you, for you're fatal then / When your eyes roll so' (5.2.37–8); Macbeth, looking at his bloodstained hands after he has murdered Duncan, asks 'What hands are here? Ha! they pluck out mine eyes' (2.2.58); and Enobarbus, speaking of Antony's defeat at Actium, declares 'To see't mine eyes are blasted' (3.10.4). Insofar as these grotesquely staring eyes are implicitly 'dilated', it seems that they are figuratively compelled by tragedy to begin that painful seeing in the dark which it demands. For not only do the tragedies trope tragic suffering as a grotesque visual excess which threatens to destroy the reason as well as darken the sight; these plays also make explicit appeals to us, often from the very beginning of their actions, to look with a difference.

Such a concern is vividly emblematized in the first scene of *Hamlet*, which opens with a group of soldiers who belong to the Danish 'watch', but whose nocturnal business of military surveillance – looking for unexpected dangers outside the walls of Elsinore – has been interrupted by the appearance of the ghost. As a result, they have had to enlist the assistance of Horatio as a different, scholarly observer in order to 'approve our eyes'. The play begins, then, with an emblematic in-turning of the collective gaze, away from what is exterior to Denmark and towards the royal revenant, whose uncanny return from beyond the grave signifies to all, however uncertain they may be of its precise meaning, that something is 'rotten' within the state. This domestic in-turning of the tragic gaze is paralleled in the other tragedies; as we shall see, it has an implicitly feminine dimension in its ambiguously 'dark' discovery or opening up of the 'rottenness' of death. For like the interior of the female body, this is a mystery which ultimately eludes the desire for straightforward visual revelation.

At the same time as the male protagonists of Shakespearean tragedy are compelled to turn or redirect eyes which have been implicitly enlarged or dilated by the figurative darkness of tragedy, so too the interrelationship of this tragic redirection of vision with that of the audience is suggested by the change which occurs in their heroic status as spectacular figures, or 'th'observ'd of all observers'. Like the wounds of Coriolanus, the valour of Shakespeare's warrior heroes has formerly caused them to be viewed as ambivalent figures of admirable horror who have themselves worn the mask of Death, since their heroic status has depended on their own engendering of horrific images of death and violence in battle. In the first act of *Macbeth*, we are informed both of the 'reeking wounds' in which Macbeth has 'bathed' with Banquo on the battlefield, 'as if they meant to memorize another Golgotha', and also of the 'strange images of death' which have been wrought by the valiant Scot in defence of his king. Coriolanus too emerges from Corioles 'as he were flay'd'; Volumnia declares that 'Death, that dark spirit, in's nervy arm doth lie' (2.1.159), and he refers to his sword as 'death's stamp'. The close affinity between Othello and Death is likewise implicit, as W. Engel has noted, in that homophonic relationship of 'moor' to *mors* which was often played on in the Renaissance.[19] And just as the one-pointed and wrathful gaze of the warlike Coriolanus is troped as a 'red eye', so we are told at the very beginning of *Antony and Cleopatra* that Antony's 'goodly eyes' have 'glowed like plated Mars' 'o'er the files and musters of the war' (1.1.2–4), while the defeated Goths 'tremble under Titus' threatening look' (1.1.137).

Yet the masks of Death which have been worn by these heroes disintegrate, along with their spectacular authority and their potent singularity of vision, in the face of even stranger images of loss, suffering and death – images that often have a potent feminine dimension. These are 'strange images of death' which figure both tragedy and death very differently, as a self-concealing, metamorphic state that eludes ocular discovery, and is closely entwined with the mutable shapes of nature. While many of these images appear far from the battlefield, others subvert the logic of warfare and of masculine action to which these heroes were formerly wedded. So Coriolanus, from his former cold imperviousness to the 'widows' eyes' which he has created in battle, assumes a 'muffled' or mourning guise on his arrival in Corioles as an exile from Rome, and is himself transformed into a 'boy of tears' when he is faced with his plangent female relatives outside the gates of Rome;

the troping of this ocular phenomenon in bodily terms – we are told that his eyes 'sweat compassion' – hints at a new synthesis of bodily with visual experience. Similarly, Macbeth is only finally afraid 'of death and bane' when he is uncannily assailed by the forces of war under the implicitly feminine mask of nature, as Birnam wood finally comes to Dunsinane. And Antony, watching his fleet's last battle against Caesar from a vantage point next to a pine tree, and half-maddened by its surrender, compares his fall to the loss of a privileged spectatorial and spectacular vantage point which was seemingly synonymous with that phallic masculine authority he had formerly possessed: 'this pine is barked / That overtopped them all' (4.12.22–3). What replaces this commanding singularity of perspective is the overwhelming sense of visual obscurity and flux that Antony terms 'black vesper's pageants', as the fallen hero imagines himself dissolving like a cloud into the world he had formerly commanded by means of spectacular power:

> That which is now a horse, even with a thought
> The rack dislimns and makes it indistinct
> As water is in water . . . now thy captain is
> Even such a body. Here I am Antony,
> Yet cannot hold this visible shape . . .
>
> (4.14.9–14)

By imaging tragedy in terms of a fragmentation or eclipse of clear vision, these plays present an inverted aesthetic parallel of that phenomenon termed *epistrophe* by the Platonists, in which a material or worldly vision was held to be replaced by an immaterial spiritual vision. For not only is the reversal of vision which is accomplished here a visual disempowerment, as it transfers the hero's formerly death-like aspect onto a very different death-like spectacle, whose semiotic obscurity figuratively unmans him; at the same time, this tragic *epistrophe* does not turn the gaze of the heroic protagonist away from material existence or the body – instead, it points to the uncanny feminine flux at the very centre of his identity and his world.[20] This is what Antony calls 'the very heart of loss', to which he has been led (or so he declares just before his bungled suicide) by a feminine darkness and mutability of both character and body: that 'grave charm', 'boggler', and 'right gipsy', Cleopatra. Therefore, like Macbeth, Antony places the blame for his altered vision upon woman's enigmatic alliance with nature, fatality and death.

The fearfulness of the corpse is traditionally associated with its stone-like rigidity and inertia; yet in contrast to the singular 'stamp' of death which was the sword of Coriolanus, the most disturbing feature of these feminine aspects of horror which confront the male protagonist of tragedy seems to be the mysterious mutability that they share with nature (since the natural world only *appears* to be dead in its annual cycle of decay and renewal). As an oxymoronic spectacle of lively death, the mutilated, dying or dead female body defies any simplicity of visual response or 'discovery' on the part of the human observer towards the sphere of matter. But this spectacle may be unsettling too because the movement towards tragedy of a female protagonist frequently coincides with the erosion of her distinctly human character, as she is figuratively reassimilated back into the natural world. The mutilated Lavinia affords a uniquely disturbing figuration of the wounded human body as both tree and deer: her uncle Marcus, finding her 'straying in the park, / Seeking to hide herself, as doth the deer / That hath received some unrecuring wound' (3.1.89–91), asks her 'what stern ungentle hands / Hath lopped and hewed and made thy body bare / Of her two branches, those sweet ornaments / Whose circling shadows kings have sought to sleep in . . . ?' (2.3.6–19). In stressing the damaged relationship to nature's protective attributes of secrecy and shade of a body that is neither alive nor dead, these figurative metamorphoses neither diminish nor alleviate the human pathos of Lavinia's speechless suffering. In later plays, however, while the idealized woman's emblematic assimilation into the sphere of nature loses none of this quality of figurative strangeness, the process is frequently marked by mystery and concealment; it also appears to demand a different response to tragic suffering, by hinting at the function of tragic fatality as a mysteriously benign solvent of the boundaries between human and natural worlds. So Cordelia is 'dead as earth', and Juliet's tomb 'gorg'd with the dearest morsel of the earth' (5.2.46), while both Ophelia and Desdemona perform quasi-ritual acts of identification with the willow tree just before their deaths. And Cleopatra's maternal embrace of the asp in death completes an elision with the 'serpent of old Nile' which was implied earlier in the play, leaving her to wonder, 'Have I the aspic in my lips?'.

But the metamorphic properties accorded to nature in classical antiquity also distinguish female characters who are the direct or indirect agents of some of the most disturbing sights in these tragedies: the 'weyard sisters', Tamora, Lady Macbeth and Goneril and Regan. These women's indecipherable uncanniness and their excessive cruelty and amorality are troped as a disturbing wildness within nature that is intimately related to the engendering of tragedy, and that appears to call into question all conventional meanings of the sign 'woman'. This is what Lady Macbeth calls 'Nature's mischief'. In *Titus*, the phenomenon is signified by the comparison of the savagely vengeful Tamora to Diana, the goddess of wild nature; in *Lear*, by the whore-horse imagery whose prominence in the first part of the play culminates with the troping of Goneril and Regan as centaur-women. Although nature's 'mischief' may be directly or indirectly contrasted with a thaumaturgic 'virtue' hidden within the natural world, and personified by the dead or injured female body, it is similarly resistant to visual apprehension, since it too is intimately associated with the darkness and obscurity of night. In consequence, the disturbing crisis of visual interpretation in relation to the female form which is expressed in Banquo's address to the three sisters is arguably relevant to the entire genre of Shakespearean tragedy:

> What are these,
> So wither'd and so wild in their attire,
> That look not like th'inhabitants o'th'earth,
> And yet are on't? . . .
> you should be women,
> And yet your beards forbid me to interpret
> That you are so.
>
> (1.3.39–47)

Breaching the heroic body

Not only do the tragedies turn the gaze of the male protagonist towards a feminine mutability which threatens both the specular and the spectacular foundations of their heroic existence; their representations of masculine death frequently stress the feminizing effects of a violent opening of the male body. Cleopatra exclaims as Antony dies after his bungled suicide, 'O see, my women, / The crown o'th' earth doth melt. My lord! / O, withered is the garland of the war, / The soldier's pole is fallen' (4.15.64–6). Michael Neill has argued that the imagery of opening or 'discovering' the self which is so prominent in *Othello* suggestively parallels the emergent science of anatomy.[21] Neill contrasts this dramatic 'opening' of masculinity with the externally-directed, performative model of heroic identity which Othello shares with other tragic heroes, stressing instead the mutable and unmanly character of the interiority which his tragic process of discovery reveals. My contention, however, is that the redirected gaze of Shakespearean tragedy differs significantly from the anatomizing perspective to which Neill compares it, and that these plays delineate death instead as a region whose opening perplexingly eludes the ocularcentric and colonialist desire to 'discover', 'map', or 'anatomize' a formerly uncharted territory. For as Neill himself partially acknowledges, what is 'discovered' within the opened body of the male hero is an obscure feminine alterity that cannot easily be measured or defined. Thus the corpse of the murdered Julius Caesar, initially troped as a hart or male deer by his friend Mark Antony, is gradually metamorphosed into a doe or hind, both by the feminine associations of the heart as centre and by the eroticized drift of words like 'bay'd', 'spoil', 'strucken', and 'lie':

> Here wast thou bayed, brave hart.
> Here did'st thou fall. And here thy hunters stand
> Signed in thy spoil and crimsoned in thy lethe.
> O world, thou wast the forest to this hart,
> And this indeed, O world, the heart of thee.
> How like a deer, strucken by many princes,
> Dost thou here lie!
>
> (3.1.204–10)

The emasculating effect of Caesar's bloody death has been analysed in diverse ways by feminist critics. Gail Kern Paster has commented of Caesar's murder that 'The assassination . . . discloses the shameful secret of Caesar's bodiliness: by stabbing and displaying his body, the conspirators cause the fallen patriarch to reveal a womanly inability to stop bleeding'; while Marie-Dominique Garnier has associated it rather with the maternal tropes of a Caesarian birth-within-death which she has shown to run through the play.[22] What is clear is that in their figurative opening or penetration of the heroic body, wounds can suggestively confuse its gender. This disturbing ambiguity of the wound – as a mark of martial prowess that is also the site/sight of its potential loss – appears to underlie the refusal of Coriolanus to show his wounds to the Roman populace, which becomes a chief factor in his escalating tragedy; Janet Adelman notes that this spectacle 'is for him the sign of boundary confusion, a dangerously feminizing self-exposure'.[23] But when this forced bodily opening is effected by a death not received in battle, the violated corpse may be configured as sodomitically 'breached'; and here Marlowe's dramatization of the violently eroticized death of Edward II was probably a decisive influence on Shakespeare's troping of the assaults on sovereign figures in *Hamlet, Lear* and *Macbeth*.

When, in *Macbeth*, Shakespeare describes what for the Renaissance was the ultimate in criminal acts – the murder of a virtuous king – he tropes it both as a classical image of female horror, the Gorgon, and also as a quasi-sodomitical entry of the royal body from behind. In announcing the murder of Duncan to the court, Macduff appeals to them to: 'Approach the chamber, and destroy your sight / With a new

Gorgon' (2.3.70–1), while Macbeth will later declare that 'his gash'd stabs look'd like a breach in nature / For ruin's wasteful entrance', and will describe the daggers of the putative murderers as 'unmannerly breech'd with gore' (2.3.111–14). In his violent death, therefore, it seems that the king has become a grotesquely feminized spectacle of nothing: this feminine breach or gap in nature is, Macduff exclaims: 'death itself . . . the great doom's image' (2.3.77). Macduff's comparison of Duncan's dead body to a representation of Christian apocalypse, or 'the great doom', represents regicide as a phenomenon, however horrific and absolute, that can be revealed and viewed. In contrast, his comparison of the royal corpse to the archaic classical figure of the Gorgon transforms that 'sovereignty of the gaze' accorded to Renaissance monarchs into an apotropaic and feminine stare that cannot be met with safety, but only regarded obliquely – in Greek mythology, those who looked directly into the face of the Gorgon were turned to stone. Accordingly, one of the deadliest spectacles of tragedy – which the audience never actually sees – is refigured as a sense of being *looked at*: by a corpse whose feminization in death reinforces its uncanny status as both more and less than human.

Yet both the figures used by Macduff of Duncan's murder emphasize the close association between tragic spectacle and judgement which pervades the entire play. In the first act, the still honourable Macbeth was 'Nothing afeard of what thyself didst make', but just as the bloody 'images' of death and horror that are engendered by his subsequent murderous actions swiftly contradict his former heroic pretensions fearlessly to control or engender death, so they also condemn both him and his wife to a 'watchful tyranny' in which their eyes can no longer, it seems, be closed by rest, since they are now haunted by the impression of an unnatural surveillance. Positioned at the centre of the play, in fact, is the 'horrible shadow' of Banquo's ghost which, like the corpse of Duncan, is similarly identified with the mysterious, quasi-feminine fecundity that marks the violently 'breached' male body, and which *looks back* at the murderer. The fearful gaze of this 'shadow' is seemingly linked with the spectral figure's ambiguous gender, as its Medusa-like 'gory locks' and uncanny but also bawdy occupation of the stool 'i'th'midst' of the Macbeths' feast hint at the survival of that predestined fecundity which is Macbeth's greatest fear. In the next act, the effect is repeated when Macbeth demands to see the occult 'shows' of the witches, for the 'horrible sight' that he is finally shown is the line of Banquo's heirs; indeed, Marjorie Garber has commented on the show of kings that: 'This is his [Macbeth's] personal Gorgon, the sign of his own futility and damnation'.[24] This ghostly line culminates with the eighth king, corresponding historically to Mary Queen of Scots, who holds a 'glass' in which appear future generations of Banquo's royal heirs. Like Irigaray's dilated eye, which mirrors only the fissures in identity, the glass gives literal shape to the effect of being looked at from beyond the grave by a fertility that transcends death. The feminine attributes of the violated dead body as an opened eye of judgement are similarly implicit in Lear's death as he gazes at Cordelia's dead face, while to the guilty eyes of Othello, even the submissive Desdemona, once dead, is the site of this vengeful and feminine eye of death: 'O ill-starred wench, / Pale as thy smock. When we shall meet at compt / This look of thine will hurl my soul from heaven / And fiends will snatch at it' (5.2.270–2). The visual ensnarement which is attributed to Cleopatra's corpse by Caesar is only slightly more benign: 'she looks like sleep, / As she would catch another Antony / In her strong toil of grace' (5.2.345–6).

Shakespeare's feminized chiaroscuro

Observing that the representation of 'innards' is predominantly 'female' in Greek tragedy, Ruth Padel has connected the classical motif of a dark feminine interiority with the continuing potency attributed by the increasingly rationalist and ocularcentric Greek culture of the fifth century BCE to the chthonic powers, to earth-darkness and to night; in Greek tragedy, Padel points out, 'darkness is where we are most likely to encounter gods'.[25] Shakespearean tragedy echoes its Greek precursors by promoting a subtle redefinition both of darkness and of the material sphere with which darkness was intimately connected. These paradoxical dark openings of the visual field involve obscure spectacles of horror as well as of desire, and may confer madness, illumination, or both. But what is persistently implied is that the uncanny site/sight of death and destruction that is both framed and defined by night is also a mysterious matrix of fertility and renewal, a region in which the annihilating blackness of tragic closure is curiously elided with the dark formlessness of new beginnings.

Although orthodox Christian theology associated darkness with the world, the flesh and the devil, the desirable female blackness which was central to the biblical *Song of Songs* was accorded a complex allegorical significance by Christian commentators, who typically identified it with the hidden Wisdom of God; at the same time, meditation upon an originary divine darkness was central to the branch of Christian mysticism termed the *via negativa* and shaped by the writings of pseudo-Dionysius the Areopagite. Yet the frequency with which Renaissance writers allied darkness and the desirable female body was also indebted to a contemporary revival of interest in some of the more obscure motifs of classical thought and culture, and primarily to representations of Love as blind which were derived from Orphic accounts of Love's birth from a primordial goddess of Night. This was a tradition which influenced several Renaissance thinkers; observing that 'Love is said by Orpheus to be without eyes, because he is above the intellect', the Neoplatonist Pico della Mirandola identified Love's parent Night with the hiddenness of a primordial deity, while Spenser described Night as the 'most ancient grandmother of all, / More old than Jove' (I v 22); later in *The Faerie Queene*, by depicting Night as veiled, Spenser implied that she was the mutable shadow of another veiled figure – Nature.[26] The associations between this primordial darkness and the dynamic properties of matter are hinted at in oxymoronic encomia to the 'dark' beauties of various sonnet-like mistresses which appear in English drama and poetry of the 1590s, where the most significant attribute of darkness is often their black eyes, like those of Sir Philip Sidney's Stella, or Romeo's Rosaline.

The affinity of The *Sonnets*' dark lady, of the tawny-skinned Cleopatra, and of the figuratively 'black' beauties of Shakespeare's comedies with this tradition is immediately striking; however, Lucrece, Tamora, Juliet, and Desdemona too are all metonymically enveloped by the darkness of night.[27] At the centre of *Hamlet*, moreover, is inscribed a highly charged allusion to a mourning oriental queen and mother, Hecuba queen of Troy, whose wordless grief and its nocturnal context is exaggerated by her 'mobled' or muffled face. Hecuba shares this attribute of self-concealment with Night, whom Lucrece describes as a 'blind muffled bawd', as well as with Love, 'whose view is muffled still' (*Romeo and Juliet*, 1.1.169). Like Night, Hecuba symbolizes the obscure interweaving of tragedy and death with beginnings, as the grieving mother of an exemplary tragic moment – the fall of Troy – which the mythological genealogies of many European nations also defined as a site of origin. This 'mobled queen' is draped in several real as well as figurative layers of darkness or self-concealment: her facial 'mobling'; her 'bisson rheum' or blinding tears; the blanket with which she has hastily draped her naked body; the night which envelops her; and also, by implication, the darkness of her skin. Of course, *Hamlet*'s Hecuba never appears on stage, but is evoked only in the First Player's declamatory speech; none the less, her 'mobled' figure casts its mimetic shadow over the entire play. Indeed, she is one of the most potent of Shakespeare's signs for that encounter with a self-concealing origin, or 'nothing', which lies at the heart of tragic suffering.

It is in the love tragedies, however, where 'amorousness' is closely entangled with blackness, fatality and death, that we find the most detailed explorations of the tragic 'turning' of an orthodox, manly or heroic vision towards a feminine darkness, as an obscure spectacle which effects a potent metamorphosis in its beholder. At the beginning of *Antony and Cleopatra,* Philo speaks scornfully of the turning, or 'bending', of Antony's gaze, from Rome to Egypt, and from martial exploits to the dark skin of Cleopatra: 'his goodly eyes . . . now bend, now turn / The office and devotion of their view / Upon a tawny front' (1.1.2–6). Yet since the specific object of Antony's tropically 'bending' gaze is left obscure and undefined, it is implied that the 'tawny front' of Cleopatra may conceal more than it reveals. This uncanny capacity of the Egyptian queen to elude any distinct form of visual apprehension, and hence to defeat the same spectatorial impulse to which she consistently appeals, even in her death, is vividly conveyed in Enobarbus' account of her spectacular epiphany on Cydnus. Here he provides a detailed description of Cleopatra's golden or sun-like entourage but lamely tells us that: 'For her own person / It beggared all description' (2.2.207–8). Enobarbus relates that the queen's pavilion was 'cloth of gold, of tissue', but he leaves the implicitly dark or 'tawny' centre of this highly contrived image of sunny radiance unrepresented, by describing the queen as 'Oe'r-picturing that Venus where we see / The fancy outwork nature' (2.2.210–11). Plutarch had observed that 'they call Egypt, since it is mostly black, Khemia, like the black part of the eye', while Horapollo attributed the metaphor to Egypt's location 'in the middle of the earth, just as the so-called pupil is in the eye'.[28] And like a dilated pupil at the centre of the 'eye' of her gilded pageant, the enigmatically obscure spectacle of Cleopatra on Cydnus reminds us yet again that the 'other' seeing of tragedy conceals as much as it reveals, by directing our attention precisely towards those aspects of experience which elude absolute comprehension. For although she herself uses the trope of Antony's absence from Egypt, it seems that in her association with that which is concealed beneath or behind the 'real' world of glistening appearances Cleopatra herself functions as a dark 'gap in nature', 'the very heart of loss', towards which, sooner or later, tragedy has reluctantly to direct its gaze.

It is not Antony but Romeo, however, who has the most direct encounter with that dilated feminine eye towards which the tragedies direct our attention, and it is this play which hints most explicitly at a more benign aspect hidden behind the 'mask' of night, through night's subtle figurative entwining of death and love. At the beginning of the play Romeo is already avoiding the sun, making himself an 'artificial night' in the cultivation of a fashionable lovesick melancholy. Only on meeting Juliet at a masked ball, however, where this second sun, like the star Sirius, 'hangs upon the cheek of night / As a rich jewel in an Ethiop's ear' (1.5.44–5), does he fully identify with the blinded and nocturnal aspects of Cupid or Love, and become truly 'consorted with the humorous night' (2.1.31). As Mercutio mockingly suggests when he declares the next day that Romeo 'is already dead, stabbed with a white wench's black eye' (2.4.13–14), this encounter with the erotic aspect of a dazzling darkness has a sinister dimension of fatality; in *Titus*, nature's attributes of masquerade and concealment will assume an even more horrifying aspect for Lavinia and Bassianus, when they discover the Gothic queen Tamora and her black lover Aaron under the 'chequered shadow' and 'sweet shade' of the forest. What his love of Juliet obscurely reveals to Romeo, it seems, is the paradoxical beauty and fatality of 'the mask of night', as a region in which death is chiastically crossed with love, shade with brightness, and endings with beginnings. For this dark 'discovery' of physical love – and of the female body in particular – culminates in that 'palace of dim night' which is the Capulet tomb. Juliet has already imagined Romeo as 'thou day in night', and as a constellation of stars that will illuminate (yet also, of course, be revealed by) the darkness of the night; what Romeo finds in the 'lantern' of the tomb is a female body which, like that of Cleopatra, perplexingly combines the attributes of light and darkness, revelation and concealment. Just as Juliet's beauty is depicted here as the lively mask of death, so too, it is implied, the mask of death and night, like the Capulet tomb, envelops a hidden luminosity and beauty. The play ends, therefore, by repeating with a funereal difference Romeo's image in Act 1 of 'those happy masks that kiss fair ladies' brows', that 'being black, put us in mind they hide the fair'. Through this implied comparison of Juliet to the *lumen naturae* of alchemists and natural philosophers, described by Giordano Bruno as 'the light which is in the opacity of matter', *Romeo and Juliet* suggests that the radiance of a hidden deity or *dea abscondita* may be secreted within the darkest of tragic spectacles.

Changing the general's colours

In its uncanny darkening of vision, Shakespearean tragedy parallels some of the most disturbing and least rational elements within classical culture; at the same time, just as did Greek tragedy, it frequently tropes that which challenges the truth of clear vision in terms of an oriental alterity. For as is implied by Romeo's comparison of night to an 'Ethiop', and also by the eerie evocation of the mourning queen of Troy in *Hamlet*, the dilated vision of these plays associates the enigmatic and feminized interiority which is hidden at the heart of tragedy with a disturbingly unspecific racial difference. This figurative nexus is central to *Othello*, whose imagery of racial alterity Patricia Parker has shown to be more intimately entwined with the person of Othello's Venetian bride than it is with the Moor himself: 'in this evocation of an ancient imperial history of male and female, Africa and Rome, Othello evokes Aeneas, male and "European," Desdemona the figure of Dido, female and Moor'.[29] Although her husband is a physical figure of blackness, it is Desdemona, as the woman suspected of adultery, who suffers most explicitly from the metaphoric associations of blackness in the play. However, Desdemona's misrepresentation and death affords an oblique testimony to the imaginative potency of blackness; as Othello's 'cunning'st pattern of excelling nature' (5.2.11) she becomes figuratively entwined with a primordial matrix whose luminous darkness 'cunningly' eludes the optics of truth.

While she has elegantly demonstrated the figurative interrelationship of Desdemona with the darkness of racial difference, Parker has founded her readings of *Othello* upon a sustained and brilliant exposition of the importance of 'close dilations' in its text, relating 'dilations' both to the opening up or 'discovery' of a matter (as in the practices of anatomy and espionage) and to the extended rhetorical treatment of a topic.[30] In an argument which is partly indebted to this subtle analysis, Michael Neill has stated that 'no play in the canon is more obsessed than *Othello* with the idea of laying open'.[31] However, when Shakespearean tragedy is considered from the phenomenological perspective espoused by Irigaray and others, it appears to accord special significance to an additional sense of 'dilation', one which is not current until the eighteenth century, but is nonetheless implicit in the plays' darkening of vision; this relates to an ocular opening which is also a darkening or concealment. As I have already noted, the darkening of the eye which results from the dilation or expansion of its pupils had an intimate association with ideas of feminine beauty in the Renaissance. Thus, while my reading of *Othello* owes an important debt to the work of Parker in particular, it differs from recent accounts of *Othello* as a play of 'discovery' by reading it instead as a play that is shrouded in darkness, and is centrally concerned with what *cannot* be seen. This tragedy's unrepresentable tragic matrix is woman's interior and sexual 'eye', or her 'honour', which as Iago himself has to admit, is 'an essence that's not seen' (4.1.16), since it is concealed within the darkness of the female body.[32] Although it is the investigative desire for an unambiguous visual knowledge or 'discovery' of this feminine secret which causes the irresistible turn towards tragedy, the signs of darkness which cluster around the female body configure it as a site of hiddenness or self-concealment that, even in death, eludes this masculine drive to unconcealment. Indeed, in the play's catastrophe, what is actually discovered – the body of Desdemona – is almost immediately 'covered'.

This concluding emphasis upon the enshrouding and concealment of the female body in death completes the play's transference of attributes between Othello and his bride, as the putative blackness and secrecy attributed to Desdemona by her Moorish husband is finally identified with that of death, or *mors*.

It is Othello's 'ensign' Iago, of course, who gradually manipulates and perverts the gaze of his master, by suggesting that vision can offer some kind of absolute truth and knowledge. As his ensign, Iago has been chosen by Othello to carry his flag or 'colours'; he is therefore 'ensigned' by profession, a character who is marked, we might initially assume, for semiotic decipherment.[33] Yet a new meaning of 'colour', as a cloak of falsehood, dates from 1592, while the play's use of 'ancient' as a synonym for 'ensign' hints at Iago's capacity for a misrepresentation allied to sexuality, since 'ancient' could also mean a bawd. And in his directorial staging of that dumb show or play-within-the-play which identifies Cassio as the new owner of Desdemona's handkerchief, Iago does indeed manipulate the ambiguity of those visual signs, 'flags', or 'colours' which he is professionally charged to display, in order to confirm his own 'colour', or web of lies. For his most important sign, one which no longer confirms but rather undoes 'Othello's occupation', is Desdemona's handkerchief. Once possessed by Iago, this property functions within the play as 'a flag and sign of love, / Which is indeed but sign' (1.1.154–5): a mark, like the treacherous ensign, both of Othello's loss of a stable self-image, and of the self-concealing resistance of certain signs to ocular interpretation.

It is therefore the ensign, rather than the master, who personifies the more conventional tragic affiliation between criminality, deception and darkness in *Othello*. Iago declares at the end of Act 1 that 'Hell and night / Must bring this monstrous birth to the world's light' (1.3.402–3); later he observes that 'When devils will the blackest sins put on / They do suggest at first with heavenly shows / As I do now' (2.3.346–8). Yet through its emphasis upon Iago's 'shows', the play locates the causes of tragedy not in the absolute meaning of particular signs, but rather in the ambiguities of representation itself, whose black or inky materiality Shakespeare plays on repeatedly in his *Sonnets*.[34] Hence Othello's bodily darkness only becomes 'devilish' after its difference has been corrupted by Iago's semiotic manipulations, which are designed to convince him that the most vicious association with darkness, obscurity and conceal-ment is that of his wife.

By advising Othello to 'Look to your wife, observe her well with Cassio' (3.3.200), Iago transforms the initially composed and even somewhat dispassionate general, who has previously been an admired yet strange spectacle among the Venetians he serves, into a parody of a spectator as spectacle, the monstrous figure with rolling eyes who appears to Desdemona as he is about to murder her, when she exclaims: 'And yet I fear you, for you're fatal then / When your eyes roll so' (5.2.37–8). By this means, Othello becomes tragically ensnared in Iago's subtle manipulation of the Western epistemology of the gaze, as a naive belief in the possibility of what he calls 'ocular proof' leads him and Desdemona to tragedy. Yet in contrast to the 'hellish' dissembling of Iago, the vilified attributes of darkness and obscurity which Iago encourages Othello to project on to Desdemona (most notably in the shape of the misplaced handkerchief) function within the play as emblematic figures of the limitations inherent in this Eurocentric system of knowledge, with its narrow code of morality and action founded upon belief in the clarity of vision. Although these signs of concealment and darkness initially unite the lovers, the same imagery will be used on Cyprus to divide them, with tragic consequences. None the less, the imagery alludes obliquely to the faint but palpable trace within the play of a very different mode of apprehension: a bodily seeing that rejects the mastery of the gaze, and is associated with the erotic and generative properties of night, with love as well as with death. As in the *Sonnets*, 'Love's other eye' is here represented as the chaotic matrix or 'cistern' in which what the lover 'discovers' is actually his own lack of any distinct identity. It is precisely his abjection of this inverted and bodily vision that leads Othello to tragedy. By this means, Shakespeare distinguishes the traditional Western association of what is black or cannot easily be seen with evil – which Iago performs as the dishonest bearer, or misrepresenter, of Othello's colours or signs – from what is implied to be blackness's more deeply hidden and potentially creative meaning.

The first act of the play hints at an indirect association between Othello's racial difference and a nocturnal mode of bodily seeing that is intimately allied to love, paralleling that embraced by Romeo and Juliet under the auspices of Blind Cupid. Iago figures the affinity between love and darkness in crude and grotesque imagery when he images the union of Othello and Desdemona in terms of the bodily 'covering' of woman in sexual intercourse with a dark and animal difference, warning Brabantio that 'you'll have your daughter covered with a Barbary horse' (1.1.109–10). The connection is expressed in more abstract and modest terms by Desdemona, when she tells the Venetian senators that she loves the Moor because of an indirect or bodily seeing: 'I saw Othello's visage in his mind' (1.3.253). But while Othello, in his support of Desdemona's plea that she be permitted to accompany her new husband to Cyprus, acknowledges the same association between love and darkness, he explicitly distinguishes love's visual 'dullness', and what in the Folio text is a 'seeling' of the eyes, from that 'speculative' activity which is integral to his profession of soldier:

> And heaven defend your good souls that you think
> I will your serious and great business scant
> When she is with me. No, when light-winged toys
> Of feathered Cupid seel with wanton dullness
> My speculative and officed instrument,
> That my disports corrupt and taint my business,
> Let housewives make a skillet of my helm
> And all indign and base adversities
> Makes head against my estimation.
>
> (1.3.269–75)

The Moor's conjunction of blackness with a famed military prowess has figuratively allied him, like Shakespeare's other warrior protagonists, with the darkness of death as *mors*. But this speech affirms his public commitment to a civic service which is ostensibly founded both on 'speculation' and on a fierce rejection of love's 'seeling' or dulling of sight, in a trope borrowed from the 'seeling' or sewing up of the eyes of an untrained falcon. However, the homophony between 'seel' and 'seal', which is played on in the *Sonnets* (73.1.8) hints at the affinity of this visual envelopment with the power and secrecy of a hidden matrix (as 'seal'). We find a similar implication, of an originary self-concealment, or 'tyring', that the artist or inventor can only struggle to apprehend, in Cassio's blazon of Desdemona as one that 'in th'essential vesture of creation / Does tyre the inginer' (2.1.64–5).

It is his over-estimation of the capacity of vision to discern the truth, together with his negative conception of love's relationship to a visual 'seeling', or seeing in the dark, that will make Othello so susceptible to the ocular manipulations of Iago. In Act 3, Iago will remind Othello:

> She did deceive her father, marrying you,
> And when she seemed to shake, and fear your looks,
> She loved them most . . .
> She that so young could give out such a seeming
> To seel her father's eyes up, close as oak –
> He thought 'twas witchcraft.
>
> (3.3.209–14)

The speech hinges on an identification of Desdemona with the same activity of 'seeling' which Othello has previously identified with Blind Cupid, and which an earlier tragic heroine, Juliet, had celebrated as a gift of 'love-performing night'. By now, however, this secretive and self-concealing attribute of love and lovers has been metamorphosed into a sign of feminine deception that only serves as additional evidence of Desdemona's infidelity.

When, in Act 1, Othello states that 'My parts, my title and my perfect soul / Shall manifest me rightly' (1.2.31–2), the statement hints at his investment in a system of signification in which he believes the signs of interiority (or what Katharine Eisaman Maus calls 'inwardness') can be accurately interpreted. But his error is immediately clear to the audience, who already know that the 'honesty' of the man he has elected to bear his own military sign, flag or colour – Iago – is illusory. The ensuing tragedy will stem from Othello's mistaken confidence in his ability to decipher the meaning of visual signs, as his ensign uses false 'shows' to act out the more conventional association between darkness or concealment and evil. For like the Turkish fleet, which apparently moves towards Rhodes rather than Cyprus at the beginning of the play, Iago stages a 'pageant' to keep Othello 'in false gaze'. What this act of betrayal hinges on is a malicious misrepresentation to Othello of what is now, seemingly, his chief flag or colour: his wife. It is specifically to his ensign's 'conveyance' that Othello entrusts Desdemona on the sea voyage to Cyprus, and as Parker has pointed out, this synonym for carrying has a recurring sense of trickery in Shakespeare.[35]

In Venice, Iago has already begun to manipulate events under that 'cover' of night which predominates throughout the play; it is on Cyprus, however, that his nocturnal manipulations come to fruition. The uncanny result of Iago's plotting is the metonymic transference of Othello's attributes of blackness to the person most intimately associated with him – his wife, with the result that Othello claims that Desdemona's imputed adultery has blackened the whiteness and purity of an honour or name on whose attribution – to Othello or Desdemona – the Quarto and Folio texts are suggestively divided: 'Her [My] name, that was as fresh / As Dian's visage, is now begrimed and black / As mine own face . . . ' (3.3.389–91). In Act 1, the Duke tells Brabantio: 'If virtue no delighted beauty lack / Your son-in-law is far more fair than black' (1.3.290–1); like him, Othello sees himself as white within, white in name and honour. However, he becomes convinced that Desdemona's exterior whiteness conceals an interior darkness. Yet while Shakespeare's text reminds us that this attribution of an interior darkness to woman has a powerful biological source, Othello's hubristic belief that he can decipher the moral implications of this bodily interiority or concealment is shown to be tragically mistaken.

On Cyprus, the influence of Iago makes Othello ever more obsessed with what can be seen – or seen through. His statement after he has murdered Desdemona that: 'Had she been true, / If heaven would make me such another world / Of one entire and perfect chrysolite, / I'd not have sold her for it' (5.2.139–42), equates his ideal, virtuous woman with a crystalline transparency or translucency. This is a model of feminine virtue which takes no account of the metonymic association between sexual love and darkness; when Desdemona tells Emilia that she would not abuse her husband 'in such gross kind' as he has suggested, she swears 'by this heavenly light!', to which Emilia retorts: 'Nor I neither, by this heavenly light: / I might do't as well i'th' dark' (4.3.64–6). Indeed, while Othello declares of Desdemona's putative affair with Cassio that 'I'll see before I doubt' (3.3.193), Iago points out that the sexual act is typically invisible to others, hidden away from the public view (and also, of course, unrepresentable on the Renaissance stage). He answers Othello's demand for 'ocular proof' of Desdemona's affair with Cassio by asking:

> Would you, the supervisor, grossly gape on?
> Behold her topped?. . .
> It were a tedious difficulty, I think,
> To bring them to that prospect. Damn them then
> If ever mortal eyes do see them bolster
> More than their own. What then? How then?
> It is impossible you should see this
> Were they as prime as goats, as hot as monkeys,
> As salt as wolves in pride, and fools as gross
> As ignorance made drunk . . .
>
> (3.3.398–408)

Since Iago cannot offer Othello this spectacle of sexual performance – a possibility that clearly fascinates Othello as much as it horrifies him – he positions him instead as the moralistic but equally voyeuristic audience to his ensign's own perverted style of dramatic production, offering him an illusory and incomplete vision of 'truth' which Othello obligingly fills out with the monstrous creatures of his own imagination. Not only does the 'ocular proof' that Othello is eventually shown by Iago not directly involve Desdemona at all, it also uses as her metonymic substitute a 'flag and sign of love': the 'handkerchief' or 'napkin' which was a love gift,

and which symbolizes, not the revelation, but the covering and concealment of woman's body. Since 'handkerchief' derives from the French
word 'to cover', it has a buried association both with the oriental veil and
also with that dark sexual activity of 'covering' alluded to by Iago in Act
1. At the same time, 'napkin' has associations with the material matrix or
'pattern' to which Othello compares Desdemona before he kills her
(5.2.11), as well as with the contrasting activities of both discovery and
concealment; the word has an etymological affinity with 'map', from the
Latin for napkin, *mappa*, while in the Renaissance 'to napkin' was to wrap
up or hide. Rather than Desdemona herself, it is this textural figure for
a revelation that is also a concealment which constitutes the centrepiece
of the dumb show that Othello finally observes in Act 4 scene 1. From
his hiding place, Othello can hear nothing, which suits Iago perfectly;
what he wants is to offer him a purely visual perspective on his own
exchange with Cassio, which will actually be about Bianca rather than
Desdemona.

One of the most notable attributes of Night as a goddess of archaic
origins is her textural muffling or covering; yet it is paradoxically the
loss of her 'covering' handkerchief or napkin which accelerates the
transference of Othello's attributes of blackness onto his wife. Indeed,
soon after the handkerchief scene, Desdemona is being addressed as
'thou black weed' (F, 4.2.68) – a trope which elides the infection of nature
with an image of woman as a dark garment of concealment. Whereas her
husband's blackness had formerly caused him to be termed a 'devil', it is
now Desdemona who is accorded the black attributes of the underworld
and death: 'You! Mistress! / That have the office opposite to Saint Peter
/ And keep the gates of hell' (4.2.92–4). And Parker has noted that a
further figurative identification with a creative version of her imputed
'blackness' is apparent in the melancholy lament sung by Desdemona
shortly before her death, since not only does Desdemona attribute this
song to her mother's maid, Barbary, whose name associates her with the
Berber 'darkness' of North Africa; the song's central motif of the willow
may also associate the unlucky bride with the abandoned North African
queen, Dido.[36] Yet while Desdemona becomes the bearer of all the
negative cultural associations of her husband's bodily blackness, in a
process that ends with her literal and fatal muffling (or napkining) in the
nuptial bed linen that has become her shroud or winding sheet, through
this misrepresentation, the play explores the intimate yet disturbing
associations between woman, the goddess of erotic love, of origins and of
endings, and the tragic paradox of seeing in the dark.

At the beginning of Act 2, Othello's forces are about to arrive on the
island, not only at night, but in the middle of a terrible storm, when the

sea 'seems to cast water' even on the stars, so that those looking out for
the Venetian ships cannot distinguish between dark sea and dark sky.
This scene of natural disorder is imaged by the observers as a return to
an originary watery formlessness; the second gentleman reports:

> The chidden billow seems to pelt the clouds,
> The wind-shaked surge, with high and monstrous mane,
> Seems to cast water on the burning bear
> And quench the guards of th'ever-fired pole.
> I never did like molestation view
> On the enchafed flood.

(2.1.12–17)

When Desdemona's ship emerges first, and almost miraculously, out of
this storm, Shakespeare stresses the centrality of woman, female sexuality
and love to these vistas of a dark and watery chaos, by reminding us both
of mythical accounts of Venus' emergence from the sea onto the island
and of the Orphic notion of Love's birth from Chaos. For Desdemona's
arrival is seemingly a second birth of Venus; the courtly Cassio speaks
of 'the divine Desdemona', greeting her on his knees, and references
elsewhere in this scene to Desdemona as 'Our great captain's captain'
and Othello's 'fair warrior' further remind us of the myth of Venus'
union with Mars, the god of war, as a result of which she was sometimes
figured with his attributes, as an armed Venus. A Venusian comparison
also informs Desdemona's witty exchange of words with Iago and Emilia
soon after she disembarks, in which she speaks surprisingly knowingly
of women and sexuality, as a bride who has apparently not yet consummated her marriage. Desdemona specifically hints here at the obscure
masquerade of female sexuality, declaring that: 'I do beguile / The thing
I am by seeming otherwise' (2.1.121–2), and asking Iago how he would
praise a woman who is both 'black and witty' – that is, sexually knowing
(2.1.131).

Parker has noted that a homophonic relationship between Venice and
Venus implicitly informs the play's focus upon a Venetian bride whose
fate is sealed on Venus' own birthplace of Cyprus. Yet further insight
into the complex function of this mythological imagery, within a play
whose plot pivots upon the gradual enshrouding of a beloved woman
in darkness and death, is afforded by two hitherto unobserved homophones of Cyprus in the Quarto text of the play; this includes spellings of
Cyprus as 'Cipres', 'Cipresse', 'Cypres', or 'Cypresse'. The 'cypress' was
the dark tree of mourning, death and concealment that was planted in
Mediterranean graveyards, and was frequently used for coffins because

of its durability. It was a seemingly contradictory attribute of the goddess of love; in Francesco Colonna's *Hypnerotomachia Poliphili* (1499), cypress trees are described as encircling another island associated with Venus, that of Cythera. But 'cypress' has a textural meaning as well, as the name for textile fabrics which were orginally imported from or through the island of Cyprus; these were gauzy materials resembling cobweb, lawn or crape, when black, they were much used for habiliments of mourning, as 'sad cypress'. Cypress appears to have become especially fashionable around the turn of the century: John Florio notes its association with a feminine veiling, as '*Velaregli*, shadowes, vailes, Launes, scarfes, Sipres or Bonegraces that women use to wear over their faces or foreheads to keepe them from the Sunne'; cypress's figurative affinity with a sexual opening that is also a concealment is suggested in Thomas Campion's lyrical evocation of the dark hours best suited to lovers, when 'the Sypres curten of the night is spread'; while in *Twelfth Night*, 'sad cypress' emblematizes the self-concealment of those marked by death or loss.[37] On Venus' island, therefore, the wider implications both of *Othello*'s nocturnal setting and of its preoccupation with veiling and hiddenness become apparent, as the island becomes the tomb-like site for a tragic encounter with the funereal and self-concealing attributes of Venus; in antiquity, the goddess had a little-discussed association with darkness, fatality and death: in particular, as Venus Libitina, the Romans accorded her rulership of sepulchres, while she was depicted as mourning the death of Adonis wholly shrouded with a cypress-like veil (Plate 6).[38]

On Cyprus, Desdemona's fate becomes mysteriously entangled with the textural traces of an obscure yet potent maternal origin that is sym-bolically positioned outside the continent of Europe. This hidden matrix is evoked primarily through the theft or 'conveyance' of the handkerchief which Othello had received from his mother; but another half-effaced maternal figure is evoked in Desdemona's willow song, which she learnt from her mother's maid. While one mother (Othello's) is Moorish and another (Desdemona's) Venetian, both are associated with an indefinite oriental alterity via a metonymic link with another woman – the Egyptian charmer who gave Othello's mother the handkerchief, and the plaintive maid called Barbary. This produces an uncanny doubling of both mothers, Venetian as well as Moorish, and hints at the suspension of ethnic differences in relation to a female creatrix.

Just as Cyprus is defined in the play as a liminal and contested zone between east and west, between Turk and Venetian, so it is here that the relationship between love and that primordial darkness or chaos which Orphic thought held to be concealed behind or beneath love becomes increasingly clear. Othello exclaims of Desdemona, 'perdition catch my

Plate 6 Venus mourning the dead Adonis. V Cartari, *Les images des dieux* (Lyons: 1610). By permission of the Syndics of Cambridge University Library.

soul / But I do love thee! and when I love thee not / Chaos is come again' (3.3.90–2). The exclamation hints at the potency within the play of 'chaos', as a primordial and watery darkness of beginnings which is elsewhere implied to be closely related to the womb. As Othello's love for Desdemona itself dissolves into chaos, the horror elicited by his belief in her adultery appears to be intimately entangled with his violent abjection of the feminine body as a dark matrix or place of origin. The result of this disgust for woman's obscure entanglement with the disorderliness of beginnings is that Othello literally puts love to death.

Botticelli's 'Birth of Venus' uses the bright colours of early Renaissance art to create a seemingly virginal and certainly coy image of the great love goddess. But Desdemona's reenactment of the birth of Venus is a more baroque and sexualized affair, framed by the darkness of the storm, and juxtaposing Cassio's Petrarchan hymn to her 'divine' beauty with Iago's bawdy references to the abhorrent difference of female sexuality. Just as her exchange with the 'critical' Iago reminds us of Venus' patronage of sexual activity, Desdemona's potential fecundity is also hinted at in this scene. For in the bride's arrival *before* her spouse (in a departure from nuptial conventions which is somewhat ominous) there occurs an early displacement of the signs associated with Othello onto his wife. When the people cry 'A sail!', Cassio declares that 'My hopes do shape him for the governor' (2.1.55); instead, the ship which has been sighted bears Iago and Desdemona. Shakespeare's allusions to sails frequently stress their potential for a feminine conception, as they become 'bellied' with the wind; the sail image consequently extends Desdemona's representation as one who is birthed to encompass the idea of a potential genetrix, able to impose form upon chaos. Othello, when he comes ashore to join Desdemona, sees their reunion, significantly and ominously, as an achieved end: 'If it were now to die / 'T'were now to be most happy'. His bride, however, replies in the language of fertility and growth: 'The heavens forbid / But that our loves and comforts should increase / Even as our days do grow' (2.1.187–93). Yet the play's first textural sign also suggestively anticipates both the ambiguous provenance and the emblematic function of the cypress / handkerchief / veil imagery; in French, 'voile' is a synonym for both sail and veil.

The misplaced matrix

Julia Kristeva has argued that 'Fear of the archaic mother turns out to be essentially fear of her generative power'.[39] On Cyprus, Othello's increasingly grotesque language tropes the womb as a dark and form-less receptacle, whose wateriness evokes those dark seas from which Desdemona's 'sail' has emerged: 'a cistern for foul toads / To knot and gender in' (4.2.62–3). The imagery echoes that contemporary conception of women's bodies as watery which has been discussed by Gail Kern Paster.[40] At the same time, the emblematic power of the handkerchief as a love- and death-token inheres to an important extent in its association both with Othello's mother and with a deadly feminine matrix; 'she dying, gave it me', and 'it was dyed in mummy, which the skilful / Conserved of maidens' hearts' (3.4.76–7). When Othello asks Desdemona about the handkerchief's whereabouts, he warns her to 'Make it a darling, like your precious eye! – / To lose't or give't away were such perdition / As nothing else could match' (3.4.68–9). This other, single eye is seemingly the dark and hidden eye of the female genitalia, and as numerous critics have pointed out, if we pursue the logic of the motif of defloration which is represented by the spotted pattern of the handkerchief, what is implicitly alluded to here is the figurative – and physical – unveiling of woman through the tearing of her hymeneal veil.[41] But it seems that for Othello the loss of virginity implies a specifically tragic fall or 'perdition'. For what Othello is tormented by on Cyprus is a feeling of loathing for the 'darkness' of the sexually experienced woman, who by the loss of her bodily veil or covering paradoxically becomes opaque rather than transparent to the masculine gaze, since she now invites a different, sexual or bodily style of 'seeing'. He tells Desdemona that his mother believed the loss of the handkerchief would _divert_ his father's gaze from her irrevocably: 'if she lost it / Or made a gift of it, my father's eye / Should hold her loathed' (3.4.59). Yet the disastrous unfettering or unveiling of this feminine generative potential seems none the less to reveal the apotropaic effects of the opened female body; not only does Othello associate the loss of the state figured by the handerchief with the opening, _through its loss_, of another eye, both single and 'precious', he also stresses the revulsion of the masculine gaze from this uncovering of a 'loathed' maternal origin. Hence this bodily loss or opening, represented as the revelation of something too fearful to look on, is seemingly comparable to the opening of that petrifying feminine gaze alluded to in the other tragedies, as a disclosure which simultaneously protects and encloses a feminine secret. A similar look, of course, will be attributed by Othello to Desdemona's corpse.

Ultimately, it remains unclear whether Desdemona's 'precious' bodily eye is ever opened, since critics are uncertain if her marriage to Othello is consummated. However, in declaring that 'when I have plucked the rose / I cannot give it vital growth again, / It must needs wither. I'll smell thee on the tree . . . ' (5.2.13–15), Othello emphasizes his failure to accept the relationship between sexuality and those cyclical processes of death and rebirth which were associated with Venus as a dark goddess of nature. In the bedchamber, the play reaches its point of utmost darkness when Desdemona's face is fatally veiled as her husband smothers her (most probably, and most ironically, on a bed positioned within the recessed 'discovery space' of the English Renaissance stage). Thus the darkness which could have facilitated an obscure, erotic seeing becomes the setting for a real, rather than a figurative and sexual, 'covering' and 'dying'.

Othello's last speech seems obliquely to allude to the failure of his former model of vision. It does so, not only in its reference to the dead Desdemona as the lost, because unrecognized, pearl (which by implication has been reconcealed in the sea after removal from the concealment of its shell), but also in its hint of a renewal of vision achieved through weeping: Othello describes himself as 'one whose subdued eyes, / Albeit unused to the melting mood, / Drops tears as fast as the Arabian trees / Their medicinable gum'. The meaning of this new 'medicinable' vision, as a mysterious yet natural by-product of his ocularcentric tragedy, seems closely related to Othello's decision 'to die upon a kiss', as his body finally covers that of Desdemona, reconcealing her pale corpse once more beneath the darkness of death, and embodying in himself a final elision of *mors* with *amor*, or Death with Cupid. But like the opacity of the sexualized female body, it seems that the complex meaning of the lovers' corpses defies visual apprehension. Indeed, Lodovico asserts that this is a spectacle fit only for the perverted eye of Iago: 'Look on the tragic loading of this bed: / This is thy work. The object poisons sight, / Let it be hid' (5.2.361–3).

5

FORTUNE'S FOOLS:
REVOLUTIONS OF TIME,
FATE AND SOVEREIGNTY

Macbeth (c.1606)

> The road is opened up in nature or matter, forest or wood (*hyle*)
> and institutes a reversibility of time and space. . . . the question
> – sexuality – is determined, defined or undefined, only in return
> and by the answer itself.
>
> (Derrida, *Writing and Difference*)[1]

> We do not mean the coursing snatchers only,
> But fear the main intendment of the Scot,
> Who hath been still a giddy neighbour to us
> . . . pouring like the tide into a breach,
> With ample and brim fullness of his force,
> Galling the gleaned land with hot assays . . .
>
> (Shakespeare, *Henry V*, 1.2.142–51)

In contrast to the category of *anagnorisis*, the Aristotelian concept of
a tragic *peripeteia* or fall has received surprisingly little attention, above
all in its implications for the relationship of the tragic protagonist to
time. Yet it is both perplexing and suggestive that Aristotle defined the
tragic crisis as a fall or change which is not a decline from a great height,
but is rather a turning about or around, from *peri-pipto*. Moreover, its
Greek etymology further suggests that this fall may have hidden erotic
connotations, since *peri-pipto* could also mean 'to embrace'. I will show in
this chapter that Shakespeare's tragedies configure the moment of tragic
peripeteia or fall as a circling backwards in time that often has a potent
erotic dimension, and which can further imply a suggestive deviation
from conventional masculine identity. This turning backwards has a
clear affinity with the Platonic concept of *epistrophe* or 'reversion', in
which the Many return to the One; however, the Shakespearean and
tragic version of return is typically inflected as a return to a material and
earthly origin.[2]

In their implication that tragic knowledge involves a new understanding of temporal recurrence, or of circularity, these plays afford a partial parallel to a suggestive passage from the *Essayes* of Michel de Montaigne, where the wise man is advised to avoid the temptation to rush forward *en ligne droit*:

> The more wee amplifie our neede and possession, the more we engage our selves to the crosses of fortune and adversities. The carriere of our desires must be circumscribed, and tied to strict bounds of neerest and contiguous commodities. Moreover, *their course should be managed, not in a straight line, having another end, but round [en rond]*, whose two points hold together, and end in our selves with a short compasse. [my emphasis][3]

Montaigne commends this apparently perverse circularity of direction because it returns the individual to the 'self', thereby freeing them from 'the crosses of fortune and adversities' which are encountered in the reckless 'carriere of our desires'. In Shakespeare's tragedies, however, rather than being freely chosen, the discovery of an identity with and in death, often figured as a temporal 'falling backwards', is enforced by a feminine-gendered Fate or Fortune. This concept of a circular temporality is inflected differently in each play; yet it is in *Macbeth*, above all, that the implications of pre-modern conceptions of temporal recurrence are explored most suggestively. For not only does the play's complex meditation upon time effect a subtle reconfiguring of the meanings of tragedy; it simultaneously offers an intriguing political comment upon the recent accession of James I, as a king whose sovereignty is implied to be closely related to the enigmatic circularity of time.

Although a disordering or differing of time has frequently been associated with Shakespearean comedy and romance, critical exegesis of the tragedies, as well as of the histories, has typically defined the temporal paradigms of these plays in relation to a familiar, 'modern' model of historical time, as diachronic or linear. Yet Marjorie Garber has brilliantly demonstrated that 'the whole pattern of history comes full circle' within the reverse order of Shakespeare's two historical tetralogies:[4]

> The fact that the first comes second and the second comes first instinctively problematizes the whole question of double time as it relates to the genre of the history play. The first tetralogy predicts the second; the second also predicts the first.[5]

Garber's account sees this curious reversal of temporality primarily as a theatrical device; yet it is also implicitly related to Renaissance interest in ancient conceptions of a cyclical or repetitive model of time, which had been shared by a majority of thinkers and intellectual systems in classical antiquity. My assumption is that the time which is 'out of joint' in Shakespearean tragedy is linear and successive time: the time which may be termed (to borrow and reapply a phrase used in Derrida's *Given Time*), 'the time of the king'. For it is not only in *Hamlet* that a tragic disjointing of time is intimately related to a crisis in masculine authority, deriving in that play from acts of regicide and usurpation. What Francis Barker has called 'an assault on sovereignty' is also a central theme in *Lear* and *Macbeth*, and Barker has suggested that this assault 'co-involves the dismantling even of time itself': the loss of a former period of temporal and historical coherence, associated with the imagined fullness of the old king's body.[6] A similar theme is adumbrated in several of Shakespeare's early histories, as well as in *The Rape of Lucrece*, where the rape destroys the moral credibility of the Tarquins as kings of Rome along with Lucrece's confidence in the 'proportioned course of time' (774). And while kingship itself is not at stake in *Romeo and Juliet*, *Othello*, and *Antony and Cleopatra*, we see there too a disruption of the diachronic ordering of time and society associated with the father's law and the father's line.

The turning backwards of time

Allied with this disjointing of linear time is a more or less explicit awareness of another patterning of time, as circular and repetitive rather than straight and linear. It is this ostensibly tragic discovery of a time that is cyclical which prompts Edmund's dying words in *Lear*: 'The wheel is come full circle; I am here', as well as Cassius's remark at the end of *Julius Caesar* that 'the time is come round'. While the tragedies' 'disjointing' of masculine inheritance calls into question an optimism in man's – and history's – onward progress, simultaneously they explore the effects of a circling back or inwards of the tragic protagonists; through this process, the greater influence upon their living and dying of a different time or timing is suggested. According to Barker, this tragic fissuring of what he calls 'chronometric' time is also a 'denaturing of time'. Yet in fact, the ostensible ordering of time and history in sequential and teleological terms which was implicit in the millenarian expectations of Christian eschatology, and which was also inspiring hopes for the gradual improvement of human society and culture in certain secularizing writers of the late Renaissance, had far less affinity with the category of nature than did that periodic, cyclical view of time and history with which it was often contrasted by Renaissance thinkers, and which by the middle ages had even begun to qualify some aspects of Christian theology.[7] As reinterpreted by the early Renaissance, the association of a circular image of time with nature could have extremely idealized associations, with the *restitutio omnium* or 'restitution of all things' which would coincide with the restoration of a lost Golden Age, or with the perfecting of nature attempted by the alchemists, who called their art the *opus circulatorium*. Both of these conceptions were indebted to the Platonic association of the circle with eternity. But the preoccupation of the Renaissance with periodicity or temporal recurrence could have less idealized associations, with the discovery of nature's inherent tendency to change and flux: a state often seen as analogous to the primal chaos. This was indeed the starting point of the 'circular' alchemical work, which commenced with a turning backwards to the original state of prime matter.[8] In a formulation which allies this circularity of nature with the most familiar attribute of fortune, Giordano Bruno remarked in *De gli eroici furori* that 'nature delights in the vicissitude which is seen in the revolution of her wheel'.[9] In the tragedies, images of cyclical time, and of turning or returning, frequently coincide with a tragic unsettling of the linear and lineal time of the king or *pater familias*, and evoke the spectre of a perpetual mutability in nature as well as in history.

It is to elude the threat of 'Nature's audit', or judgement, which he allies figuratively with the cycle of the seasons, as well as with the ambiguous bodily depredations of time's 'hours', that Shakespeare urges the young man of the *Sonnets* to beget an heir. In his narcissistic focus on the erotic pleasures of the present moment, by enjoying 'the hours and times of your desire' (57.2), it seems that the youth has fallen prey to a dimension of time which is often figured in feminine tropes: to 'sluttish time' (55.4), to the 'dial hand' of beauty (77.2), and to 'Time's hours' (or whores); this familiar homonymic association between 'hours' and 'whores' may allude to the classical conception of the Hours as the 'porters' or guardians of heaven's gate.[10] The poet warns the youth that 'If all were minded so, the times should cease' (11.7), and while he continues, intermittently, to praise him, it seems the beloved has now become a feminized figure of the past rather than a vital link in the chain of masculine inheritance: 'Thus is his cheek the map of days outworn. . . . In him those holy antique hours are seen' (68). In the tragedies (and also in *Titus* and *Lucrece*), a sudden break in 'the time of the king' is integrally related to an analogous disruption of the expected course of patrilineal succession. This preoccupation obviously addresses one of the most pressing questions of the day: the ending of the Tudor dynasty with the reign of Elizabeth I. But alongside repeated disruptions or deferrals of succession, often as a result of the actions of feminine figures who pervert or disregard woman's procreative role by aligning themselves with death rather than with birth, the tragedies are also preoccupied with various forms of temporal repetition which are equally unsettling of the established order. Unlike Renaissance myths of the Golden Age, these motifs do not image cyclical recurrence in terms of exact resemblance, and hence as involving a restoration of traditional or Saturnian forms of masculine authority; instead, they trope what Coriolanus calls the 'slippery turns' of the world as a process of repetition that involves a distinctly feminine difference, or vicissitude, since it is attributed to the fickle goddess Fortuna.

In her essay 'Women's Time', Julia Kristeva explicitly associates woman with a differing of conventional temporality, arguing that she has a close connection both with cyclical time or temporal repetition (presumably because of the periodicity of her bodily cycles), and also with that timeless time which Christian thought typically opposes to linear or historical time: this 'monumental' time has affinities with the 'other' time of myth, as well as with the Christian concept of eternity.[11] These associations are derived primarily from that feminine figuration of the Nietzschean thought of eternal return which has recently been illuminated by Ned Lukacher;[12] however, they are also consistent with the close connection between classical ideas of cyclical time and the ultimate subjection of human life, above all at the moment of death, to forces wholly beyond its control. Such influences could be variously defined: as Fortune or fate, as the motions of the soul, or as the process of natural decay. In Shakespeare's historical tragedies, moreover, this temporal differing is typically associated with the rule of tyrannical or disturbingly wanton female rulers or consorts – Tamora, Gertrude, Lady Macbeth, Goneril, Regan and Cleopatra – who appear to image in their persons the fickleness, even the inherent doubleness, of cyclical time and of Fortune. At the same time, in *Romeo and Juliet*, *Othello* and *Hamlet*, temporal dislocation is also allied with an imagined or real discovery of woman's sexual autonomy or wantonness, as one who, like Fortune's wheel and the cycle of the years, 'can turn, and turn, and yet go on / And turn again . . . ' (*Othello*, 4.1.253–4).[13]

The idea of time as a sphere or wheel, and hence of its cyclical recurrence, had been pervasive in Greek and Roman antiquity.[14] The concept is already dimly present in Hesiod's *Works and Days*, but it was given pre-eminent authority among the ancients by its appearance in the works of both Plato and Aristotle. In the *Timaeus*, the Demiurge's creation of the soul of the world is described as incorporating two intersecting yet opposed *circular* motions, which cross one another in the form of the Greek letter *chi*:

> . . . he cleft the structure so formed lengthwise into two halves, and laying the two so as to meet in the centre in the shape of the letter X, he bent them into a circle and joined them, causing them to meet themselves and each other at a point opposite to that of their original contact: and he comprehended them in the motion that revolves uniformly on the same axis, and one of the circles he made exterior and one interior. The exterior motion he named the motion of the Same, the interior that of the Other. And the circle of the Same he made to revolve to the right by way of the side, that of the Other to the left by way of the diagonal.[15]

This stress on the dual circularity of motion within the created universe has important implications for Plato's conception of time, since Timaeus subsequently asserts that:

> Time then has come into being along with the universe, that being generated together, together they may be dissolved . . . and it was made after a pattern of the eternal nature, that it might be as like to it as possible.[16]

This highly influential text defines time as the moving image of eternity, the motion in question being that of the heavenly bodies.[17] It emphasizes, however, that the planetary orbits are not perfect circles but spirals. And especially significant for the concerns of this chapter is Timaeus' curious observation that the planets occasionally circle round in the reverse direction; this conception of their *tropai* or 'turnings back' presumably referred to the phenomenon of the apparent retrograde movement of the planets.

Aristotle's version of time was similar to Plato's, although far more pragmatic. He wrote in the *Physics*:

> we say that human affairs and those of all other things that have natural movement and become and perish seem to be in a way circular, because all these come to pass in time and have their beginning and end as it were 'periodically'; for time itself is conceived as 'coming round' . . . Hence, to call the happenings of a thing a circle is saying that there is a circle of time; and this is because it is measured by a complete revolution . . . [18]

The continuing influence of a broadly Platonic view of time in Augustan Rome is evidenced in Book VI of the *Aeneid*, where Anchises describes to Aeneas the fate of departed souls, who must wait:

> till lapse of days, when time's cycle is complete [*perfecto temporis orbe*], takes out the inbred taint and leaves unsoiled the ethereal sense and pure flame of spirit. All these, when they have rolled time's wheel through a thousand years, the god summons in vast throng to the river of Lethe, in sooth that, reft of memory, they may revisit the vault above and conceive desire to return again to the body.[19]

But probably the most detailed account of cyclical recurrence known to the ancient world was that of Stoicism, which (in a doctrine thought to have been derived from Pythagorean thought) maintained that following its periodic destruction by fire or water, the universe would be exactly recreated. Like that of Plato, this perspective was combined with an emphasis upon the influence of the stars; from the time of Cicero, Stoic thought was closely interwoven with beliefs in astrology disseminated from the Near East. Yet while only the material, or 'sub-lunary' sphere was ultimately subject to impermanence and flux in Platonic and neo-Platonic accounts of time, no such distinction was made by the Stoics who deemed spirit to be immanent in the material world, and were consequently sceptical about the possibility of individual immortality. Instead, Stoicism held that a manly and active virtue, defined as a life in conformity with nature and fortune, was the only way to transcend the cycles of flux and vicissitude. Like previous Greek thinkers, Stoicism related these cycles to the capricious feminine figures of Necessity (Ananke), Fate (Heimarmene), and Fortune (Tyche), and above all to the stars.[20]

The classical model of time as a cyclical process was well known to the middle ages. For example, the mythology of Saturn was explained by Macrobius as follows:

> It is said that Saturn used to swallow his children and vomit them forth again, a myth . . . pointing to an identification of the god with time, by which all things in turn are created, destroyed, and brought to birth again.[21]

Here the idea of temporal recurrence is allied with a masculine deity of time; however, it was also frequently imaged by medieval artists and writers as the attribute of a feminine deity or power, in the form of

Fortune's wheel. Whereas for the ancients the power of Fortuna (or Tyche for the Greeks) was often synonymous with that of the gods, in the medieval context her activity was normally subordinated to the will of God, or to Christian Providence (as in Boethius' *De Consolatione Philosophiae*). But during the Renaissance, traditional Christian conceptions of temporality and providence were implicitly challenged by attitudes derived from classical, especially Stoic sources. Central to this change was a renewal of interest in pagan concepts of Fortune, in which she was accorded a much more extensive control over the sphere of fate and destiny, sometimes as one of the Fates, sometimes as what Alberti described as a 'supreme goddess'.[22] Thus just as Seneca maintained that 'Thou canst not wander from thy Fortune, she will beseige thee, and whether thou goest a great traine will follow thee',[23] so an exemplary late Renaissance text such as Montaigne's *Essayes* worked numerous variations on the theme of submission to Fortune's embrace (or of *allant entre ses bras*):

> Good and bad fortune, are in my conceit two soveraigne powers. 'Tis folly to thinke, that humane wisedome may acte the full part of fortune . . . I say moreover, that even our wisedome and consultation for the most part followeth the conduct of hazard.[24]

The doubleness of Fortune alluded to here, which was derived from one of her classical representations as dual or bi-frontal, recurs frequently in Renaissance explorations of her significance (Plate 7). So too does an interest in her association with the vicissitude of temporal cycles, which was already implicit in two of her medieval attributes: the wheel and the armillary sphere. This connection with time led not simply to the identification of Fortune with Occasio or the opportune moment, but also to her interpretation by thinkers such as Machiavelli as the force and logic of history.

Hence at the same time that the 'rediscovery' of classical civilisation by Italian humanism gave a new impetus to ideas of temporal recurrence, it simultaneously renewed interest in feminine figurations of cyclical time. While Fortune was the most prominent of these personifications, several Renaissance mythographers were also intrigued by the potent image of a feminine-gendered Eternity which they discovered in Claudian. Richard Linche observed that:

> *Trismegistus, Plato* and the Pythagorickes, called Time the Image of Eternitie: in that it is revolved in it selfe, and admits no date.

Plate 7 The double or chiastically 'crossed' figure of Fortuna. Achille Bocchi, *Symbolicarum quaestionum . . . libri quinque* (Bologna: 1555), symb. lxiii. By permission of the Syndics of Cambridge University Library.

Whereupon for the more ample and copious manifesting thereof, we will heare the opinion of *Claudius* in his Stiliconyan comends, who there makes a description by a Serpent, that compasseth round with her bodie the denne or cave wherein she lyeth, in such sort, that making as it were a circle, she holdeth in her mouth the end of her taile: by which is signified

110

the effect of time, which in it selfe alwaies goeth round: which description is taken from the Ægyptians, who before that the use of letters and of writing was invented, signified the circumference of a yeare by a Serpent, with her taile betweene her teeth: For that in times there is the like coherence and depencie, for the end of one yeare or time passed, is the beginning of the other succeeding.[25]

The cyclical model of time was related to the 'dial' of hours and days – to the calibration of time in circular form – as well as to the revolving wheel of the seasons. We can therefore see its survival in the popular and especially rural emphasis upon calendrical time, above all in the continuing observation of certain festive days and times whose influence on *Romeo and Juliet* I have already discussed. There was of course a long-standing connection between 'playing' and this popular version of circular time; even when, in post-Reformation England, public playing no longer related to the seasonal and festive cycles of the year, it was still at such times that plays or masques were usually performed at court.

In astronomical and astrological terms, cyclical time was measured by that moving circle of the fixed stars which was familiar to the Renaissance in the image of the armillary sphere. It was this association of cyclical time with the circling movement of the stars which had produced the classical view of history as shaped by the intervention of divine forces; while this concept anticipated yet also differed from the Christian account of a linear temporality directed by Providence, and leading towards the *eschaton* or last days, observing the planets remained important even for religious ceremony: the Geneva Bible of 1579 is prefaced by instructions to the Protestant clergy as to how to calculate Easter and other holy days with reference to 'the Cycle of the Sunne' and 'the change of the Moone'.

In the Renaissance, the astrological conception of the 'Great Year' of the world, dependent on the return of the stars to their places, was shared by many influenced by Platonism or Hermeticism. The *Asclepius* had declared that 'in heaven time runs by the return of the coursing stars to the same places in chronological cycles'.[26] But the effects of cosmic influences upon the cycles of human history could be variously defined. On the one hand, as interpreted in Virgil's influential 'Eclogue IV', the notion of the world's cyclical renewal could be defined in broadly Platonic terms, as leading to a *renovatio temporum* when divine justice (as the Roman goddess Astraea), assisted by Diana Lucina as a goddess of birth, would bring around the Golden Age again, under the benign rule of the god Saturn as Time. The deployment of this conception in the service of the personal cult of the Renaissance prince or monarch has been extensively studied. Lorenzo the Magnificent took for his motto *Le temps revient*, while Lorenzo di Pierfrancesco de' Medici adopted as his emblem the *ouroboros*: a serpent with its tail in its mouth.[27] Similarly, Elizabeth Tudor adopted as one of her emblems the armillary sphere, an attribute of Fortuna which had been a badge of her mother, Anne Boleyn; her reign was likewise authorized by its representation as a triumphant 'turn' or return to a restored Golden Age. In this formulation, the specificity of historical time was assimilated into the repetitive dimension of myth.

On the other hand, a more pragmatic and less optimistic conception of temporal recurrence informed the Renaissance reappraisal of classical historians such as Polybius and Tacitus, each of whom had seen history in terms of cycles. The sixteenth-century French historians Jean Bodin and Louis Le Roy both agreed with the Stoics that each temporal cycle must end in *ekpyrosis* or cosmic dissolution, although neither author considered that this end was either imminent or desirable; Bodin in particular aimed to prolong the state by teaching the need for government to conform to the fundamental principles of nature.[28] But the Stoic notion of temporal vicissitude had already been applied more pessimistically in several early Renaissance historical texts which remained influential in the late sixteenth century. Machiavelli's *Discourses*, Pomponazzi's *De Fato*, and the historical writings of Francesco Guicciardini all related the rise and fall of states and empires to a temporal periodicity which invariably eluded the mastery of worldly governors. Pomponazzi wrote in his study of fate:

> He who before, at one time, was a beggar, at another time will be a king or a master . . . Cities and countries which were large and powerful later become small and weak . . . Thus it all seems to be a game of the Gods.[29]

Within Renaissance humanism, therefore, broadly idealized conceptions of temporal recurrence (which ostensibly served the absolutist aspirations of Renaissance monarchies) coexisted with much more fatalistic and pessimistic attitudes towards both cyclical time and the power of fate or fortune. The latter attitude produced various pragmatic emphases upon the correct use of 'swift-gliding' time, and on the role of a masculine *virtus* in tempering or combating the feminine principle of *fortuna*. This complex and multiple perspective survived throughout the sixteenth century, and is well evidenced in the works of Niccolò Machiavelli, for whom *fortuna* appears often to have been synonynous with *i tempi* – the times. While his counsel to the man of *virtù* to master fortune is often cited, Machiavelli could also express a bitter scepticism on the same subject; in 1512, after the failure of the Florentine republic, he wrote in a letter to its exiled leader, Piero Soderini:

> Anybody wise enough *to understand the times* and the types of affairs and to adapt himself to them would always have good fortune, or he would protect himself always from bad, and *it would come to be true that the wise man would rule the stars and the Fates.* But because there never are such wise men, since men in the first place are short-sighted and in the second place cannot command their natures, it follows that *Fortune varies and commands men and holds them under her yoke.* [my emphasis][30]

Shakespearean peripeteia and tragic periods

Classical ideas of temporal recurrence were therefore widely disseminated among Shakespeare's contemporaries; they exercised a decisive influence upon the poetry of Samuel Daniel, and were also implicit in Spenser's translation of Du Bellay, *The Ruines of Rome*: both were sources for Shakespeare's *Sonnets*.[31] In Shakespeare's tragedies, although the significance which is accorded to temporal repetition varies widely, a 'turning backward' or returning of time is often inflected as feminine, whether through its association with the influence of unruly women (whose sexual parts are often punned on as 'circles'), or in the persons of male protagonists who, like the youth of the *Sonnets*, have deviated in important respects from the norms of masculine authority. Tamora in *Titus* is the first and most grotesquely exaggerated example of time's relationship to unruly women, who as a grisly personification of *tempus edax*, the devouring womb of Time, will 'Like to the earth swallow her own increase' (5.2.191). Through Tamora, a feminine and bodily tomb – also implicitly allied with the deadly pit in the forest – is opposed to the masculinized family tomb with which the play begins: that of the aged and peculiarly Saturnian figure of Titus. The striking parallelism, as well as difference between these two characters serves to remind us that, as both womb and tomb, it was Saturn's consort, the earth (Rhea), who was presumably the original, feminine and chthonic source of his mythology; in the play, the Gothic queen has become the consort of the Roman emperor Saturninus, whose imperial title Titus has declined. In this association with Saturn and Rhea, as also in her comparison to Dido and Diana in Act 2 of the play, Tamora's grotesque characterization hints at a close connection between the female characters of Shakespearean tragedy and the mythic attributes of repetitive time.

As recently redescribed by François Laroque, festivity in Shakespeare's plays is usually 'rushing headlong in the opposite direction to the course of [linear] time', since it typically involves looking backwards rather than forwards.[32] This paradox aptly sums up the quality of frantic temporal acceleration in *Romeo and Juliet*, a play whose preoccupation with festivity is closely linked with images of a sexual, as well as calendrical turning and returning. The lovers' challenge to paternal authority, which begins in the festive context of Capulet's 'old accustomed feast', is set by Shakespeare in the 'dog days' of late July: a period analeptically defined in relation to the pagan culture of ancient Egypt, where the appearance on the dawn horizon of the Dog Star, Sirius, identified by the Egyptians with the goddess Isis, had heralded the annual inundation of the Nile.[33] In this, the hottest time of the year, 'is the mad blood stirring', observes Benvolio (3.1.4). The retrograde effect of these 'canicular' passions upon the conventional forward motion of time, as well as their connection with an active feminine sexuality, is aptly suggested by Mercutio's witty conceit that 'the bawdy hand of the dial is even now upon the prick of noon'.

In Act 1 scene 2, Benvolio advises Romeo to 'Turn giddy, and be holp by backward turning', in order to escape from his Petrarchan enthralment by Rosaline; in the very next scene, Juliet's future loss of her maidenhead is ribaldly imagined by the Nurse as a falling 'backward'. This apparently perverse act of turning back is performed by both lovers in Act 2 scene 1. It is now, after Capulet's ball, that Romeo climbs into the Capulet orchard, determined that he can no longer 'go forward' but must instead 'turn back, dull earth, and find thy centre out' (1–2). The motif of returning or going back subsequently overdetermines the lover's first exchanges, as Juliet leaves the balcony twice, only to return, calling Romeo back like a falcon to her lure, or like a fettered bird:

> 'Tis almost morning, I would have thee gone:
> And yet no farther than a wanton's bird,
> That lets it hop a little from her hand,
> Like a poor prisoner in his twisted gyves,
> And with a silken thread plucks it back again,
> So loving-jealous of his liberty.
>
> (Q1, 2.2.176–81)

By linking the re-turning of the lover to his mistress with his binding by a silken thread, Juliet's speech implies a connection between the threads of the Fates and the lovers' mutual and irresistible desire to call each other 'back'. A similar conception, of turning or revolving back, informed the beginning of the alchemical work, as well as the medieval image of Fortune's wheel; when Romeo leaves for exile in Mantua, Juliet exclaims: 'Be fickle, Fortune: / For then I hope thou wilt not keep him long, / But send him back' (3.5.62–4). The tragic catastrophe does indeed hinge on Romeo coming back, too early once again, to Verona and to Juliet's tomb, after the letter sent to him by Friar Lawrence has itself been returned, undelivered.

A graphic image of tragedy's relationship to the circular motions of fate occurs in the First Player's speech in *Hamlet*, where he blames the inconstancy of the goddess Fortune for the fall of Troy: ' "Out, out, thou strumpet Fortune! All you gods, / In general synod, take away her power, / Break all the spokes and fellies from her wheel, / And bowl the round nave down the hill of heaven, / As low as to the fiends!" ' (2.2.484–8). Several other allusions in the play stress the cyclical motions of time as well as Fortune. Thus the Player King tells his Queen that:

> Full thirty times hath Phoebus' cart gone round
> Neptune's salt wash and Tellus' orbèd ground,
> And thirty dozen moons with borrowed sheen
> About the world have times twelve thirties been,
> Since love our hearts, and Hymen did our hands,
> Unite commutual in most sacred bands.
>
> (3.2.145–50)

While these lines link the crisis in the royal marriage with the cycles of the sun and moon, the same cycle of thirty years is used again in the gravedigger scene, when in response to Hamlet's question: 'How long hast thou been a grave-maker?', the First Clown replies:

> Of all the days i'th' year, I came to't that day that our last king Hamlet o'ercame Fortinbras . . . It was the very day that young Hamlet was born – he that was mad and sent into England. . . . I have been sexton here, man and boy, thirty years.
>
> (5.1.134–154)

This reference to Hamlet's birth as having coincided with a major event in Danish-Norwegian relations anticipates the sudden reversal of Danish supremacy that will coincide with his death, as young Fortinbras receives the 'dying voice' of young Hamlet. In seeking to revenge his dead father, Hamlet is indeed proceeding in a direction which, as Claudius expresses 'is most retrograde to our desire' (1.2.14). But of course the temporal cycle that interests the 'mad' Hamlet – whose reason is 'like sweet bells jangled out of time and harsh' (Q2, 3.1.159) – is the 'fine revolution' that is the body's return to earth, through the processes of human decomposition assisted by 'my Lady Worm'. 'As thus: Alexander died, Alexander was buried, Alexander returneth into dust . . . ' (5.1.198–200). Similarly, the *Corpus Hermeticum* had observed that 'the recurrence of earthly bodies . . . is [the dissolution] of their composition, and this dissolution causes them to recur as undissolved bodies – immortal, in other words'.[34] These are the same processes that figuratively embraced in Cleopatra's dying 'joy o' the worm'. Earlier in the play, Cleopatra had been closely identified with the fickleness of the 'housewife' Fortuna; yet in the mordant embrace of figurative serpent by real serpent, her highly emblematic death suggests the familiar image for circular time and Eternity: the coiled serpent with its tail in its mouth.

In *King Lear*, the overt, if not the deepest, cause of the tragedy is closely related to Lear's whimsical decision not to maintain his own residence after abdication, but instead to progress around the country, visiting each of his daughters 'by due turn': 'Ourself by monthly course, / With reservation of an hundred knights / By you to be sustained, shall our abode / Make with you by due turn' (1.1.133–6). Although Lear has previously invoked Apollo in his dispute with Kent, and as a king would have been most closely associated with the planetary symbol of the sun, his abdication seems to have effected a lunar metamorphosis, whose alchemical significance has been suggestively explored by Charles Nicholl.[35] Valeriano had linked the moon explicitly with Fortuna or Tyche in his *Hieroglyphica*, observing that 'Luna is *Tyche* because she is guardian of bodies, which are swayed by alterations of fortune'.[36] It is his lunar processing about the country, together with his own changeable behaviour, that makes Lear vulnerable to the equally capricious whims of his two daughters, who appear thereby to emblematize the doubleness and mutability of Fortune; their incongruous roles as housekeepers to the king also parallel traditional descriptions of Fortune as a 'housewife'. Culminating in Lear's fit of 'the mother', the circular and repetitive pattern of his extended *peripeteia* enacts, not a process of generation, but rather a Saturnian consumption of the self in relation to family. In cursing Cordelia, Lear exclaims that 'The barbarous Scythian, / Or he that makes his generation messes / To gorge his appetite, shall to my bosom / Be as well neighboured, pitied and relieved, / As thou my sometime daughter' (1.1.117–21). Since the tragedy ends with the extinction of his own royal blood-line, it seems that Lear as the wrathful 'dragon' has himself assumed the shape of the tail-eating serpent, which the alchemists interpreted as that necessary destruction which must precede the accomplishment of their 'work': 'He quickly consumes his venom, for he devours his poisonous tail. / All this is performed on his own body . . . '.[37] (A similarly alchemical conception of the self-destructive dragon may underlie the several comparisons of Coriolanus to a dragon.) By the last act, however, as Lear is taken away to prison with Cordelia, he can assert that: 'we'll wear out / In a walled prison packs and sects of great ones / That ebb and flow by the moon' (5.3.17–19).

In *Othello*, as in *Hamlet*, a central theme of the tragedy relates to the male protagonist's encounter, through a real or imagined apprehension of woman's mutability and infidelity, with a disturbing flux and vicissitude in nature. Othello declares of Desdemona that 'when I love thee not / Chaos is come again' (3.3.91–2); his belief in her adultery with Cassio produces an inner reversal whereby he effectively turns away from the courtly civilities of peacetime and marriage, back to the brutality and violence of his military past. Intimately entangled in this tragic *peripeteia* is the 'antique token' of the handkerchief, which is described as a cipher of the interweaving of death with breeding and desire, and of the ancient past with the present. Not only mysteriously 'hallow'd' silkworms, but also several women have played a magical part in the spinning and transmission of this web of fate:

> That handkerchief
> Did an Egyptian to my mother give,
> She was a charmer and could almost read
> The thoughts of people . . . She, dying, gave it me
> And bid me, when my fate would have me wive,
> To give it her . . .
> 'Tis true, there's magic in the web of it.
> A sibyl that had numbered in the world
> The sun to course two hundred compasses,
> In her prophetic fury sewed the work;
> The worms were hallowed that did breed the silk,
> And it was dyed in mummy, which the skilful
> Conserve of maidens' hearts.
> (3.4.57–77)

In his 1592 treatise on silkworms Thomas Moffett notes the myth that 'the mysterie of weaving silk' was given to Venus by its first discoverer,

Saturn, or Time, in exchange for her assistance in his seduction of the nymph Phillyra.[38] As in the myth of Pyramus and Thisbe, also retold by Moffett (because the unhappy lovers' blood was supposed to have stained the fruit of the mulberry tree, upon which the silkworm feeds), the metonymic entwining of passion with the production of silk produces a tragic metamorphosis, for after giving birth to a monstrous offspring which is half man and half horse, Phillyra is metamorphosed into a linden tree. Similarly, in *Othello*, the silken favour functions not only as a trope for the sexual favours which Desdemona is supposed to have conferred on Cassio, but also as a potent image of the operations of time and fate in the play; thereby it reminds us of the subtle entangling of the threads of Fate with the body of woman. As he succumbs to his own tragic metamorphosis of identity through jealousy, Othello exclaims: 'this forked plague is fated to us'.

Eulogized by Cassio on her arrival in Cyprus as a goddess whose safe emergence from a storm-tossed sea implies an association, not only with Venus and the Virgin Mary, but also with the Renaissance image of Fortuna (who was linked with tempests, and often represented by a sail), Desdemona's loss of the handkerchief appears to confirm her loss of control over that fate or 'daimon' which Joel Fineman has deciphered in her name.[39] At the very beginning of the play, Iago tells Brabantio that his daughter has performed 'a gross revolt, / Tying her duty, beauty, wit and fortunes / In an extravagant and wheeling stranger / Of here and everywhere' (1.2.132–5); the trope suggests that it is Othello who is to be Desdemona's ill star or daimon, like a 'wheeling' planet whose deviation from its proper orbit Desdemona has imitated. In Act 5, however, Othello attributes his murder of Desdemona to a feminine planet, the moon, which he imagines to have turned aside from her usual course: 'It is the very error of the moon, / She comes more nearer earth than she was wont / And makes men mad' (5.2.108–10).

In his suicide, Othello continues the circling backwards of his tragic *peripeteia*, defining his death as a repetition – with a difference – of an event from his past: 'in Aleppo once, / Where a malignant and a turbanned Turk / Beat a Venetian and traduced the state, / I took by th' throat the circumcised dog / And smote him – thus!' (5.2.350–4). Lodovico's exclamatory response – 'O bloody period!' – completes the speech's suggestive interweaving of death with writing; yet while modern editors usually see this phrase as imaging Othello's death as an end or full stop, the older meanings of 'period', from the Greek *periodos*, included a going round or circuit, a cycle or period of time, and the orbit of a heavenly body. As if to emphasize this motif of periodicity, Othello, like Desdemona before him, does in fact speak once more before dying: 'I kissed thee ere I killed thee: no way but this, / Killing myself, to die upon a kiss' (5.2.356–7). In this final chiastic crossing of 'killing' with 'kissing', there is a suggestion that the tragic ending may simultaneously be read as another beginning.

'Macbeth' and multilayered time

It is in *Macbeth*, however, that we find the most detailed dramatic exploration of time's multilayered character and ambiguous directionality. In several of Shakespeare's histories, tragedies and Roman plays (as well as in the poetry and drama of many of his contemporaries), we can identify the existence of what can be termed 'double time', whereby the particular historical time of the play is implicitly paralleled or repeated by recent or near-contemporary political moments. In Elizabethan plays such as *Titus*, *Richard II*, *Henry IV* and *Hamlet* (as well as in a Jacobean play such as *Antony and Cleopatra*), more or less buried allusions to the reign of Elizabeth I can be discerned, while contemporary interest in a British *renovatio temporum*, inspired by the recent accession of King James, informs both *Macbeth* and *Lear*. But parallels to several recent political events are especially explicit in *Macbeth*; in particular, by suggesting how the time of early Scottish history intersects not only with the present political situation, but also with the events of some forty years previous, the play's exploration of topical interest in James' lineage and hereditary claim to the English throne encompasses significant allusions to the controversial life and death of his mother, Mary Queen of Scots, whose assumed involvement in the murder of her first husband and royal consort, Lord Darnley, had led many Protestants to characterise her as a 'quean' or harlot. Yet *Macbeth*'s temporal focus also extends more widely, encompassing implicit allusions to classical myth, biblical typology and Celtic antiquity along with its contradictory prophetic focus upon a future which is now the present.

In consequence, the play functions as a curious temporal palimpsest, in which a variety of different times coexist within the dramatic process. At the centre of this process is a group of characters who are defined in the play as both more and less than women. On the one hand, represented in the play as a dense and paradoxical elision of Christian demonological lore with pagan conceptions of fate, fortune, and sibylline prophecy, is the feminine trinity of the 'weyard' sisters, which personifies the disturbing ambiguity of this 'weyard' but also 'weyward' pattern within nature as well as human history.[10] On the other hand is Macbeth's 'fiend-like' queen, whose incitement of her husband to regicide affords an implicit personification of Fortune's 'housewifery', and whose barely

119

veiled comparison to Mary Queen of Scots is one of several devices whereby the apparent distinction between Banquo's line and Macbeth's kingship is implicitly questioned.

Among several references which link Lady Macbeth with Mary, the most notable is the ironic association of the Macbeths' castle with 'temple-haunting' martlets, or housemartins: the martlet was a badge of Mary Stuart, which she had inherited, through her mother, from the House of Lorraine, and which James had in fact retained upon his Great Seal.[41] (Curiously, the martlet also appeared on the arms of Shakespeare's mother's family, the Ardens.) In classical tradition these birds were associated, through their near-relatives the swallows, with Aphrodite as a household deity, and also with the vengeful mother Procne in Ovid's *Metamorphoses*, transformed into a swallow after she had murdered her son as revenge for her husband Tereus' rape of her sister Philomel. In its emblematic position on the battlements of the Macbeth's castle, therefore, the martlet prefigures the importance to the tragedy of a transgressive maternal desire or sexuality. The play subsequently draws out the implications of the emblem, by allying the language of 'accounting' used by this treacherous 'hostess' or housewife not only with ideas of judgement but also with an active or whorish female sexuality, as well as by the porter's comic figuration of the Macbeths' castle as simultaneously Hell and a brothel-house.[42] These images trope Macbeth's crime as an abuse of housekeeping, husbandry or stewardship. And like the fall of the first Adam, the final responsibility for this fall into a false housekeeping or whoredom rests with woman.

But it is in the curious parallelism of its first and final acts that the play directs our attention most explicitly to the mysterious doublings of role and circumstance which distinguish Macbeth's history. In Act I scene ii, the 'bloody' captain emphasizes the disdain of Fortune that Macbeth has shown in his defeat of Macdonwald. In 'unseaming' this rebel 'from the nave to the chops', it is implied that Macbeth has achieved a Herculean defeat of the 'nave' (and 'knave', or rebel) which is at the centre of Fortune's wheel. In his next words, however, the captain alludes to the wild weather that accompanies the sun's springtime 'reflection' on its tropical turning back to the place of the vernal equinox (1.2.25–8), and in the description of Macbeth's ensuing encounter with the reinforced Norwegian forces and the Thane of Cawdor we find the first suggestion of the extent to which Macbeth's history will repeat *through inversion* the events with which the play begins:

> Norway himself, with terrible numbers,
> Assisted by that most disloyal traitor,

The Thane of Cawdor, began a dismal conflict;
Till that Bellona's bridegroom, lapp'd in proof,
Confronted him with self-comparisons,
Point against point, rebellious arm 'gainst arm,
Curbing his lavish spirit: and, to conclude,
The victory fell on us;–

(1.2.51–9)

Like the earlier image of the conflict against Macdonwald 'As two spent swimmers, that do cling together / And choke their art', this account stresses the resemblance of the opposing forces, hinting thereby at the affinity – soon to be confirmed by the sisters' greeting – between Macbeth and the traitorous Cawdor. These events are closely paralleled at the end of the play, in the final combat between Macbeth and Macduff. Just as Macbeth had fought Macdonwald to secure Duncan's throne, so Macduff is now fighting against Macbeth on behalf of Duncan's son Malcolm. And like that of Fortune's 'nave', Macdonwald, whose head Macbeth had 'fix'd' upon the battlements, Macbeth's destiny is now fixed: 'They have tied me to a stake: I cannot fly, / But bear-like, I must fight the course' (5.7.1–2). In this bear imagery, there are hints of Christian eschatology's expected ending of time after the final encounter between Christ and the Antichrist or Great Beast. While in the first act both Macbeth and Banquo were indirectly compared with Christ, since their valour seemed almost to 'memorize another Golgotha' (1.2.41); it is now Macbeth who assumes the bestial place of Christ's final antagonist, and Macduff who is both like and yet unlike Christ, since he 'was not born of woman' in the conventional sense. At the same time, however, the bear image suggests a further temporal reversion: to a prehuman or animal state equivalent to the *nigredo* of alchemy. The suggestion that the climax of the tragedy is a return to originary chaos is compounded by the illusory movement of the wood, which as *silva* similarly allies judgement with a return of, or to, the state of primal matter. And the implication that the play's conclusion has mysteriously involved a return to a previous temporality is given a final emphasis by Macduff, who when he re-enters with Macbeth's head, greets Malcolm with 'Hail, King! for so thou art'. For as his own repetition of this greeting is itself repeated by the assembled nobles (*Macduff* Hail. King of Scotland! / *All* Hail, King of Scotland!) there is a third eerie echo of the weyard sisters' triple greeting of 'Hail' to both Macbeth and Banquo. And so, with 'Thrice to thine, and thrice to mine, / And thrice again, to make up nine / Peace! – the charm's wound up' (1.3.35–7).[43]

Central to Macbeth's tragedy is his preoccupation with what seems to be a fated inability to perpetuate his kingship through lineal succession. Indeed, the play defines his tyranny as specifically opposed to the diachronic as well as synchronic order represented by kinship. Thus in his second meeting with the witches, Macbeth conjures them to answer him although the consequence may be that 'the treasure / Of Nature's Germaine tumble all together, / Even till destruction sicken' (4.1.58–60). Yet his own tragedy will reveal that a deeper pattern underlies his bloody 'breaching' of that resemblance which is nature's 'germaine', as kinship or germinal seed. For what the overall structure of the play disturbingly suggests is that, by returning Scotland to a state analogous to the primal chaos, the violent disordering of nature performed by Macbeth's tyranny actually enables a different kind of return or temporal repetition, since ultimately it will make possible the reuniting of Britain by Banquo's descendant James. In this respect the heirless Macbeth is actually the 'harbinger' of 'He that's coming' (1.4.45, 1.5.66); although he is 'so far before / That swiftest wing of recompense is slow to overtake thee' (1.4.16–17). When Ross comments that, 'Things at the worst will cease; or else climb upward / To what they were before' (4.2.24–5), he is envisaging this change as an exact repetition or *renovatio* of a recent past; yet the audience's knowledge of the sisters' prophecy concerning Banquo invests the restoration of Duncan's line with which the play ends with a disturbing quality of transience. Macbeth observes of the prophecy to Banquo that 'If't be so, / For Banquo's issue have I fil'd my mind; / For them the gracious Duncan have I murdered . . . ' (3.1.63–5). Thereby the play draws out very clearly the striking ambiguity of Macbeth's importance to the Stuart claim, which like Macbeth's own career was closely entangled with prophecy.

The idea of the restoration of a lost Golden Age had promoted a new interest in the quasi-mythic past of Renaissance states, which led British historians as well as poets to focus on a distant national past associated with Britain's legendary Trojan founder, Brutus. In 1551, John Bale had noted in *The first two partes of the Actes, or unchast examples of the Englysh votaryes*:

> As I was in wrytinge this matter an old Prophecy of Merline came unto my remembraunce. That after the manyfolde irruptions of straungers, the kinges of thys realme shuld be ones agayn crowned wyth the Dyademe of Brute, and beare his auncient name, the new name of straungers so vanishinge awaye.[44]

Fifty years later, Sir John Harington noted the survival of a similarly ancient prophecy in the unpublished manuscript of his *Tract on the Succession to the Crown* (1602): 'A King of Brittish blood in Cradell crownd / With Lyon markt shall joine all Brutus' ground / Restore the crosse and make this Ile renown'd'. This prophecy was explicitly linked with James in a marginal comment added to the Harington manuscript by the then Archbishop of York, Tobie Matthew, who noted that 'The K of Scotts' is said to have a Mole like a Lyon'.[45]

While contemporary interest in a British *renovatio* informs both *Macbeth* and *Lear*, only *Macbeth* specifically alludes to the genealogical claim of James to the throne of a united Britain. This was derived most recently from the marriage of James IV of Scotland to Henry VII's daughter Margaret; yet a more ancient Stuart claim was traced from Banquo, since according to Renaissance chroniclers, Banquo's son Fleance had wedded a Welsh princess after his flight from Scotland (Plate 8).[46] But in fact *all* of the key protagonists of the play were James's ancestors; not only were the Kings of Scotland before the Stuarts married into their line (with the marriage of Walter the Steward to Marjorie, daughter of Robert Bruce) descended directly from Duncan and his son Malcolm, Macbeth, as Duncan's cousin, was also part of this family. James' inheritance of both the English and the Scottish thrones consequently depended upon his ties of blood to several women, including not only his ancestor Marjorie Steward (as the heir to Duncan and Malcolm's royal line) but his Catholic mother, Mary Queen of Scots, and his Protestant cousin, Elizabeth, Queen of England. It was possibly because of this dependence upon different modes of inheritance through the female line that the Stuart dynasty was represented as capable of a phoenix-like parthenogenesis via an almost miraculous process of historical survival and renewal; in *The Triumphes of King James the First*, George Marcelline observed that 'this house of *Stewart* in *Scotland*, is as a *Phoenix* among the Nobility . . . for since the year of grace, 1057, from the raigne of *Malcolme*, even to this present, it hath flourished ful of prosperity and honour'.[47] The same attribute of 'phoenix' had been used by James in a poem lamenting the death of his cousin Esmé Stuart d'Aubigny (who may also have been his first lover).[48]

The phoenix impresa had been inherited by James' mother, Mary Queen of Scots, from her mother, Marie de Guise. Yet his mother's controversial reign had engendered much speculation about James' legitimacy, and Mary was almost completely effaced in the many encomia written to celebrate his accession to the English throne. Instead, like Macduff, James was represented by the panegyrists as a monarch who was 'not born of woman', but who instead had inherited the throne

Plate 8 The Stuart family tree, derived from Banquo. John Leslie, *De origine moribus, et rebus gestis Scotorum libri decem* (Rome: 1578). By permission of the Syndics of Cambridge University Library.

through a parthenogenetic regeneration of English sovereignty, whereby the dying English phoenix, Elizabeth, had miraculously transmitted the kingdom to the reborn British phoenix, James.[49]

Although the phoenix was of indeterminate gender, the use of this emblem to celebrate the Stuart line hints at its brief deviation (in the person of a female monarch) from a strictly patrilineal line of succession. Similarly, *Macbeth* associates both Banquo and Fleance with the mysteriously self-sufficient fecundity of another emblem of temporal renewal: the serpent. Macbeth decides to murder Banquo and Fleance because: 'We have scorch'd the snake, not kill'd it: / She'll close, and be herself' (3.2.13–14); the imagery of 'closing' links the idea of circular time, as represented by the *ouroboros*, with breeding.[50] The imaging of genealogical survival as a serpentine renewal or 'breeding' that is paradoxically associated, not just with death, but also with the 'return' of judgement as revenge is later applied to Fleance after he escapes: 'There the grown serpent lies; the worm, that's fled, / Hath nature that in time will venom breed, / No teeth for th'present' (3.4.28–30). The cyclical fertility of this process is troped as feminine; yet the association of Banquo's lineage with an almost mystical form of self-generation and renewal effects a figurative displacement of both the female body and the maternal role, paralleling the troping of Macduff as one 'not born of woman'. Thereby it appears to confirm the displacement of queens / queans from this privileged model of kingship and temporality. The device also gives a new and erotic inflection to the panegyrists' definition of James' rule, as a phoenix-like turning backwards or *renovatio* of time that simultaneously represents a (historical) addition to the previous (mythic) pattern.

Yet Macbeth's serpent imagery also suggests an implied secrecy or 'closeness' in the renewal of royal blood through Banquo's line; in an earlier scene, speaking to the men whom he has enlisted to murder Banquo and Fleance, Macbeth describes the gifts of Nature as being 'clos'd' within different individuals:

> . . . the valu'd file
> Distinguishes the swift, the slow, the subtle,
> The housekeeper, the hunter, every one
> According to the gift which bounteous Nature
> Hath in him clos'd; whereby he does receive
> Particular addition, from the bill
> That writes them all alike . . .
>
> (3.1.94–100)

What is implied in this figuration of a natural differing of individual ability is nature's role in the secret dispensations of fate. Both 'addition' and 'bill' ally this gifting by nature with ideas of judgement and election, already introduced by the imagery of 'auditing' and 'accounting' in Act 1 scenes 6 and 7. It is this potential, presented in the play as due not to the predestination of the Christian God, but rather to a fated 'closeness' or intimacy with nature, which is distinguished by the surplus or 'addition' of fruitful seeds that the witches seemingly have the ability to see: as Banquo expresses it, they 'can look into the seeds of time, / And say which grain will grow, and which will not' (1.2.51–8).

'Posteriority' and genealogical survival

Hecate refers to Macbeth as a 'wayward' son; yet while in one sense Macbeth's tragedy illustrates the potential for 'recoiling' in a formerly virtuous nature (another much-used contemporary term for a fall from grace was 'backsliding'), it can also be related to his resistance to turning back as *conversio* or repentance: 'I am in blood / Stepp'd in so far, that, should I wade no more, / Returning were as tedious as go o'er' (3.4. 135–7). In contrast, the implication that James' rule may mysteriously be defined as much by concepts of turning backwards as by extension into the historical future is aptly suggested by the two appearances of the murdered Banquo in the second half of the play, as a ghost or *revenant* whose likeness will continue to haunt or dwell within the line of kings which are his heirs. The imagery which describes these apparitions has a strikingly erotic nuance, in a development of the implicit sexual ambiguity of that 'ditch' in which the murderers have left Banquo's body with 'twenty trenched gashes'.[51] Just as Duncan's death has previously been imaged as a 'breach in nature' (2.3.111), an 'unnatural deed' (2.4.11) 'performed' upon 'th'unguarded Duncan' (1.7.70–1), so the figuration of Banquo's death as a sexual violation is further suggested in the 'gory locks' and 'blood-bolter'd' hair of the ghost.[52] The paradoxical connection here, between a murderous assault and a procreative sexuality (blood, hairs), is made explicit by the pun on hairs / heirs at the end of the play, when Old Siward declares of his dead son that 'Had I as many sons as I have hairs, / I would not wish them to a fairer death' (5.9.14–15).[53] Moreover, when, some lines after this account of his murder, Banquo's ghost sits on the 'stool' reserved for Macbeth, we may discern a covert allusion to the 'bank' or seat concealed in Banquo's name (which was inscribed by Simon Forman as 'Bancko' in his account of seeing the play performed); this allusion also hints at a possible combination of supernatural with erotic significance in that 'banke and

Schoole of time' upon which Macbeth has desired to 'jump' the life to come.

The Bankside or other side of the river Thames was associated with a disorderly sexuality because of the brothels which were situated there, and the erotic association of 'banks' figures prominently in the literature of the period. But it is the additional association of 'bank' as seat with the backside or arse that is suggestively evoked by Banquo's uncanny occupation of Macbeth's place 'i'th'midst'. This innuendo is extended by the hidden pun on faces/faeces/*fesses* [French for buttocks] in Lady Macbeth's whispered reproach to her husband: 'Shame itself! / Why do you makes such faces? When all's done, / You look but on a stool' (3.4.65–7). The effect of Banquo's ghostly return is consequently to elide James' noble ancestor with the throne/stool in a way which points up the affinity between throne and closet-stool or privy, and further hints at the colloquial association between privy and 'jakes' or Jacques (which as Sir John Harington obligingly pointed out in *The Metamorphosis of Ajax*, was the French equivalent of James). If we can read these references as oblique allusions to King James' presumed sexual preferences, then what may further be implied is that a certain backwardness or 'posteriority' is now a privileged attribute of Stuart kingship, the mark both of its procreative difference and of its vulnerability. This seems ironically to confirm Macbeth's observation that 'the greatest is behind'.

Yet while at one level the play identifies James as one who, as a descendant of Banquo, is to benefit from the women's prophecy, through its subtle exploration of ideas of doubling it frequently calls into question the perceived difference between Macbeth and Banquo. Thereby it suggests that the different destinies of Duncan's two 'captains' are in an important sense merely the two aspects of Fortune, whose double and chiastic nature is vividly represented in the striking emblem from Achille Bocchi's *Symbolicarum Quaestionum* which is Plate 7. Patricia Parker has shown that a 'preposterous' pattern which hinges on ideas of doubling or 'cozening' is present in several of Shakespeare's comedies and histories.[54] What we are offered in *Macbeth* is indeed an extended meditation upon those curious doublings or chiastic reversions which occur not only in natural ties of blood or kinship, but also in the temporal process. Through this motif, ideas of political *renovatio* and genealogical inheritance are given a new inflection, as the paradoxical relationships between the several characters who are twinned within the drama are framed by a final inhuman act of 'cozening', accomplished by the forces of nature, fortune and time. In Act 5 of the play, these powers are emblematized both by the apparently uncanny movement of the forest and by the revelation of Macduff as one who was born *before his time*, since he 'was from his mother's womb untimely ripped'. But their duplicity has already been shown, in the riddling utterances of the 'weyard' sisters to Macbeth and Banquo. The three sisters demonstrate this knowledge, not only in their chiastic language of equivocation, where 'the battle's lost and won' and 'fair is foul, and foul is fair', but also in their winding dance, which, like that of the anti-masque of hags in Jonson's *Masque of Queenes*, was presumably anti-clockwise, and whose description as an 'antic round' further hints at their association with the ambiguous circularity of time.[55]

It is in their encounter with the 'weyard' and 'wayward' sisters that the contrasting destinies of Macbeth and Banquo are explicitly repre- sented in terms of a chiastic twinning which points up both the difference within seeming resemblances, and the resemblance within apparent differences: 'So all hail, Macbeth and Banquo! / Banquo and Macbeth, all hail' (1.3.68–9). Yet this chiastic structure of reversal pervades the entire text. For it is as a cozening or deceitful 'cousin' to Duncan that Macbeth makes manifest the deadly difference which is concealed within lineal doubling, as well as within the 'Germaine' or seeds of time. In this respect, the murder of one cousin by another must have evoked memories of several other deaths involving prominent cousins in recent history. The accession of James had certainly reopened memories of the execution in 1587 of his mother, Mary Stuart, by the (ostensibly reluctant) order of her cousin Elizabeth, as a result of that other cousin's presumed involvement in plots against the English queen's life and throne. A more recent tragedy involving cousins, whose effects were still reverberating in early Stuart culture and society, was the execution in 1601 of the Earl of Essex, who had similarly plotted to depose his monarch and 'cousin'. But the historical event to which the murder of Duncan by the Macbeths appears almost too explicitly to allude was the violent murder of James' father, 'King' Henry Stuart or Lord Darnley, in which his wife and cousin Queen Mary was held by Protestant propagandists to have been implicated; commentators on his reign would subsequently criticise James for failing to revenge this double crime.[56]

We can plausibly decipher an additional, biblical, resonance to this tragic concern with cozenage and kinship, which Parker has pointed to as a subtext in both *The Comedy of Errors* and *The Merry Wives of Windsor*; this is one which is especially apt given the frequent use of the Latin form of James' name, *Jacobus*. Eulogized on his accession as another Jacob, who like his biblical forebear was now the father of an elect nation, this only son was consequently associated with the biblical account of the twin brothers, Jacob and Esau, who 'strove together' within their mother Rebecca's womb:

And the Lord said to her, two nations are in thy wombe, and
two maner of people shalbe devided out of thy bowels, and the
one people shalbe mightier then they other, and the elder shal
serve ye younger.
Therefore, when her time of deliverance was fulfilled, beholde,
twinnes were in her wombe.
So he that came out first was red, and he was all over as a rough
garment, and they called his name Esau.
And afterwarde came his brother out, and his hand held Esau
by the hele: therefore his name was called Iaakob.[57]

Early Protestant commentators interpreted this story as an allegory
of predestination; the Geneva Bible's gloss on the first stage of the twin
brothers' rivalry, when Esau sells Jacob his birthright for a mess of a
pottage, was that 'ye wicked preferre their worldlie commodities to Gods
spiritual graces: but ye children of God do ye contrary'. This contrariness
of the elect is further emphasized, as Patricia Parker has pointed out, in
the emphasis upon that 'preposterous' temporal reversal which is implicit
in Jacob assuming priority over his elder brother, as a result of his
devious acquisition of his father's blessing by masquerading as Esau.[58]
The determination by biblical commentators to associate Esau and his
heirs, the Edomites, not only with the unregenerate, but specifically with
the Great Beast of *Revelation*, seems to have been due not only to Esau's
striking attribute of redness, but also to his hairiness; this distinctive
feature of the elder brother was a vital element in the biblical story, since
Jacob had concealed his own smooth hands with goatskin in order to
obtain the blessing which his blind father was reserving for Esau as the
eldest son. In *The Triumphs of King James*, James is compared to Jacob, as
one destined to triumph over the Great Beast of irreligion or Catholicism
represented by 'That rejected *Esau* (otherwise called *Edom*) which
signified the Red Dragon, that old usurper, that Tyrant over so many
nations, the Pope himselfe'.[59]

The association of Esau with tyranny and usurpation, as well as with
a red or bloody bestiality and evil, suggests obvious parallels to
Shakespeare's representation of Macbeth. (The Tudor morality play,
The Historie of Jacob and Esau, had also defined Esau as a watcher, who
in his commitment to hunting 'scarcely sleepeth .xii. good houres in two
weekes'.[60]) Duncan observes of her husband to Lady Macbeth that
on the journey to their castle, 'We coursed him at the heels, and had
a purpose / To be his purveyor: but he rides well; / And his great love,
sharp as his spur, hath holp him / To his home before us' (1.6.21–4). Yet
whereas Duncan, unlike Jacob, was unable to catch Macbeth's heel,

Banquo's eventual supplanting of Macbeth has been predestined, not by the God of Christanity, but by fate or fortune as embodied by the 'weyard' sisters. And while the tyrannical Macbeth is distinguished by his loose and ill-fitting royal garments, by his red and blood-stained hands, and by his curiously animal-like 'fell of hair' (5.5.11), these attributes of redness and hairiness are implicitly borrowed by and transferred to the bloody-haired Banquo.[61] That Banquo's hair only becomes a significant attribute after his death suggests that it has important implications for his 'ghostly' or spiritual displacement of Macbeth, as a twin-like type of Jacob who is destined to return through his bloody *hairs*: that is, in the persons of his numerous Stuart heirs. At the same time, however, the traces of this biblical analogy within the play hint at the relevance of its exploration of 'doubling' as both twinning and cozening to the new relationship of the kindred realms of England and Scotland, following James' accession to the English throne; this was of course a topic which was being hotly debated in 1606.

An image which was used frequently in debates over the union of the two kingdoms was of two brothers; in *The Joieful and Blessed Reuniting the Two Mighty & Famous Kingdomes, England and Scotland* John Thornborough described England and Scotland as 'two branches of one vine', arguing that the two nations were destined 'to grow up and agree together; seeing nature hath made them all of one kinde, forme, complexion, habit and language'.[62] Similarly, in a parliamentary debate on 19 February 1607, Thomas Hedley would argue that the union was 'a Question between Two Brothers . . . Both Son to one Father'; a month later, the King's speech on the subject declared his hope and expectation that his accession to the English throne and the union of the two countries should 'as two twinnes . . . have growne up together'.[63] But the play points tellingly at the perceived inequalities within this 'brotherly' relationship. In the persons of Macbeth and Banquo, we are offered contrasting views of kingship: on the one hand, of a tyrannical king of Scotland who represents an especially degenerate and unsanctified moment of Scottish history; on the other hand, of one whose 'royalty of nature' and 'grac'd person' is ultimately to accomplish, through his heirs, a mysterious 'addition' – a doubling and even tripling of the realm of Scotland, through its assimilation into a reunited Britain. The last king in the pageant of Banquo's heirs which is shown to Macbeth by the weyard sisters:

> bears a glass,
> Which shows me many more; and some I see,
> That twofold balls and treble sceptres carry.

Horrible sight! – Now I see, 'tis true;
For the blood-bolter'd Banquo smiles upon me,
And points at them for his.

(4.1.119–24)

While this show focuses upon Banquo's assocation with a future *British* sovereignty, in an obvious compliment to James and his hopes for Union, it is striking that Macbeth, like the rebel Macdonwald, is ultimately supported only by Irish mercenaries: 'wretched Kernes'. Moreover, it is striking that he shares some of his most distinctive attributes with the Irish 'wood-Karne'.[64] In John Derricke's *Image of Ireland*, the Irish were described 'with glibbed heddes like Mars him selfe, their malice to expresse: with Irefull hartes and *bloudie hands*, soone prone to wickedness' [my emphasis]; Barnaby Rich claimed that the Irish 'are grown into such a habite of savage tyranny, that nothing is more pleasing to the greatest number of them, then civill warres, murthers, massacres, whereunto they are commonly inclined'.[65] Not only did English observers comment critically on the Kernes' 'long crisped bushes of heare which they term glibs', they were also suspicious of the large loose garments worn by the Irish: an attribute that may help to elucidate the troping of Macbeth's kingship in terms of clothing ('now does he feel his title / Hang loose upon him, like a giant's robe / Upon a dwarfish thief', 5.2.20–2); Irenius observes in Spenser's *View* that the capacious Irish mantle 'is a fit house for an out-law, a meet bed for a rebel, and an apt cloak for a theife'.[66] Such descriptive parallels are consistent with the observation of British antiquarianism that 'all the Inhabitants of *Ireland* were first of all called *Scots*, as Orosius shews; and our *Annals* relate, that the *Scots* passed more than once out of *Ireland* into *Albium* . . . '.[67] In the context of the contemporary debate upon Union, therefore, we may see Macbeth as representing the deep-seated English fear of a return to an archaic Celtic barbarism and paganism, which might enter into England by the back door as it were of Union. In one of his least favourable comments upon the ancient Britons, Camden had quoted Gildas' reference to the opinion of both pagan and Christian authors that Britain was at that time '*a province plentifull of tyrants*. Neither will I speake of their ancient religion, which is not verily to be counted religion, but a most lamentable and confused *Chaos* of Superstitions'.[68]

Both the 'paltering' language of the weyard sisters and the ghostly occupation of Macbeth's stool by Banquo hints at a disturbing affinity between the two 'captains'; however, it is the show of kings that presents us with a final chiastic repatterning of kingship. Here, the complex and inverted relationship between the two friends and antagonists is mediated through the ghostly presence of a queen. For while at first sight the pageant of Banquo's royal heirs appears to exclude all reference to the controversial woman from whom James had inherited both the crown of Scotland and his claim to the throne of England, the eighth king actually occupies the place of his mother, Mary Queen of Scots, in James's royal genealogy, since he was himself the ninth Stuart monarch descended from Banquo. This eighth 'king' bears a 'glass' which functions both as a mirror, and as a prospective, or magic glass. In its surface, the court performance of the play (which Paul believes to have been its first performance) would implicitly have invited James to see himself, as Banquo's next heir.[69] Yet this act of self-recognition also implies that, like the youth of the *Sonnets*, James is his 'mother's glass', and is consequently linked through association with those controversial aspects of her reign to which the earlier part of the play had obscurely alluded. And finally, as a king who is looking in the 'glass' presented by this play within the play, James, like Banquo in the banquet scene, is effectively occupying the place of Macbeth, who sees not his own heirs but those of Banquo in the glass. What occurs in and through the glass of the eighth 'king' is consequently one further and especially significant doubling of kingship, in which, like the opposing aspects of Fortune, the apparently dichotomous destinies of Macbeth and Banquo, Macbeth and James, are crossed and interrelated. This subtle reversal of time and destiny is accomplished in relation to a queen who may bear yet another attribute of Fortune – the crystal ball or sphere (Plate 9). The suggestive identification of the two kings – past and present, Scottish and British – is made explicit by the First Witch's speech at the end of the scene, in a Folio addition now usually attributed to Thomas Middleton:

Ay, Sir, all this is so: – but why
Stands Macbeth thus amazedly?–
Come, sisters, cheer we up his sprites,
And show the best of our delights.
I'll charm the air to give a sound,
While you perform your antic round;
That this great King may kindly say,
Our duties did his welcome pay.
(4.1.125–32)

On the one hand, therefore, *Macbeth* explores the association of that kingship which is not able to perpetuate itself through lineal succession with recurring cycles of triumph and betrayal, in which the continuing influence of the 'rebel's whore' Fortune can be clearly discerned. Yet

Plate 9 'Fortuna', attributed to a mannerist painter of Antwerp, c. 1530 40.
Strasbourg, Musée des Beaux-Arts.

on the other hand, through its subtle use of chiasmus or doubling, the play appears simultaneously to suggest that the new British kingship represented by Banquo's heir is mysteriously dependent upon its opposite, yet originating shadow – the tyrannical, bloody and effeminate image of a Scottish or Celtic king.

6

CORDELIA'S BOND AND BRITANNIA'S MISSING MIDDLE

King Lear (c.1606)

Nature nous a mis au monde libres et desliez; nous nous emprisonnons en certains destroits.

(Montaigne, *Essais* III, ix)[1]

Because woman is silent about herself, she creates an excess of mystery and obscurity, turns herself into an indecipherable riddle.

(Elizabeth Bronfen, *Over her Dead Body*)[2]

Just as the crisis of the succession had informed much of the drama, as well as the political thought of the last decade of Elizabeth's reign, so what might be termed the crisis of the accession of James I left its distinct imprint on early Jacobean drama, in numerous plays which more or less obliquely interrogated not only the identity of the new king, but also that of his new kingdom. It was around 1606, when the debate about the Union of England and Scotland was at its height, that Shakespeare made two, and possibly three, powerful interventions in this reopened debate upon the question of kingship, for along with *Macbeth* and *King Lear*, he may also have written *Antony and Cleopatra* in this period.[3] This latter possibility should serve to remind us that (like James's own rhetorical attempts to define his kingship in patriarchal terms) Shakespeare's dramatic meditations upon masculine rule invariably cast a long and feminine shadow behind them; yet in fact the implication of the ruler's sovereign power with certain feminine tropes is already subtly delineated in *Lear* and *Macbeth*, plays whose historical proximity is further strengthened by their tropical affinity.

While we can discern the defining influence of a Scottish queen in *Macbeth*'s exploration of the relationship of kingship to temporality, a very different queen, Cordelia, is of central importance in *King Lear*'s strikingly scatological refiguration of James's new British kingdom. And here too a morally compromised kingship is implied to have an unsettling association with a suggestively feminized anality: a breach or fissure in the body politic that marks the site of the uncanny. Like that of Macbeth, Lear's is also a 'breached' or divided kingship; yet while it is the chiastic crossing or doubling of kingship, by and through certain feminine figures associated with Fortuna, which animates the political relevance of *Macbeth*, the political heart of Lear's tragedy is the king's sacrifice of the centre or seat of his 'breached' kingdom or sovereignty. In *Lear*, moreover, the Janus-aspect of rule, as represented by Lear's two elder daughters, leads to tragedy precisely because it is *not* properly mediated and united by a third figure. By implication, this 'jointing' or 'bonding' should have been the role of Cordelia, who both by her name and in her fidelity to a filial 'bond' seems to emblematize the intended centre of Lear's bequest of a tripartite British sovereignty. But instead, as the malcontent Edmund moves insidiously to occupy the political vacuum that has been engendered by Cordelia's 'Nothing', by becoming the lover of both her sisters, the rejected territorial middle which was seemingly to have been Cordelia's jointure is figuratively 'digested' and, it is implied, excreted by her brothers-in-law. What it becomes is a discarded waste/waist land, whose spectral uncanniness signals the concealment of the animating spirit or soul of royal power within the centre of the land.

In my exploration of this muddied yet potent dramatic terrain, I will show how, through the elision of its tragic geography with the figure of a disinherited or propertyless queen, the play not only develops Shakespeare's earlier figurations of queens in relationship to images of a 'holed' or fissured state, it also makes a subtle and very witty contribution to contemporary figurations of Britain and the Union in masque, entertainment and antiquarian text.

Rejointing the kingdom

On 20 October 1604, James officially claimed the title of King of Great Britain; the theme of union consequently enjoyed considerable importance over the next few years, not only in political discussion, but also in courtly compliment. Several of these comparisons focused on James as a second Brutus, who was reuniting the kingdom which his legendary predecessor had supposedly divided among his three sons.[4] Yet the idea of a 'joint' or 'bond' between things was more usually personified as female, and in the King's 1603 entry into London, Ben Jonson imagines the future destiny of 'this land' of Britaine as the 'navill', middle, or *omphalos* of the world; in much other courtly panegyric it is similarly the feminine personification of his new kingdom, as Britannia, that is most closely associated with the idea of Union. The troping of kingship as a three-legged seat, or joint stool, in *Henry IV Part I* suggests that the association of kingship or sovereignty with an implicitly feminine act of joining preceded the Jacobean Union debate; however, the use of the trope in both *Macbeth* and *King Lear* shows that it had now acquired an especial topicality.[5] While the seat or stool of kingship has an especially ambiguous effeminacy in Act 3 scene 4 of *Macbeth*, in the 1608 Quarto of *Lear* it is explicitly identified by the deranged king, during the mock trial scene, with a female ruler:

Lear: Arraign her first, 'tis Goneril – I here take my oath before this honourable assembly – kicked the poor King her father.
Fool: Come hither mistress: is your name Goneril?
Lear: She cannot deny it.
Fool: Cry you mercy, I took you for a joint-stool.

(3.6.46–51)

The figurative association of an idealized image of woman with the middle or between can be attributed to a variety of factors. It may be partially explained by the exchange of women between families in marriage (a bond which was cemented above all by the 'jointures' or dowries that accompanied them); in her marriage to Antony, Octavia is used to create an 'unslipping knot' between Caesar and Antony, as 'the piece of virtue which is set / Betwixt us, as the cement of our love / To keep it builded (2.2.134, 3.2.28–30). In a more bawdy context, Renaissance texts often refer to a woman's hymen, broken in her first sexual intercourse, as the virgin 'knot', while frequently alluding to the feminine associations of the place 'between', whether as an anal or genital orifice.[6] And in this sense, the 'knotted' or intact virginal body could also be troped as a piece of enclosed land, a *hortus conclusus* in which the feminine boundary or between functioned as a bond or limit, just as the chaste body of the married woman could be imaged in terms of a 'bond of chastity' (*Cymbeline*, 5.5.206).[7] But the feminine figuration of the middle also had a philosophical basis. Platonism had troped the feminine-gendered soul, as *psyche* or *anima*, as a bond or *vinculum* between heaven and earth: 'And God set the soul in the midst thereof [of the universe] and spread her through all its body and even wrapped the body about with her from without'. This notion of soul's occupation of 'the midst' survives in late Renaissance vitalism, which typically sees all of matter as informed by a principle equivalent to the world soul.[8] In Ben

Jonson's 1606 masque *Hymenaei*, this unifying activity of soul is explicitly linked to the Roman queen of the gods, Juno, as an emblem of Union that is combined with the imagery of encircling or enclosing: 'She that makes soules, with bodies, mixe in love, / Contracts the world in one' (ll. 141–2).[9]

In such contexts, a *feminine* activity of bonding or jointing coexists problematically with the conventional Aristotelian equation of *femaleness* with that bodily and material sphere that needs to be joined with its opposite, whether as husband or heaven. In the field of Shakespeare criticism, a metonymic association between the tropes of Renaissance 'joinery' and the 'unruly matter' of women has recently been brilliantly analysed by Patricia Parker in her study of *A Midsummer Night's Dream*.[10] Yet while Parker defines the place of women in this figurative association in relation to an Aristotelian conception of the rude *materia* that must be shaped and ordered by diverse modes of 'joinery', my reading of the Jacobean imagery of jointing or bonding in *Lear* allies this trope to the uncanny joinery associated with Cordelia as an emblem of soul's perplexing conjunction of spirit with primal or unshaped matter. The Renaissance fondness for quibbling on the near-homophony between the French words *âme* and *ane/asne*, the soul and the ass (an animal who provided a familiar metaphor for the backside, bottom or buttocks), which Shakespeare explored in the unlikely union of the ass-headed Bottom with the fairy queen Titania, well illustrates his sense of the strange affinity between this feminine activity of joining and the apparently unredeemable stuff of waste matter whose diverse medicinal properties were nonetheless stressed in contemporary herbals.[11] *Lear* plays on a similar proximity between the spiritualized figure of Cordelia, the 'asinine' folly of her royal father, and that wasted, unenclosed region which is her 'digested' jointure.[12]

During the reign of Elizabeth the English body politic was consistently imaged as feminine; indeed, Claire McEachern has recently emphasized 'the absolutely fundamental quality of gender to national identity in this period', observing at the same time that 'the figure of our country as "she" is a commonplace of national affect'.[13] But while in its oft-cited description by John of Gaunt in *Richard II*, England (here equated with Britain) is troped as a birthplace, as 'This nurse, this teeming womb of royal kings' (2.1.51), the classical association between the island and death, as the other world, or the isles of the blessed dead (the Elysian Fields, the Fortunate Isles or the Garden of the Hesperides), was more commonly cited in the period, in a pun which emphasized the homology between queen Elizabeth and her realm, as a feminized otherworld: 'The place *Elysium* hight, and of the place, / Her name that governs there *Eliza* is'.[14] This ancient association of Britain with an otherworldly paradise, *divisus ab orbe* (divided from the world) yet nonetheless 'sited in the middest of the temperate zone', as Camden noted in his *Remaines*, reappears in panegyrics to James and his family (especially in the Jacobean masque). Yet when the state was seen as disfigured by political conflict and corruption, these images of the British otherworld at the edge, or end, of the known world could acquire a rather darker dimension through Britain's association with a darkly chthonic and typically feminine materiality that evokes, not the Elysian fields, but rather Hades (the classical underworld through which only the heroic dead could pass to Elysium) and this was the region which had been scatologically troped by Rabelais in his *Tiers Livre* as '[queen] Proserpina's close-stool'.[15] In Shakespeare's texts, it is typically in relation to the figures of displaced or disorderly queens that these darker, chthonic associations of the island kingdom are most clearly explored.

It was probably due in part to political caution that in contrast to contemporary poetic emphasis upon the queen's identification with her kingdom, Shakespeare's Elizabethan dramas focus primarily upon reigning monarchs who are male. However, early in his career, Shakespeare created two excessive and transgressive figures of female sovereignty whose disordered desires are linked with a disordered realm; through their figurative association with Diana, both these queens appear to refer obliquely to Elizabeth. The grotesque portrait in *Titus Andronicus* of Tamora, the defeated queen of the Goths, hints at the presence of an obscure and dangerous political allegory upon the ageing Queen, in its comparison of Tamora to the classical deity to whom Elizabeth was so often compared – a deity, moreover, who was mythologically linked with Prosperina, queen of the underworld. Tamora's new Roman kingdom (acquired through a marriage which may hint at Elizabeth's 'Roman' contamination of the purity of the English Reformation) is reconfigured as tragically fissured, as the queen's metonymic association with a gaping pit (finally metamorphosed into her own devouring mouth) elides Rome both with the pagan Hades and the female genitals. And in *A Midsummer Night's Dream*, the temporary disobedience to her lord of Titania, the fairy queen, allies a climactic reversion to natural chaos, in which the rivers 'have overborne their continents' (or bounds), with a disorderly female sexuality that is bawdily emblematized by her erotic union with a double ass or arse: the ass-headed Bottom.

In *Henry VI*, *Richard III*, and *Richard II*, queen consorts also assume an especial emblematic potency, as images of a chaotic and fissured body politic. *Richard II* creates an especially vivid chain of figurative association between a queen's grief, imaged as an internal breach, and the disordered 'state', 'seat' or 'bank' of England. When she hears of Bolingbroke's return to usurp the throne, the tropes used by Richard's queen subtly identify her with that seat, both as the 'teeming womb of royal kings' but also as the place from which kings are passed or rejected, for in what seems to be something of a breach birth, Bolingbroke is delivered as the monstrous 'heir' to her own fearful conceits; in other words, as the next king, whose emergence confirms Richard's deposition:

> So, Greene, thou art the midwife to my woe,
> And Bolingbroke my sorrow's dismal heir;
> Now hath my soul brought forth her prodigy,
> And I, a gasping new-deliver'd mother,
> Have woe to woe, sorrow to sorrow join'd.
>
> (2.2.62–6)

In this trope of the grieving queen who births an unacceptable or illegitimate offspring, English sovereignty, as the mother of English kings, is elided with a personification of sorrow; indeed, the imagery used by Richard's French-born queen hints at a second-meaning and interlingual pun on *grevé*, French for grieved, and *crevé*, the bursting open of the bowels; the double character of this 'delivery' is certainly implied when the queen ends by redefining the prodigious birth as an act of joining.[16] The doubleness attributed here both to the queen and, through her, to English sovereignty (which accords with a trope used elsewhere in the play, of Richard and Bolingbroke as weighed in a scale), is refigured at the end of Act 3, when she learns in a garden of Richard's deposition. At this point she is metonymically related not only to the disordered garden of the kingdom, which the 'wasteful king' has neglected (just as, Bolingbroke implies in Act 3 scene 1, he has his queen), but also to its impending restoration, since it is now to be 'trimm'd and dress'd' by a new monarch as gardener. The trope seems confirmed by the gardener's concluding reference to the queen's 'State' (which is capitalized in the Folio text): 'Poore Queene, so that thy State might be no worse, / I would my skill were subiect to thy curse', and by his decision to plant 'a bank of rue' where her tear has fallen, in 'remembrance of a weeping queen' (3.4.102–7). Thus the grief of Richard's queen, associated in the previous passage with a portent of the state's future imaged as a tear, breach or division, is now fixed as an emblem of the reparation of England's torn past, in a bank of remembrance which converts grief to fruitfulness.

The manifold divisions in the state of England created by the Wars of the Roses are imaged in *Richard III* by the mournful presence of three tragic queens: Anne, Richard III's queen; Elizabeth, Edward IV's queen; and Margaret, Henry VI's queen; at the end of the play, moreover, Richard is attempting to create yet another queen, by proposing marriage to his niece Elizabeth of York. An emblematic association between these royal women and the mysterious cycles of both fruitfulness and decay in 'England's lawful earth', which they collectively personify, is suggested at several points in the play, as these consorts and mothers of England's suns/sons become infernal Furies united against Richard, whose treachery has turned 'the sun to shade' (1.3.266). In *Hamlet*, however, while Gertrude is described by Claudius as 'Th'imperial jointress of this warlike state' (1.2.9), a similar 'disjointing' of the state and its accustomed rituals, associated with her hasty second marriage, is imaged in terms of a disturbing excess of natural fecundity, in which generation is already corrupt or decayed. As a figure for the corrupt Danish state, the 'unweeded garden / That grows to seed' is also the queen herself, whose 'enseamèd bed' combines the punning associations of *seam* (joint), *seem* (appear), and *seme* as seed (from the Latin *semen*), as an erotic locale of seeding, joining or 'union' which is also a 'rank' or foul-smelling locus of deception: a 'nasty sty' or wasteland ruled over by Claudius the 'mildewed ear' or 'moor'. In the last scene, this false or corrupt union becomes a literal agent of death, in the pearl or 'union' with which Claudius attempts to poison Hamlet, but by which both he and Gertrude die. Yet just as Hamlet's own quibbling and mercurial language gradually accords a more positive valency to those processes of bodily and worldly corruption represented by 'my Lady Worm', so in *Lear* also a similar imagistic nexus, of a 'disjointed' kingdom reduced to waste and foulness as a result of a feminine copiousness which is bodily as well as verbal, is ultimately given a rather different inflection.

When we take a closer look at Shakespeare's Elizabethan queens, therefore, it seems that the real queen's easy identification, as a female ruler, with the feminine-gendered body politic of England was rather too close for comfort. In contrast, Richard Helgerson contends that on the accession of James, 'Britannia and the British monarch, so firmly identified with one another as to be virtually interchangeable through most of Elizabeth's reign, now occupied separate and mutually hostile camps'.[17] Helgerson's assertion may seem superficially illogical: after all (and in spite of earlier English propaganda to the contrary) it was only now that an English monarch could unequivocally claim rulership of the whole island; moreover, as scholars of the Union debate have clearly shown, James was far more committed to the idea of Great Britain as a unified realm than were his English Parliaments.[18] Yet while James was widely complimented on his accession to rulership of the whole kingdom of Britain, for example in the anagram devised by Camden, that 'Charles James Steuart / Claims Arthur's seat', *King Lear* points to the perception in this period of a striking figurative divergence between the monarch and his realm or 'seat'. This divergence is attributable in large part to the continuing personification of the body politic, or the sovereignty of the kingdom, as female. But it was also undoubtedly influenced by James's own highly polemical definition of his kingship, which he argued was not constricted by the bonds of earthly law.

James's feminine 'seat'

Commenting on James's predominantly feudal conception of kingship, C. H. McIlwain observed that:

> [T]here is one aspect of the feudal relation [of governor and governed] that is conspicuous by its absence in James's politics. Of the reciprocal duties of *dominus* and *homo*, so prominent in the medieval conception of English kingship, there remains not a trace: it has been replaced entirely by the Roman conception of the king *legibus solutus*, placed so immeasurably above his *subditi* that he can in no way be bound by earthly law to the performance of any duties to them.[19]

We can plausibly associate the absence of the language of reciprocal obligation (or 'bonds') from James's model of kingship with his seeming lack of interest in the traditional medieval trope of kingship as a marriage between male ruler and feminine-gendered realm. Although he used a conjugal figure in his first address to Parliament, in 1604, declaring that 'I am the Husband, and all the whole Isle is my lawfull Wife, I am the Head and it is my Body', the bond of marriage was not James's preferred metaphor for the relationship of what he termed 'a free and absolute *Monarche*' to his realm. (And while he was to redeploy the imagery of marriage in several of his appeals for Union, the 'marriage' envisaged there was between two kingdoms, not between monarch and realm.) More commonly, James troped what he considered his divinely-sanctioned kingship as fatherhood, defining himself not as the spouse of his realm but as its benign *paterfamilias*, its 'natural father and kindly Master'.[20] This emphasis upon the realm as child left its gender strangely indistinct; thus, in one of his appeals for the union of the two kingdoms, James could speak of the desirability of a Union between two brothers. Moreover, in the context of his ideology of absolutism, James's exaggerated infantilizing of the state had disturbing political implications. In *The*

True Law of Free Monarchies (1598), he had insisted that 'the king is over-lord over the whole lands', that his subjects were 'but his vassals, and from him holding all their lands as their over-lord', that Parliament was his servant, to be summoned and dismissed as it pleased him, and that 'the king is above the law, as both the author and giver of strength thereof'.[21] While there is some dispute among historians on the extent of distrust between James and his early Parliaments, his absolutist stance undoubtedly intensified the interest of those concerned to protect the common law in the ancient precedents being excavated by antiquarian research.[22] My contention is that literary interest in the idea of Britannia often fulfilled a similar function.

For in spite of (or perhaps, we may even infer, because of) the new monarch's explicit desire to subordinate his realm(s) to his royal prerogative, during the early years of James's reign the semi-autonomous identity of his island kingdom was accorded an unprecedented level of figurative development in diverse works by poets, dramatists and antiquaries. Since several of these texts were associated with royal entries, masques, or other court performances, their emphasis upon Britain ostensibly compliments the king, by alluding to his desire for Union. But such texts also develop the allegorical identity of the island in ways which often suggestively contradict James's apparent desire to curb the imaginative, as well as the political, autonomy of his new kingdom, since they frequently distinguish the fixed centre or 'seat' of British sovereignty – in other words, the land itself – from the monarch. Thus while Parliament was forcefully rejecting the king's appeal for Union on diverse grounds which included the fear that a change of name would jeopardize the integrity of the English legal system, and with it a specifically English sovereignty, a very different version of Britannia was being defined in these literary and historical texts. It is now widely recognized that in the drama of 1604–8, 'liberties were directly taken with the king's image without recourse to conceal-ment'; however, little attention has been given to the ways in which, during the same period, the liberty of the realm was being textually dilated or enlarged through this reinscription of the monarch's island 'seat'.[23]

In contrast to the early Jacobean Parliaments' fierce rejection of the name of Great Britain, antiquarian research had already imaginatively reincorporated the English body politic into the greater and more ancient realm of Britain or Albion several decades before the accession of James. In these antiquarian texts, emphasis upon the island's traditional attribute of whiteness was sometimes associated with an implicitly feminine beauty, as in this account by Humphrey Lhuyd:

[O]ur Brytaynes called this Iland *Prydain* in their language, which the Latines for the hardnesse and evill sounde thereof, have reiected, and have called the countrey *Britannia*, and the people *Britanni*, for the more gentle and pleasant soundes sake ... *Pryd*, amongst us signifieth comlinesse or beutie: *Cain*, signifieth white. So yt by ye ioyning of these two wordes together, and taking away C, in composition, for the better soundes sake: is made *Prydain*, that is to say, a white, or excellent bewtie, or comelinesse.[24]

It is notable, moreover, that Lhuyd's etymological account derives the present name of the island from a linguistic 'ioyning' imposed by its Roman colonists. However, most sixteenth-century authors of antiquarian and chorographical works exhibited little interest in the island's feminine personification. Camden was unusual, therefore, in making several allegorical references to Britain as a feminine figure. In his introduction to *Britannia*, he alludes to the ancients' amazement at the fertility of the land, 'the ground enriched so with all sorts of corne, that Orpheus hath reported it to be the very seat of Ladie *Ceres*', and observed that 'This plentifull abundance, these goodly pleasures of *Britain*, have persuaded some, that those fortunate Ilands, wherein all things, as Poets write, doe still flourish as in a perpetuall spring tide, were sometime heere with us'.[25] Subsequently, in his discussion of the possible derivation of the island's other legendary name of Albion from the Greek *alphon*, white, Camden mentions another of its classical personifications:

For environed it is with white rockes, which Cicero termeth *mirificas moles*, that is, wonderous Piles: and hereof it is that upon the coined peeces bearing the stamp of Antoninus Pius and Severus, Britaine is pourtraicted sitting upon rocks in woman's habit.[26]

This seated figure, armed with a spear or trident as well as a Celtic shield with a central point, was to become the traditional image of Britannia in later centuries. It is this Roman image which is positioned at the top of the decorative frontispiece added to *Britannia* for its 1594 and all later editions (Plate 10). Later, in *Britannia*'s Gloucestershire chapter, when Camden describes the source of the Isis, we encounter a Ceres-like personification of Britannia, as a goddess crowned with wheat, but also adorned with the mythological golden fleece:

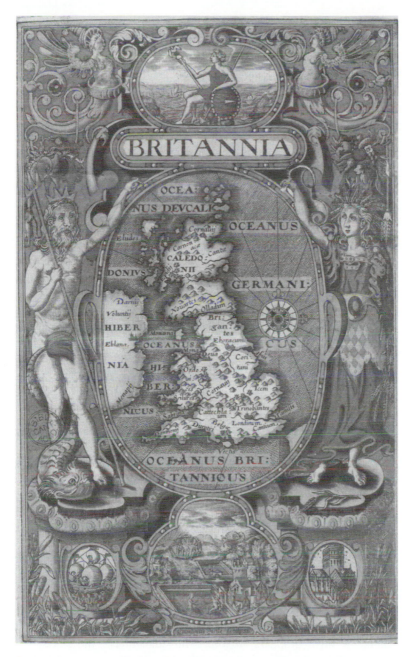

Plate 10 Frontispiece, William Camden, *Britannia* (London: 1611). By
permission of the Syndics of Cambridge University Library.

And here bedight in gold,
Among them [the rivers] glitt'reth Britannie with riches
manifold
of goulden fleece; a coronet of wheat-ears she doth weare,
And for her triumph over France, her head aloft doth reare . . . [27]

In its striking fusion of the imagery of 'ears' and 'reare' (often given
bawdy connotations at the time) with an encircled and fertile head,
Camden's English text hints at a potent sexual – and double-sexed
– dimension of this fecund national deity. Yet this second figure of
Britannia was demurely clad when it too was incorporated into
Camden's frontispiece, where it was placed on the right side of the
decorative arch which framed the page; opposite it was a naked figure of
Neptune. Just as both of Camden's two initial figures of Britannia preside
over an intersection of land and water (whether as sea or river), so the
visual polarity here between Neptune and Britannia as corn-goddess
points to the subtle interrelationship of the island of Britain with the
sea which bounds or encircles it. And this motif of the interdependence
of land and water in Britannia's identity is repeated in Camden's third
allegorical personification of Britain, which he added to the 1607, first
folio (and first Jacobean) edition of his work, in the context of his
extension of a poem describing the marriage of the two rivers, Tame and
Isis. The watery nuptials are performed by 'BRITONA, hand-fast-
maker shee', who:

All clad in laurell green,
Plays on the harp what ever acts
Our auncestors have seene.
She singes how BRITANNY from all
The world divided was,
When Nereus with victorious Sea
Through cloven rocks did passe . . . [28]

This emblematic link between Britain and a process of uniting or joining
stresses the affinity between political and marital union. Yet the island is
also mysteriously founded on a geographical division ('from all the
world'), whose breaking of earthly boundaries has a suggestive eroticism,
in the forceful passage through a cleft of this extremely fertile sea-god, to
whom the mythographers attributed fifty daughters. And since, as I
mentioned above, antiquarian researches into the ancient customs of the
British were to fuel some of the resistance to James's conception of

kingship and law, it is striking too that Camden's only Jacobean figuration of Britannia also emphasizes her close affinity with the past, as a receptacle and instrument of historical memory.

In the many representations of Britannia that appeared in royal panegyrics during the first part of James's reign, feminine personifications both of place and of sovereign power were often given significant emphasis. Thus a female Genius of London, devised by Thomas Dekker, was to have welcomed James on his royal entry into the city on 15 March 1604, although this opening device was unacted. By representing London as a female, Dekker was clearly in disagreement with the other poet employed for the entry, Ben Jonson, whose own version of the city Genius was virtually the male twin of this figure. However, in the first of those Arches of Triumph for which Jonson was responsible, at Fenchurch, on which were positioned twelve emblematic personages, 'the highest person advanc'd therein' was a female figure entitled 'Monarchia Britannia', whose close connection with London as the 'seate of empire' Jonson acknowledges; she was 'here placed as in the proper seate of the empire: for, so the glorie and light of our kingdome M. Camden, speaking of *London*, saith shee is'.[29] But the most fully developed feminine personification of the new kingdom in this entry was devised by Dekker for the fourth Arch, at Soper Lane. This was '*Arabia Britannica*, a Woman, attyred all in white, a rich Mantle of Greene cast about her, an imperiall Crowne on her head, and a Scepter in one hand, a Mound in the other; upon which she sadly leaned . . . '[30]

Given the predominance in this entry of feminine personifications of the new British sovereignty, it is hardly surprising that while some of the attributes of the former monarch, such as her phoenix emblem, were promptly transferred to James, others, which were more explicitly gendered, were awarded instead to his queen, Anna of Denmark. Yet it was probably not simply her symbolic identity both as a crowned consort and as the mother of a future king that encouraged Anna's close association with Britannia in royal panegyrics produced during the early part of the reign; there was also the happy coincidence of her name, which she herself preferred to be written as Anna. Whether as Anne or Anna, however, the queen's name could conveniently be linked with the tail or end of the restored national identity, as Britain or Britannia; at the same time, those familiar with Geoffrey of Monmouth's *Historia Regum Britanniae*, which was still an important, albeit much criticized source text for research into ancient British history, would have known that Anna is the name Geoffrey accords to Arthur's sister (called Morgause in other versions of Arthurian myth), who becomes queen of Scotland and the mother of British kings.

In the speeches written by Jonson for the seventh and last Arch of Triumph in the royal entry, Anna was complimented by the observation that the day (15 March) was held sacred to the Roman deity Anna Perenna as well as to the deity of the month, Mars. Yet by allying that rejection of martial ambition which was to be the keynote of James's foreign policy with the new queen's 'strong and potent vertues', the speech distinguishes Anna from Anna Perenna as the spouse of Mars. Jonson's compliment to Anna attributes to the pacific influence of this 'greater ANNE' the enthronement of yet another feminine aspect of British sovereignty, peace, who can now 'sit in that bright state she ought'. Alongside this suggestive association between Anne/Anna and the seat of sovereignty, the device also stressed the zodiacal imagery of joining through encirclement, noting that the Roman Anna 'fills the yeare, / And knits the oblique scarfe that girts the spheare'; this imagery was to recur constantly in encomia to Anna as a personification of British sovereignty and hence of Union, thus in the dedication to Anna of John Dowland's *Lachrimae* (1605), she is complimented as that 'joint' (*juncta*) which unites three kingdoms (Scotland, England and Ireland) and three protective deities (Juno, Pallas and Venus).

The queen's association with Union was developed in those early Jacobean masques in which Anna usually took the leading parts, and of which several critics now see her as a prime mover.[31] The masque's most developed female personification of Union appears in *Hymenaei*, performed at the Twelfth Night revels of January 1606, where the Roman deity Juno appears as a figure of 'UNIO'; this device compliments James, but it also implicitly associates queen Juno, as spouse to Jupiter, with Anna, who did not perform on this occasion. Yet as early as Samuel Daniel's *A Vision of Twelve Goddesses* (1604) diverse emblems of binding are accorded to the twelve goddesses who come to bless the new kingdom (led by Anna as Pallas); some years later, in Jonson's *Masque of Beautie* (1608), queen Anna personated Harmonia, whom Jonson compares to the principle of unity (or union) within nature: 'the *worlds soule*, true *harmony*'; a year later, in his *Masque of Queens* (1609), Anna's company of queens dispels an anti-masque of witches which threatens 'to loose the whole henge [bond or joint] of things'.[32]

Anna was the protagonist of an especially subtle representation of Union in a masque which she not only commissioned, but whose plot she helped to shape. In Jonson's first masque, the *Masque of Blackness*, performed at court on 6 January 1605, Jonson hints at a figurative association that was to be more fully developed in *Lear*: between the new British monarchy and the darkness yet fecundity of a primal matter figured both as feminine and as racially other. The masque compliments the new king by defining his sun-like person as the only power which can whiten the black beauties of the daughters of Niger; however, it also implies that the quest of these Aethiopian nymphs for Britain is for a realm with which they have discovered a symbolic affinity (like that which the similarly complected queen of Sheba felt for Solomon, to whom James was frequently compared). In fact, Camden had cited Pliny's observation that:

> There groweth an herbe in Gaule like unto Plantaine, named Glastum, that is Woad, with the juice whereof, the women of Britaine, as well maried wives as their young daughters anoint and die their bodies all over; resembling by that tincture *the colour of Æthiopians*, in which maner they use at some solemne feasts and sacrifices to goe all naked.[33] [my emphasis]

While the masque compliments James himself as Albion, since it is the termination or 'end' of the island's new name, '-tania', which has guided the nymphs' quest, their arrival in Britain seems to be closely connected with its restored appellation as Britannia. And although the nymphs' 'reverence to the place' may be partly explained by their descent from Oceanus, the watery protector of Britain or Albion, the masque also tells us that as 'the first form'd dames of earth' their blackness gives them an especial association with earth; this appears to be expressed through the 'indenting' which they mark upon the island of Britain in their dancing. Moreover, while the bleaching of these black beauties by James's sun-like powers is anticipated at the end of the masque, it is not yet accomplished; the masque consequently hints at the existence of an as yet unassimilable difference within British sovereignty: a feminized as well as racial difference which is seemingly linked with the restoration of its ancient name.

The wasted middle of 'Lear'

While clearly shaped by the same climate of opinion which motivated the masques, Shakespeare's play can arguably be read as the dramatic antimasque to these productions. In *Lear*, as in the masques, female figures of sovereignty enjoy an especial importance in the play's analysis of the new identity of Britain. But the play's exploration of Union operates primarily through negation, both through the kingdom's dismemberment or division, and in the effective unmapping of its centre, as the emblematic mound or feminine seat of sovereignty upon which Lear had hoped 'to set my rest' becomes a literal and figurative dunghill

– the setting for tragic suffering and death. Yet in this focus upon the hole or void at the middle of Lear's Britain – the gap which is so aptly imaged by Cordelia's inaugural 'Nothing' – the tragedy also implies that the apparent refuse or 'waste' of pre-history can engender a new under-standing of British sovereignty, not only by illuminating its implication in an extensive web of human relationships or 'bonds', but also in stressing the uncanny limits of all worldly power.

I noted above that although *King Lear* was formerly thought to have been composed between 1605 and 1606, there has been a recent shift of opinion on this point, with the result that some time in 1606 is now agreed by several critics to be the most likely date of composition; this would place its composition not only after the *Masque of Blackness*, but also after *Hymenaei*. Most critics agree that some revisions were made specifically for the court performance of the play, given on St Stephen's Night, 26 December 1606, although further revisions to the play could have been made as late as 1608, the date of the first, Pied Bull, Quarto of the text. Not only does this date make it possible that *Lear* was written after, rather than before *Macbeth*, it also bring its composition much closer to that of *Antony and Cleopatra* (if J. Leeds Barroll is right in his redating of the latter play), whose imagery of 'the three-nooked world' of empire H. Neville Davies has shown to intersect strikingly with 'the British union of three in one'.[34] But it is notable too that *Lear* was written at a time when the physical location of queens, both past and present, was assuming a heightened but problematic significance for James.

In the first place, the corpses of three queens – Elizabeth Tudor, her sister Mary Tudor, and their cousin Mary Stuart, were currently providing the new monarch with important symbolic capital. For it was in 1606 that an elaborate tomb in Westminster Abbey for Elizabeth was completed, whose inscription acknowledged that it also, some-what strangely, housed her Catholic sister. At the same time, work had probably already commenced on an even more ornate tomb situated nearby, for James's mother Mary.[35] In her recent discussion of Elizabeth's tomb, Julia M. Walker has noted that, rather curiously, at least some of the cost of Elizabeth's tomb was met, not by James himself, but from the household accounts of his wife, Queen Anna.[36] Walker argues in this essay that the building of her monument involved the removal of Elizabeth's body from the more central position in the royal chapel of her grandfather, Henry VII, in which it had been buried, which was near the altar, to a more marginal or supplementary location in the north wing of the chapel, where its location was to be balanced by the tomb of Mary Stuart in the south wing. Walker points out that this disinterment affords an interesting parallel to the removal of Cleopatra's body from her monument at the end of *Antony and Cleopatra*; however, James's displacement of a great queen from the centre of her ancestor's sepulchre to its periphery may also have an echo in the subject matter of *King Lear*.

Furthermore, it was in this same year of 1606 – when *Lear* was most probably composed, and Elizabeth's tomb was completed – that Queen Anna set up a separate household (or 'seat') of her own – at which time, it is presumed, marital relations between the royal couple completely ceased. This event must also have influenced contemporary perceptions of the monarch, whose preference for the company of men was by now fully apparent to his new court. (In 1607, James was to replace his favourite, Lord Hay, with a new rising star, Robert Carr.) Hence while the genealogical authority of James's monarchy was being more securely bolstered by work on the parallel tombs of Elizabeth and Mary Queen of Scots, the continuing extension of this royal genealogy by a third and living queen was simultaneously being compromised. Sir Anthony Weldon would later observe of this notably restless monarch: 'he was ever best, when furthest from his queene, and that was thought to be the first grounds of his often removes, which afterward proved habituall'.[37]

James's concern in his discourse of Union was to unite two realms: England and Scotland. But by choosing to treat the legend of King Lear and his three daughters, Shakespeare was able to juxtapose the current motif, prominent in most Union tracts, of a British *duality* (which after the disinheriting of Cordelia is imaged in the division of the realm between Cornwall and Albany and their wives) with an alternative triadic structure, implicit in the king's original intention of dividing his kingdom in three, as had Brutus. Although from the seventeenth century onwards reference to the threefold aspect of Britain was usually taken to include Ireland, the association of the island of Britain itself with the mystic number three had been stressed in several ways. Thus in the legend of Brutus as told by Geoffrey of Monmouth, this founding father of Britain had divided his kingdom among his three sons: the tripartite division was into Wales (Cambria), Scotland (Albany), and England (Loegria). And at the beginning of Camden's *Britannia*, he noted the island's triangular shape as observed by the ancients:

> Britain . . . lieth against Germanie and France trianglewise; by reason of three Promontories, shooting out into divers parts: to wit, BELERIUM, in the Cape of S.Burien, in Cornwall, Westward; CANTIUM, in the Foreland of Kent, into the East; and TARVISIUM or Orcas, in the point of Catnesse in Scotland, Northward.[38]

In *Lear*, since Goneril and Regan are already married to the Dukes of Albany (Scotland) and Cornwall, the implication is that the third jointure which was to have been Cordelia's is the land lying *between* those two dukedoms, a region seemingly more or less synonymous with the region ending in Britain's eastern, Kentish promontory or 'angle'. This region, once called Loegria or Logres, the Anglo-Saxons would name England. (It is in fact near the centre of this third region of Britain that Geoffrey of Monmouth describes Cordelia as having buried her father, in an underground chamber under the river Soar, just to the south of Leicester; in *Richard III*, Shakespeare describes Leicester – the city that Geoffrey asserts to have been named for Lear – as 'the centry of this isle' (5.2.11).) Most of the action of the play appears to be set in this region, and specifically between Gloucester's castle and Dover.[39]

It was a more contemporary version of this English regional difference, of course, that James's early parliaments were so anxious to protect. *Lear* appears to support this concern, since it is implicitly due to his neglect of the subtle difference of England as a mysterious territorial 'joint' or centre (with which Kent, Edgar and Gloucester also appear to be associated), as well as by his rejection of its intended 'jointress', Cordelia – of whom France significantly declares, 'She is herself a dower' – that Lear creates 'the gor'd state' alluded to at the end of the play. Thereby he opens up a 'division', 'breach' or void in the midst of his kingdom; into this 'nothing' that is implicitly created by the loss of Britain's feminine soul, both king and subjects fall. But while the political dimension of *Lear* is overtly focused upon a catastrophic partition or 'breaching' of British national identity; in its interest in the rejected yet fecund product of this breach – the realm's lost middle – the play appears also to qualify the royal conception of Union, by warning against the neglect of what is implied to be the uncanny difference of the archaic centre, *omphalos* or seat of British sovereignty. *Richard II* had imaged this difference at the heart of kingship as the 'hollow crown' within whose centre 'keeps Death his court'; in *Lear*, however, in a development of the trope which I have noted in *Macbeth*, the scatological subtext of the play not only figures the king as an ass/arse; it also appears to metamorphose the joint-stool of kingship into a close stool or *chaise percée*.

The association of the tragic protagonist or hero with an interstitial, uncanny, and implicitly feminine site that joins opposites (culture and nature, man and god) and has the capacity to confer a supernatural blessing or curse upon the land has been identified as a central motif of Greek tragedy; in *Lear*, however, it is due to the king's initial neglect of this in-between realm – and its mysterious difference – that tragedy occurs. Only after he has sacrificed Cordelia's 'opulent third' to the appetites of Cornwall and Albany does Lear discover the worthlessness of those two 'parings' of his divided kingdom which are synonymous with his elder daughters, and the contrasting value of what he has lost. Yet the play suggests that an understanding of this loss, which is symbolized both by Cordelia herself and by that territorial jointure which I read as a metonym for the disinherited queen, cannot be acquired directly; instead, it is communicated through the obscure and riddling language that is initially exclusive to the Fool. This sibylline style of communication may have been intended to resemble that of the ancient Gallic peoples, of whom Diodorus Siculus had commented that 'when they meet together, they converse with few words and in riddles, hinting darkly at things for the most part, and using one word when they mean another'.[40] During Lear's madness, similarly 'dark' sayings will be employed by Poor Tom, and are finally adopted by the king himself.

The complex importance of the lost third or 'middle' of Lear's kingdom is emphasized in several of the Fool's riddles, where it is variously defined, yet always in ways which suggest that the relationship of this middle to nothing is not in fact accidental, but rather of fundamental importance. The digested jointure is first imaged as the 'meat' of a broken egg which has been eaten up:

Fool: Nuncle, give me an egg and I'll give thee two crowns.
Lear: What two crowns shall they be?
Fool: Why, after I have cut the egg i'the middle and eat up the meat, the
          two crowns of the egg.

                                                            (1.4.148–52)

In its anticipation of Lear's desire for the storm to split the 'moulds', 'germens' or seeds of nature, this broken egg and its consumed meat tropes the vital centre of the kingdom in terms of generation and birth. But the kingdom-as-egg subsequently mutates into a lost 'wit' that is now 'nothing' (or mad?), with a possible quibble on the white of the egg as well as on 'wit' as bawdy slang for the genitals – hinting thereby at the eclipse of both Lear's manhood and intelligence in relation to a feminine 'nothing':

Fool: Thou hast par'd thy wit o'both sides and left nothing i'the middle.
          Here comes one o'the parings.
[*Enter Goneril*]

                                                            (1.4.177–9)

A scene later, the connection of the middle with negation is refigured in facial terms, as it is equated with the nose. This riddle stresses the structural importance of the nose in maintaining a mode of visual distinction; but it hints too at the significance in the play of the most primitive sense, that of smell, which is also needed, it seems, in order to be able to 'smell out' corruption, as Lear does in his madness:

Fool: Thou canst not tell why one's nose stands i'the middle on's face?
Lear: No.
Fool: Why, to keep one's eyes of either side's nose, that what a man cannot smell out he may spy into.
Lear: I did her wrong.

(1.5.19–23)

And here Lear's failure to understand what the Fool's riddle means ('Thou canst tell . . . ? No') also allies this trope of the middle, through homophony, with the idea of negation, as 'no(se)'.

The bond of British sovereignty

Hence it is primarily through her absence rather than her presence, and above all in the muddled and mutable landscape of her digested jointure, that the play indicates the importance of Cordelia as a subtle refiguration of sovereignty as the 'bond' or 'knot' of Union. It is she alone who loves her father 'according to my bond'; moreover, she is the only one of Lear's daughters to be accorded the title of 'Queen' in the play. This is ostensibly because she is Queen of France; yet according to Geoffrey of Monmouth, Cordelia also ruled Britain for five years after Lear's death. In *King Lear*, however (in a manner not dissimilar to the situation of James's mother, Mary Queen of Scots, in her long period of English imprisonment), this British queen is seemingly a queen over nothing: disinherited, absent from her French kingdom, and with her historical rule over Britain obliterated. Her lack of territory, together with her initial association with the idea of 'nothing' – or (k)notting – confirms that Cordelia's association with the idea of bonding or jointing is highly paradoxical, and this is further suggested, both by the events which take place in the otherworldly and seemingly unbounded landscape of her digested jointure, and by the final focus of the play upon her dead body. It is through Cordelia's relationship with negation, loss and death, therefore, that *Lear* redraws the idea of Union to encompass a paradoxical (k)not or (w)hole at the centre of this putative national unity.

It seems especially significant in connection with the play's imagery of bonds that Cordelia's name is homonymically related to the French *cordelier*, meaning 'tier of knots' – a word which is punned on in the *Heptaméron* of Marguerite de Navarre. This word was commonly applied to the Franciscan monks, who wore knotted girdles or *cordelières* around the *waist* of their habits; early in the sixteenth century, the *cordelière* had also become a badge of French royalty when it was bequeathed to Marguerite's brother, François I, by their mother, Louise of Savoy.[41] Yet as is noted both by Marguerite and by her protégé Rabelais, Franciscans had a persistent reputation for libertinism in this period, and certainly the image of the *cordelier* had a suggestive duality, for while *lier* meant to tie, *delier* was to loosen or untie; in its indirect association of Cordelia with the knots or cords of Union, Shakespeare's play draws out this duality. It does this by a variety of means: her emphasis on her 'bond', her initial language of negation and refusal, the wasted middle of the play, Lear's own imagery of 'unbuttoning', and the unhistorical account of her hanging, which he probably owed to Spenser's *The Faerie Queene*. And while the explicitly erotic associations of the untied knot of the female body are displaced onto her two sisters, Cordelia herself, as the *cor/de* (heart, cord, knot) which has been both *lié* and *delié*, tied and untied, becomes, at the end of the play, the ultimate nothing: the queen as corpse or 'cors'.

When, in *Antony and Cleopatra*, Cleopatra urges the asp to untie with its teeth 'this knot intrinsicate / Of life', her troping of death as an untied knot is notably sexualized. Although the erotic dimension of loosening or untieing is never explicitly associated with Cordelia, in its negative imaging of Lear's archaic British sovereignty, as a forgetting or elision of true Union, the play allies the king's death-like passage through Cordelia's digested jointure – now imaged as an under- or otherworld location – with grotesque visions of woman's uncanny and multi-faceted bodily difference. Such visions are first given shape in Poor Tom's imagery of the 'nightmare'; however, Lear's fantasy of his elder daughters' sexual license will subsequently figure the 'nothing' concealed at the waist or centre in terms of a transgressive female sexuality which is also (like Proserpina's close-stool) a stinking gateway to Hell or the 'nether' world:

> Behold yon simp'ring dame,
> Whose face between her forks presages snow,
> That minces virtue and does shake the head
> To hear of pleasure's name –
> The fitchew, nor the soiled horse goes to't with a more

riotous appetite. Down from the waist they are centaurs,
though women all above. But to the girdle do the gods
inherit, beneath is all the fiend's: there's hell, there's
darkness, there is the sulphurous pit, burning, scalding,
stench, consumption! Fie, fie, fie! Pah, pah! Give me an ounce
of civet, good apothecary, to sweeten my imagination. There's
money for thee.

(4.6.116–27)

Here the loosened knot or waist of a lost feminine virtue is elided with
images of natural and supernatural disorder, as a fecal dirt or waste in
which the semi-bestial identity of whores, or 'soilèd horses', is stressed.
And just as the Fool had riddlingly compared Lear's lost middle to the
nose, so the infernal as well as excremental character of this sexualized
inner landscape is troped above all in terms of smell. But while it appears
to focus primarily upon the infernal aspects of the wasted middle, Lear's
speech about his centaur-daughters also points to the disturbing
ambivalence of the centre. Thus it is in the muddied English landscape
which I read as Cordelia's 'digested' dowry that this dark material
corruption, in quasi-alchemical fashion, gradually engenders something
like understanding in a triplicity of men – Lear, Edgar and Gloucester –
thereby confirming the remark of Erasmus about 'things really worth
having', that 'their excellence they bury in their inmost parts, and
hide'.[42]

At the political level, *Lear*'s figuration of Cordelia as the forgotten
middle, or bond of British sovereignty, appears to warn of the dangers of
neglecting the deeper meaning both of the political Union and of the
unacknowledged relationship of sovereignty to the wasted or disinherited
elements of society – a bond which also encompasses a relationship to
suffering and death. The play suggests that Union consists above all in
a recognition of the mutual bond of obligation, as well as the human
affinity, between a king and his subjects; in making such a recognition,
a ruler by implication acknowledges the limit or boundary of earthly
power. Cordelia's response to her father's momentous question in Act 1
scene 1, 'What can you say to draw / A third more opulent than your
sisters?' (1.1.85–6), is 'Nothing'; when pressed, she glosses this 'nothing'
with reference to her 'bond': 'Unhappy that I am, I cannot heave / My
heart into my mouth. I love your majesty / According to my bond, no
more nor less' (1.1.91–3). As subsequently defined by Cordelia, her
'bond' is a tie of reciprocal affection which secures, but also limits, what
a father can demand of his daughter; but since it also functions as a mean
between the extremes of 'more' and 'less', and since Cordelia here

addresses her father as 'your Majesty', we may reasonably attribute an additional, political dimension to the bond. In his *De Republica*, the sixteenth-century French jurist Jean Bodin, usually cited as an apologist for absolute monarchy, had written:

> Those who state that princes are loosed from laws and contracts give great injury to immortal God and nature, unless they except the laws of God and of nature, as well as property and rights protected by just contracts with private persons.[43]

That Cordelia's emphasis upon an ostensibly familial bond also has implications for the ties of mutual obligation between king and subject is made clear by Kent's appeal to Lear, after his banishment of Cordelia; this expands the meaning of 'bond' in terms of a quasi-feudal service to a monarch, but also stresses the association of this bond (like that of Cordelia) with what is 'plain'. While Kent refers to Lear as one 'Whom I have ever honoured as my king, / Loved as my father, as my master followed, / As my great patron thought on in my prayers' (1.1.141–3), he states that he is now motivated by another bond, to plainness: 'To plainness honour's bound / When majesty falls to folly' (1.1.149–50). Later, in his encounter with Oswald, Kent will refer suggestively to 'the holy cords . . . / Which are too intrince t'unloose' (2.2.72–3). Kent is thus closely connected with that imagery of joining which is focused on Cordelia, and this would certainly be consistent with the equation of Cordelia's jointure with England and its Kentish promontory. In his rejection of Cordelia and Kent, Lear rejects those very cords or bonds – the claims of the heart or 'bias of nature' – whose honouring the play implies to be central to true sovereignty. As we saw earlier, James had defined his kingship similarly, as *de legibus solutus*, or 'loosed' from the bonds of laws and contracts. Thus the play's theme of bonds and joints appears also to encompass that thorny question of the monarch's relationship to natural law which was currently being debated by jurists and parliamentarians.

This point is literally pushed to its limit when, in his madness, Lear finally arrives at an identification with what is plain, simple and lives closer to nature than to art: the lowliest and most despised of his subjects, who are personated in different ways by the disguised Kent and Edgar. The disinherited or landless class had been especially dependent upon the common, or wasteland, before the spread of enclosure, and like the sexualized female body, it was often metonymically associated with bodily or animal waste and its foul smell; in his disguise as Poor Tom, Edgar moans that he 'eats cowdung for sallets', while Oswald refers to him as a 'dunghill', and Cornwall orders that the body of the servant who has opposed the blinding of Gloucester be thrown 'upon the dunghill'. What Lear discovers, therefore, is that 'The art of our necessities is strange, / And can make vile things precious' (3.2.70–1).

When Lear first begins to understand the unkindness of Goneril, he exclaims: 'O most small fault, / How ugly didst thou in Cordelia show, / Which like an engine *wrenched my frame of nature / From the fixed place*, drew from my heart all love / And added to the gall' (1.4.258–62) [my emphasis]. The imagery suggests that Lear's rejection of natural affective ties has caused the loss not just of his emotional centre (Cordelia as love), but also of the seat or fixed centre of his kingship, which is punningly implied to have been acquired instead by Gaul, or France. The loss of Cordelia has already been emblematized by Lear's decision to stay alternate months with Goneril and Regan, although he had originally intended to 'set my rest / On her [Cordelia's] kind nursery' (1.1.124–5). But where the restless Lear finally ends up, after his other daughters' rejection, is in the digested territorial middle whose difference he has failed to acknowledge or protect. For it is on a journey from the west to the east of England, from Gloucester's castle to Dover, where he is reunited with Cordelia, that the king can find no 'rest', but must undergo instead a quasi-apocalyptic process of self-purgation which is bodily, as well as psychological, and which hints at the affinity of the particular realm which he traverses, like some classical accounts of archaic Britain, or like the Arthurian wasteland, with an otherworldly dimension inhabited by the dead. A central motif of the Arthurian narratives was indeed the mysterious interdependence between a highly specific 'Waste Land' and Arthur's 'British' kingdom (of which Logres / England was often imaged as the inner realm); *Lear*'s oblique exploration of the ancient identity of England or Logres appears to define Cordelia's lost dowry in a similarly dichotomous fashion, as a 'centre/centaur' which, like Lear's grotesque imagery of his two horse/whores-daughters, perplexingly unites a primordial bestiality – or barbarism – with insight into the ultimate unity of all human experience.

Noting that the coins of the pro-Roman British king Cunobelinos or Cymbeline were engraved with the two-faced Roman god Janus (to whom James was himself compared), Camden had speculated that this was

> because even at that time Britaine began to cast off, and leave their barbarous rudenesse. For we read, how Ianus was the first, that changed barbarous maners into civill behaviour, and therefore was depainted with two fore-heads, to signifie, that he had of one shape made another.[44]

This comment attributes the civilizing of Britain to Roman influence; yet Camden's frequent juxtaposition of pejorative comments from diverse authors on the barbarism of the early Britons with more sympathetic accounts serves as a reminder that classical commentators were often as intrigued by, as they were critical of, the perceived alterity of the British race (together with their near-relatives the Gauls) – as is suggested by their frequent identification of Britain with the otherworld. Tacitus, for example, had observed that even when conquered, the Britons 'are restive under wrong, for their subjection does not involve slavery',[45] while Diodorus Siculus praised the Britons' simple habits and modest living, implying by his assertion that 'they preserve in their ways of living the ancient manner of life' that their lifestyle resembled that of man in the Golden Age. In the Janus-faced or fissured location of Lear's madness, where Poor Tom riddlingly elides the monstrous giants of ancient British legend with the chivalrous Child Rowland of medieval romance, the 'chaos' of British antiquity is configured in a similarly ambiguous fashion, as combining extremes of physical cruelty and suffering with exceptional opportunities for learning and revelation:

> Child Rowland to the dark tower came,
> His word was still 'Fie, foh and fum,
> I smell the blood of a British man'.
>
> (3.4.178–80)

Barely British: the uncased king

Even before Lear's tragic *anagnorisis* in the storm, his division of the kingdom has resulted in a dual loss of protection. In the first place, his 'riotous' train, which is seemingly associated with a former covering or concealment of his tail or seat (since it follows behind him), is reduced and finally abolished by Goneril and Regan. The Fool's riddles suggest that this was an inevitable consequence of Lear's humiliating 'breaching' of the kingdom, which has made its seat or centre vulnerable; by implication, 'when thou gav'st them the rod and putt'st down thine own breeches' the king revealed himself as a bare arse or ass who, like that beast of burden, was now destined to suffer or 'bear' (1.4.164–5). Simultaneously, the sisters also refuse Lear the physical shelter or protection formerly due to his crown – a 'case' or 'house' for his head:

Fool: Canst tell how an oyster makes his shell?
Lear: No.

159

Fool: Nor I neither, but I can tell why a snail has a house.
Lear: Why?
Fool: Why, to put's head in, not to give it away to his daughters and leave his horns without a case.

(1.5.25–30)

Fool: He that has a house to put's head in has a good headpiece.

(3.2.25–6)

In his loss of both train and housing we can discern suggestive allusions to the inherent duality of Lear's sovereignty, as both the royal 'superflux' or superfluity on which his power was based and the shell / shelter which protected and defined it. The Lear that remains shares in the disturbingly empty attributes of his rejected middle, for as the Fool puts it, he is now 'an O without a figure', 'a shelled peascod' or empty 'codpiece' (1.4.184–90) Yet only by losing the outward appearance of a king is Lear forced to re-examine that inner lacuna which the loss has exposed: the rejected seat or centre of his sovereignty which was Cordelia's jointure. In this strange imagery of shelling, there seem to be some highly covert jokes at James's expense: Randle Cotgrave notes in his *Dictionary of the French and English Tongues* that *escossé* is French for a shelled peascod, whose husk, hull or cod is *escosse* (a feminine noun), and in the next line lists its near-homonym, *Escossois*: a Scot; moreover, the emblematic badge of James's patron saint, Sant'iago or Saint James (and also the badge of the 'unhoused' medieval pilgrims who had travelled to his shrine in Spain) was a scallop or cockleshell. And just as James frequently abandoned his London palace or seat, his family and his ministers in his restless pursuit of the pleasures of hunting, so Lear is described by Goneril as having 'put himself from rest' as he is forced out into the storm.

Lear initially experiences the stormy night as 'tyrannous', troping the wildness of nature as the barbarous misuse of royal power by his two tyrannical daughters. But that there is a more profound significance to this 'foul weather' is suggested by the spectral appearance of Edgar as Poor Tom, of whom the Fool exclaims, 'here's a spirit'. The association of Edgar's disguise with the Bedlam beggars whose vagrancy was often attributed to the enclosure of the waste or common land has been much discussed.[46] Yet Poor Tom declares that he has travelled 'o'er bog and quagmire', and the region in which he appears is explicitly wasted or unbounded: 'for many miles about / There's scarce a bush' (2.2.491–2). The only trace of enclosure appears in Tom's several references to the hawthorn (from which enclosing hedges were usually composed) and

160

these stress that this boundary is not secure, but permeable to the elements: 'through the sharp hawthorn blows the cold wind' (3.4.45–6). While at one level Tom undoubtedly resembles both a Bedlam beggar and also a quasi-penitential figure, the historical setting of the play suggests that Edgar's disguise is additionally intended to evoke a still more archaic or 'barbarous' state of man, before the existence of private property, in which the bareness of ancient British life is combined with images of a British otherworld inhabited by spirits.

Thus several features of this disguise parallel descriptions of the archaic British past by ancient writers and antiquarians. Edgar declares, 'My face I'll grime with filth, / Blanket my loins, elf all my hair in knots / And with presented nakedness outface / The winds and persecutions of the sky' (2.2.180–3), and the Folio text stresses the flooded situation of his hovel: 'Fathom and half, fathom and half: Poor Tom!' (3.4.37–8). Diodorus Siculus had stressed the simplicity of the British way of life, describing the British tribes as 'autochthonous' or sprung from the earth; he also observed of their near-relatives the Gauls that 'the treatment of their hair [with caked mud] makes it so heavy and coarse that it differs in no respect from the mane of horses';[47] while Herodian, in his description of Britain, had claimed that:

> Most of Britain is marshland because it is flooded with continual ocean tides. The barbarians usually swim in these swamps or run along in them, submerged up to the waist. Of course they are practically naked and do not mind the mud because they are unfamiliar with clothing . . .[48]

It is interesting to note, also, in Poor Tom's 'knotted' hair, an association of the imagery of knots with a reversion to the state of nature by Gloucester's disinherited heir and the king's own godson, who on the death of Cordelia and Lear will implicitly divide the burden of sovereignty with Albany. Certainly Poor Tom plays a crucial part in the play's refiguration of the bond of sovereignty. Before his departure into the storm, in his final appeal to Goneril and Regan to let him keep at least part of his retinue, Lear has declared that 'Our basest beggars / Are in the poorest thing superfluous; / Allow not nature more than nature needs, / Man's life is cheap as beast's' (2.2.453–6). But in the storm, Lear not only loses his mind, as he runs 'unbonneted' or 'bareheaded', the example of Poor Tom also inspires him to 'tear' off his clothes – 'Off, off, you lendings: come, unbutton here' (3.4.106–7) – in a physical baring implied to be synonymous with a reversion to man's primal and childlike origins. At the same time, Lear's language gradually acquires the riddling quality of that used by the Fool and Poor Tom, whom he terms a 'Noble philosopher'. Thereby Lear performs a suggestive mimesis, not just of the 'windowed raggedness' of Poor Tom as 'unaccomodated man', but also of that combination of physical bareness with an obscure and riddling wisdom which classical commentators had attributed to the ancient Britons. Significantly, Cordelia has herself been figuratively bared at the very beginning of the play, 'dismantled' of 'many folds of favour' upon her disinheriting (1.1.218–19); this reinforces the implication that it is the play's imagery of the loosening of bonds which is the paradoxical key to the deeper meaning of sovereignty as Union.

In fact, Lear's 'unbuttoning' parallels the effect wrought upon Cordelia's lost jointure by the storm, for just as the common land was not defined by the bonds or boundaries of private property, and just as Camden had stressed the dependence of his Britannia(s) on water as well as land, so the lightening and flood-waters of the storm combines a further dissolution of territorial bonds or boundaries with a fertilizing effect. It is also notable that Camden sited his wheat-crowned Britannia very near to Gloucester, at the source of the river Thames or Isis; given the location of the storm in the vicinity of Gloucester's castle, we might associate this flooding not just with rain water, but also with the flooding of Britain's chief river, which passes through London and finally reaches the sea in Kent, just north of Dover. Certainly the plausible proximity of *Lear*'s composition to that of *Antony and Cleopatra* can provide an additional and very helpful context against which to read this aspect of its tragic (e)scatology, for when viewed in this way, the chaotic and flooded middle of the play seems closely associated with that imagery of 'Nilus' slime' which pervades the Egyptian world of *Antony and Cleopatra* – another mutable landscape which combines corruption with fecundity, allying 'dungy earth', 'slime and ooze', and 'vilest things' with the disturbing difference of a queen who resists assimilation by the history of imperialist conquest. F. T. Flahiff has suggested that the site of Lear's madness during the storm most closely resembles a bog, fen or quagmire;[49] this watery landscape certainly parallels the view of classical commentators, such as Herodian, that Britain (like Ireland) was an extremely marshy or boggy region, where the firm boundaries of land were unstable and constantly at risk.

The connection of this flooded landscape with Cordelia, as yet another weeping queen who nonetheless has the potential to reconcile, or joint, the divided body politic, is made clear in the Quarto text. Here, soon after the storm, her grief at her father's suffering is described in emblematic detail:

Kent: Did your letters pierce the queen to any demonstration of
             grief?
Gentleman: Ay, sir. She took them, read them in my presence,
             And now and then an ample tear trilled down
             Her delicate cheek. It seemed she was a queen
             Over her passion who, most rebel-like,
             Sought to be king o'er her.
Kent: O, then, it moved her?
Gentleman: Not to a rage; patience and sorrow strove
             Who should express her goodliest. You have seen
             Sunshine and rain at once, her smiles and tears
             Were like a better way. Those happy smilets
             That played on her ripe lip seemed not to know
             What guests were in her eyes, which parted thence
             As pearls from diamonds dropped. In brief,
             Sorrow would be a rarity most beloved
             If all could so become it.

                                                              (4.3.9–24)

In these 'ample' tears, we can perhaps decipher a watery refiguration
of the potency of that 'ample' territorial third which Cordelia has lost.
For a scene later, she compares her tears to the fertilising and revelatory
effect of watering the earth, praying that 'All blest secrets, / All you
unpublished virtues of the earth, / Spring with my tears' (4.4.15–17).
And certainly the storm-watered wasteland of the play's middle,
across which not only Lear, but also the blinded Gloucester led by
Edgar travel from Gloucester's castle to Dover, provides the uncanny
matrix, or breeding ground, in which elements that have been ejected
and refused both by the old and the new political order – Edgar and
Kent as well as Lear and Gloucester – can slowly reassemble before they
emerge from concealment, mysteriously acquiring new insights through
their exploration of this 'rank' geography.

Is this the promised end?[50]

Although it is described by Cordelia as a pitiful sight, the report
of Lear's fleeting appearance in the cornfield at Dover offers an apt
image of the curious intermingling of rankness, or waste, with fertility
and healing which has been wrought by the dissolving effects of the
storm. For Lear is now figured both in terms of water and natural
growth:

Alack, 'tis he. Why, he was met even now,
As mad as the vexed sea, singing aloud,
Crowned with rank fumiter and furrow weeds,
With hardocks, hemlock, nettles, cuckoo-flowers,
Darnel, and all the idle weeds that grow
In our sustaining corn.

(4.4.1–6)

After the storm, in fact, the play is quite thickly strewn with references
to herbs, whose diverse utility, recognised by the 'barbarous' Britains as
well as other ancient peoples, were listed in herbals of the time. These
modest emblems of the healing fruitfulness of what appears at first sight
to be nature's waste include the flax used to treat Gloucester's eyes;
the 'weeds' in Lear's garland; the samphire which Edgar describes to
Gloucester as being gathered on the Dover cliff; and Lear's 'password',
sweet marjoram. Thus Henry Lyte noted that samphire could 'open the
stoppings of the stomach', and that flax seed 'appeaseth all paine' and
can quicken and cleare the sight', while Pliny's *Natural History* claimed
that sweet marjoram 'counteracts the stings of scorpions'.[51] Similarly,
although the 'rank' smell of some of the 'weeds' in Lear's garland –
notably fumitory as well as hemlock – and the painful or poisonous
effects of nettle and hemlock, together with the apparent uselessness of
'idle' darnel, seem to confirm a negative view of 'waste', all these plants
could also be read as signs of fruitfulness, since they typically grew in
moist and fertile ground; moreover, all were held to have some benefical
effects. Thus fumitory assists weeping, eases syphilis, and 'drives forth all
hurfull humours', especially rage; docks soften, ease or purge the belly,
and were used to treat gonorrhea, as well as nettle stings; furrow grass
healed wounds; both nettle and cuckoo flowers 'provoketh urine', while
nettle was cited by some authorities as an antidote to hemlock; darnel
could draw forth thorns and ease a headache; and even hemlock itself
was held to be a reasonable pain killer if applied as a 'plaister'.[52] As a
complex emblem of the ambivalence of seeming waste, therefore, Lear's
garland appears to signal a turning point in his suffering. When Pliny
described the ancient practice of making such garlands, he noted that:

> No crown indeed has been a higher honour than the crown of
> grass . . . This crown used to be made from green grass pulled
> up from the site where the besieged men had been relieved
> by someone . . . whatever plants had been found on the site,
> however lowly and mean, these gave the honour its nobility.[53]

Although Lear's madness has yet to be cured, his garland of weeds hints at the way in which seemingly insignificant details are gradually woven or knotted together by Shakespeare's text into a subtle pattern of meaning. But what appears to be his rebirth after the long passage through the otherwordly location of Cordelia's jointure does not occur until Lear is briefly reunited with his third daughter, when he explicitly compares his state to the sufferings of the soul after death:

> You do me wrong to take me out o'the grave.
> Thou art a soul in bliss, but I am bound
> Upon a wheel of fire that mine own tears
> Do scald like molten lead . . .
> You are a spirit, I know; where did you die?
> (4.7.45–9)

The imagery which Lear uses to describe his suffering is drawn from classical and Christian ideas of hell or the underworld; but the troping of his sufferings in this territorial middle as a death and rebirth may also be indebted to the main doctrine attributed to the ancient Britons and Gauls, which was much commented on by the ancients as well as by Tudor and Stuart antiquarians. This was the belief disseminated by their Druidic priests in the immortality of the soul, compared by some ancient authors to the Pythagorean doctrine of metempsychosis, whereby 'death is no more, / Than *middle point* twixt future life and that which went before' [my emphasis].[54] Combined with Lear's imagery of unbuttoning (which is significantly repeated at his real death), the imagery of his re*union* with Cordelia consequently hints at the positive associations of the untieing or unjointing associated with the middle – as a form of release resembling the unjointing or (k)notting of death, but one which may also be a prelude to a form of rebirth, as a revelation or reuniting. Yet if this is so, then what are the implications for the disturbing end of the play of this highly individual figuration of death as an *interitus* or middle?

Only when he comes onstage for the last time, with Cordelia's dead body in his arms, does Lear finally literalize his tragic affinity with the ass as a beast of burden, or one that 'bears' as well as 'bares': as the last lines of the play observe, 'the oldest hath borne most'. When they are taken to prison after the defeat of Cordelia's troops, Lear tells Cordelia that they will 'take upon's the mystery of things' (5.3.16); the diverse symbolism of the ass/arse in this epoch includes that of the *asinus portans mysteria*: an unsettling elision of Christian with pagan imagery, whereby the ass bears a mystery that is not only foolish or obscene, but also holy.[55] Lear's subsequent entry with her hanged body therefore reminds us that Cordelia herself is the play's central riddle. Indeed, the uncertainty surrounding her dead body, suggestively doubled by the looking glass which Lear has demanded, ensures that, like so many of Shakespeare's female corpses, Cordelia remains a mystery even in her death. We are consequently left to wonder if this is in fact 'the promised end', or instead, a *disfigured* 'image of that horror': an image in which the apparent finality of tragic endings is – once again – subtly differed.

NOTES

1 Disfigured endings

1 Jacques Derrida, *Margins of Philosophy*, trans. Alan Bass (Brighton: Harvester Press, 1986), p. xxviii.
2 English Renaissance writers frequently pun interlingually on 'grief' and *grevé / crevé*. See Frankie Rubinstein, *A Dictionary of Shakespeare's Sexual Puns and their Significance*, 2nd edn (London: Macmillan, 1989), p. 117. I am indebted to Ann Lecercle for first drawing my attention to this pun.
3 Ann and John O. Thompson, *Shakespeare, Meaning and Metaphor* (Brighton: Harvester 1987), p. 43.
4 The critical 'digestion' of the implications for English Renaissance studies of Mikhail Bakhtin's discussion of carnival and the grotesque body in *Rabelais and his World*, trans. Hélène Iswolsky (Bloomington: Indiana University Press, 1984), has now spanned some fifteen years, with notable studies by critics such as Peter Stallybrass and Allon White, Leah Marcus and Neil Rhodes. Interestingly, the most influential responses to Bakhtin have focused on the work of Ben Jonson. For a recent discussion of this ongoing reassessment of Bakhtin's thought by Renaissance critics, see Bruce Boehrer, *The Fury of Men's Gullets: Ben Jonson and the digestive canal* (Philadelphia: University of Pennsylvania Press, 1997), pp. 14–19.
5 Michael Neill, *Issues of Death: mortality and identity in English Renaissance tragedy* (Oxford: Oxford University Press, 1997), p. 45.
6 Patricia Parker, *Shakespeare from the Margins: language, culture, context* (Chicago: University of Chicago Press, 1996), *passim*.
7 George T. Wright, *Shakespeare's Metrical Art* (Berkeley: University of California Press, 1988), p. 164. Wright further notes that there are four related style changes in Shakespeare's later plays: feminine endings appear more frequently; the verse in which they appear is usually blank; the verse phrasing breaks more often after the sixth syllable (or later), rather than after the fourth or fifth; and most of the lines are enjambed. 'These four developments make the line-ending seem less of a boundary than it is in earlier sixteenth-century verse' (p. 163).
8 Julia Kristeva, *Black Sun: depression and melancholia*, trans. Leon S. Roudiez (New York: Columbia University Press, 1989), p. 27.
9 Julia Kristeva, *Powers of Horror: an essay on abjection*, trans. Leon S. Roudiez (New York: Columbia University Press, 1982).

10 Elizabeth Bronfen, *Over Her Dead Body: death, femininity and the aesthetic* (Manchester: Manchester University Press, 1992), p. 181.

11 Philippe Ariès, *The Hour of Our Death*, trans. Helen Weaver (London: Allen Lane, 1981), p. 23. In this monumental study of changing attitudes to death in Western culture from the middle ages, Ariès notes that, by the end of the sixteenth century, not only were actual customs and ideas about death undergoing profound and far-reaching changes, 'a vast transformation of sensibility' was also in progress: 'where Death had once been immediate, familiar, and tame, it gradually began to be surreptitious, violent and savage'.

12 Gisèle Mathieu-Castellani, *Emblèmes de la mort: la dialogue de l'image et du texte* (Paris: Nizet, 1988), p. 165.

13 Bronfen, *Over her Dead Body*, p. 113.

14 As Lynda Nead points out in *The Female Nude: art, obscenity and sexuality* (London: Routledge, 1992), ch. 1, the precise etymology of the Latin word *obscenus* is doubtful. But since its explicit meanings of indecency, lewdness, and filth were closely associated with the 'private' parts – the genitals and anus – she suggests that the word may also imply a meaning of *ob-scenum*, or what lies outside of the formal sphere of aesthetic representation.

15 Ibid., p. 7.

16 Ann Thompson comments wryly that 'one does not know whether to laugh or cry when one comes to examine the traditional editorial procedures for dealing with obscenity in Shakespearean texts'. 'Feminist Theory and the Editing of Shakespeare: *The Taming of the Shrew*', in *The Margins of the Text* (ed.) D. C. Greetham (Ann Arbor: University of Michigan Press, 1997), pp. 83–103 (p. 95).

17 Concern with a similar question is implicit in the detailed analysis by Ann and John O. Thompson of Shakespeare's diverse bodily metaphors in *Shakespeare, Meaning and Metaphor*, op. cit.

18 For the importance of the metaphor of 'trash' in Shakespeare's last play, which she shows to be figuratively interwoven with 'lime' and 'slime', see Ann Lecercle, ' "Trash" dans *La Tempête*', in *Shakespeare: La Tempête: études critiques* (ed.) Claude Peltrault (Besançon: Presses Universitaires de Franche-Comté, 1994), pp. 169–84.

19 See for example Jacques Derrida, *Margins of Philosophy*, op. cit., where he defines the task of deconstruction as a stretching obliquely (*lôxos*) of the word or *logos* (p. xv); Jean-François Lyotard, *Discours, Figur* (Paris: Editions Klincksieck, 1978), especially cover and p. 180; and Luce Irigaray, *Speculum of the Other Woman*, trans. Gillian C. Gill (Ithaca: Columbia University Press, 1985), a text whose anamorphic or angled perspective I have explored in 'The Burning Glass: paradoxes of feminist revelation in *Speculum*', *Engaging with Irigaray* (eds) Margaret Whitford, Naomi Schor and Carolyn Burke (New York: Columbia University Press, 1994), pp. 229–46.

20 For a discussion of this problem, see Philippa Berry, 'Rebirthing the Concept of Renaissance: the cultural impact of paganism in the English Renaissance', in *The Texture of Renaissance Knowledge* (eds) Margaret Tudeau-Clayton and Philippa Berry, forthcoming.

21 Parker, *Shakespeare from the Margins*, especially pp. 185–211.

22 On these largely neglected yet very important aspects of Renaissance punning, see Gilian West, 'The Second-meaning Pun in Shakespeare's

Emotional Verse', *Studies in Philology*, xc, 3 (Summer 1993), pp. 247–76, and Mathias Bauer, '*Paronomasia celata* in Donne's "A Valediction: forbidden mourning"', in *English Literary Renaissance*, 25, i (Winter 1995), pp. 97–111.

23 Marie-Dominique Garnier, ' "A Tongue with a Tang" (I ii 46): différence et répétition dans *La Tempête*', in *Q/U/E/R/T/Y: Arts, Littératures et Civilisations du Monde Anglophone*, 3 (October 1993), pp. 13–18.

24 Gordon Williams, *A Dictionary of Sexual Language and Imagery in Shakespearean and Stuart Literature*, 3 vols (London: Athlone, 1994), I, p. 42. In *Sodometries: Renaissance texts, modern sexualities* (Stanford: Stanford University Press, 1992), Jonathan Goldberg has illuminated the unexpected 'sodometries' of this period, in the form of 'relational structures precariously available to prevailing discourses'. Yet the definition of sodomy as an act not only meriting capital punishment, but also imaginatively allied with treason, heresy and other forms of subversion has required recent queer theory of the Renaissance to differentiate between 'homoerotics' and 'sodomy' in ways which remain somewhat confusing, and which also fail to clarify the relevance of this recurring imagery of anal intercourse to both sexes; as Bruce R. Smith notes in *Homosexual Desire in Shakespeare's England* (Chicago: University of Chicago Press, 1994): ' "sodomy" could cover a variety of heterosexual acts' (p. 11). In 'Is the Fundament a Grave?', however, Jeffrey Masten suggests how we might usefully explore the rhetorical connection of death with the anus, in a re-examination of the multiple forms of knowledge which the Renaissance configures in relation to anality (*The Body in Parts: fantasies of corporeality in early modern Europe* (eds) David Hillman and Carla Mazzio (London: Routledge, 1998), pp. 129–46). It is hoped that the present study can make a further contribution to this work of cultural and sexual redefinition.

25 On the connection of Othello with the carnival beast of the ass or donkey, see François Laroque, *Shakespeare's Festive World*, trans. Janet Lloyd (Cambridge: Cambridge University Press, 1991), p. 296.

26 Karen Silvia de Leon-Jones, *Giordano Bruno and the Kabbalah: prophets, magicians and rabbis* (New Haven: Yale University Press, 1997), p. 113. See also Nuccio Ordine, *Giordano Bruno and the Philosophy of the Ass*, trans. Henryk Baranski (New Haven: Yale University Press, 1997).

27 François Rabelais, 'Le Quart Livre' in *Les Cinq Livres* (eds) Jean Céard, Gérard Defaux et Michel Simonin (Paris: Librairie Genérale Française, 1994), xliii, ll. 39–40: 'Et meurent les hommes en pedent, les femmes en vesnent. Ainsi leur sort l'âme par le cul' (p. 1099).

28 The dissemination in the late sixteenth century of new philosophies of nature which challenged Aristotelian physics is described in Brian P. Copenhaver and Charles B. Schmitt, *Renaissance Philosophy* (Oxford: Oxford University Press, 1992), ch. 5, 'Nature against Authority: breaking away from the classics'.

29 Michel Jeanneret, *Perpetuum mobile: métamorphoses des corps et des œuvres de Vinci à Montaigne* (Paris: Editions Macula, 1997), *passim*.

30 Parker, *Shakespeare from the Margins*, especially ch. 3.

31 *Batman upon Bartholome his Booke* (London: 1582), XI, v, p. 166.

32 Thomas McAlindon, *Shakespeare's Tragic Cosmos* (Cambridge: Cambridge University Press, 1991).

33 For an account of classical 'pneumatism' see Gérard Verbeke, *L'Evolution de la doctrine du pneuma du Stoicism à St. Augustin* (Louvain: Institut superieur de

philosophie, 1945). The Stoics regarded *pneuma* as the original matter or substance from which all individual things have emanated in purposeful design.

34 Cicero, *The Nature of the Gods* (De natura deorum), trans. Horace C. P. McGregor (Harmondsworth: Penguin, 1972), II, 29–30, pp. 134–5.

35 Lucretius, *De rerum natura*, trans. W. H. D. Rouse, revised Martin Ferguson (London: Heinemann, 1975), I, ll. 1–23.

36 Charles Dempsey, *The Portrayal of Love: Botticelli's Primavera and humanist culture at the time of Lorenzo the Magnificent* (Princeton: Princeton University Press, 1992), p. 51.

37 This is the view of Howard Jones in *The Epicurean Tradition* (London: Routledge, 1989). Yet Jones, a philosopher, does not scrutinize in detail the sixteenth-century literary texts that he asserts borrowed elements of style rather than intellectual content from Lucretius.

38 Copenhaver and Schmitt, *Renaissance Philosophy*, pp. 288–9.

39 Giordano Bruno, 'De l'infinito universo et mondi', in *Dialoghi italiani* (ed.) G. Aquilecchia, 2 vols (Florence: Sansoni, 1983) I, p. 360. Cited and trans. in Hilary Gatti, *The Renaissance Drama of Knowledge: Giordano Bruno in England* (London: Routledge, 1989), p. 106.

40 Jeanneret, *Perpetuum mobile*, p. 39.

41 Arthur Golding, *Ovid's Metamorphoses Englyshed* (London: 1567), ll. 5–18.

42 Cicero, *The Nature of the Gods*, II, 58, p. 146

43 Until Harvey's 1628 discovery of the circulation of the blood, it was generally assumed that only the veins carried the blood proper, and that the arteries of the body transported and distributed what was regarded as 'spiritous blood', that is, blood informed by *pneuma*; indeed, the Greek word for artery means 'carrier of air'. Even Galen, although he rejected the Stoic notion of *pneuma* as innate in the living body, believed that the blood was transformed into vital *pneuma* in the left ventricle of the heart. See F. David Hoeniger, *Medicine and Shakespeare in the English Renaissance*, (London: Associated University Presses, 1992), pp. 91–4. I am indebted to Jayne Archer for researching this information.

44 Laroque, *Shakespeare's Festive World*, op. cit.

45 In *Ancient Philosophy, Mystery and Magic: Empedocles and Pythagorean tradition* (Oxford: Clarendon Press, 1995), Peter Kingsley notes that Graeco-Egyptian alchemists had access to pre-Socratic ideas by various routes and channels, and points out that there was a distinctive blending of Empedoclean, Pythagorean, and alchemical traditions in some parts of the late classical world (pp. 55–68).

46 Michael Sendivogus, *Novum lumen chemicum* (Prague: 1604), trans. by John French as *A New Light of Alchemy* (London: 1650), p. 58.

2 Double dying and other tragic inversions

1 Elizabeth Bronfen, *Over Her Dead Body: death, femininity and the aesthetic* (Manchester: Manchester University Press, 1992), p. 295.

2 Fredrick Ahl, *Metaformations: soundplay and wordplay in Ovid and other classical poets* (Ithaca: Cornell University Press, 1985), p. 17.

3 Porphyry, *The Cave of the Nymphs in 'The Odyssey'* (New York: SUNY Press, 1969), p. 30.

4 See in particular Mario Digangi, 'Asses and Wits: the homoerotics of mastery in satiric comedy,' *English Literary Renaissance*, 25, ii (Spring 1995), pp. 179–208 (especially pp. 198–9).
5 Jonathan Goldberg, '*Romeo and Juliet*'s Open Rs', in *Queering the Renaissance* (ed.) Jonathan Goldberg (Durham, N.C.: Duke University Press, 1994), pp. 218–35 (p. 228).
6 ibid., p. 227.
7 See Jeffrey Masten, 'Is the Fundament a Grave?', *The Body in Parts: fantasies of corporeality in early modern Europe* (eds) David Hillman and Carla Mazzio (London: Routledge, 1997), pp. 129–46.
8 For diverse accounts of double dying and the second death (called by the Greeks *deuteros thanatos*), see Plutarch's 'Of the Face appearing within the Roundle of the Moon', where he identifies the goddesses Ceres and Proserpina with the two stages of death (*The Philosophie Commonly called the Morals*, trans. Philemon Holland (London: 1603), p. 1182); Pico della Mirandola, *Commentary on a Canzone of Benivieni*, trans. Sears Jayne (New York: Peter Lang, 1984), who associates the second death with the lover's full mystical union with his 'celestial' beloved (see note 54 on pp. 174–5); and Macrobius, who in his *Commentary on the Death of Scipio*, trans. William Harris Stahl (New York: Columbia University Press, 1952), affirms that:

> There are two deaths of the creature, that is, of man, one afforded by nature and the other by the virtues. The man dies when the soul leaves the body in accordance with the laws of nature; he is also said to die when the soul, still residing in his body, spurns all bodily allurements under the guidance of philosophy, and frees itself from the tempting devices of the lusts and all the other passions.
>
> (pp. 138–9)

9 David Armitage, 'The Dismemberment of Orpheus: mythic elements in Shakespearean romance', *Shakespeare Survey*, 39 (1986), pp. 123–33.
10 The probable recusancy of Shakespeare's father, John Shakespeare, has now been widely discussed. For a recent elaboration of this argument, see Richard Wilson, 'Shakespeare and the Jesuits', *Times Literary Supplement*, 19 December 1997, pp. 11–13. The association of Shakespeare's mother's family, the Ardens, with a network of noble families tainted by recusancy – the Throckmortons, the Catesbys, the Brownes and the Montagues – is noted by H. S. Bowden, *The Religion of Shakespeare* (London: Burns and Oates, 1899).
11 I discuss the mediating properties of soul/the world soul according to Platonic and Neoplatonic thought in *Of Chastity and Power: Elizabethan literature and the unmarried queen* (London: Routledge, 1989), ch. 1.
12 For the interest of a majority of late sixteenth-century natural philosophers in a concept analogous to or identical with the worldsoul, see Brian P. Copenhaver and Charles B. Schmitt, *Renaissance Philosophy* (Oxford: Oxford University Press, 1992), ch. 5. The idea of an enlivening worldsap is discussed in Charles Nicholl, *The Chemicall Theatre* (London: Routledge & Kegan Paul, 1980), pp. 124–5. In *The Anatomy of the World* (1611), Donne compares Elizabeth Drury to this balm or 'balsamum', declaring that, with her death, the world is dead, because 'shee / Thy intrinsique balme, and thy preservative, / Can never be renew'd'.

13 William Gilbert, *De magnete* (London: 1600), Book 5, ch. 12.

14 Michel de Montaigne, 'An Apologie of Raymond Sebond', in *Essayes*, trans. John Florio (London: 1603), II, xii, p. 317.

15 Giordano Bruno, *De la causa, principio e uno*, cited and trans. in John Charles Nelson, *Renaissance Theory of Love: the context of Giordano Bruno's 'Eroici Furori'* (New York: Columbia University Press, 1958), p. 264.

16 Giordano Bruno, *The Expulsion of the Triumphant Beast*, trans. Arthur D. Imerti (New Brunswick, N.J.: Rutgers University Press, 1964), p. 53.

17 Sir Philip Sidney, *The Countess of Pembrokes Arcadia* (ed.) Maurice Evans (Harmondsworth: Penguin Books Ltd, 1977), III, p. 490.

18 On the association of May Day with the making of floral garlands by young women, see Ronald Hutton, *The Stations of the Sun: a history of the ritual year in Britain* (Oxford: Oxford University Press, 1996), p. 237.

19 See 'The Sound of *O* in *Othello*: the real of the tragedy of desire', in Joel Fineman, *The Subjectivity Effect in Western Literary Tradition: essays towards the release of Shakespeare's Will* (Cambridge, Mass.: MIT Press, 1991), pp. 143–64.

20 Porphyry, *The Cave of the Nymphs*, p.13. The association, he claims, gave rise to the ancient custom of calling brides 'nymphs', 'because they are wed for genesis', and the related custom 'of pouring on them bath water taken from springs or streams or fountains which are always running' (p. 15).

21 François Laroque, *Shakespeare's Festive World*, trans. Janet Lloyd (Cambridge: Cambridge University Press, 1991), p. 47. For detailed accounts of this carnivalesque connection between the soul and flatulence, see Claude Gaignebet, *Le Carnaval* (Paris: Payot, 1974), ch. 7. Gaignebet elucidates the association of Carnival with 'le surgissement des esprits, venus de l'au-dela, qu'il faudra renvoyer dans leur demeure' which he traces back to Ovid's *Fasti*, (p. 21). The at least partial survival of this tradition in post-Reformation England is evident from Ben Jonson's masque for Twelfth Night 1618, *Pleasure Reconcil'd to Virtue*, where the Bowle-bearer declares:

> Beware of dealing with ye belly, the belly will not be talked to, especially when he is full: there is no venturing upon *Venter*, then; he will blow you all up: he will thunder indeed la: Some in derision call him the father of farts: But I say, he was ye first father of great ordynance, and taught us to discharge 'em on feastivall daies ...
> (*Works of Ben Jonson* (eds) C. H. Herford and P. and E. Simpson, 11 vols (Oxford: Clarendon Press, 1925–52), VII, ll. 57–63).

22 For an account of this bizarre carnival practice, see Gaignebet, ibid., on 'le soufflet'.

23 Cicero, *De natura deorum*, II, ix, 23–32; Ficino, 'In Plotinum', in *Opera omnia* (rpt. Turin: 1959), II, 2, p. 1746, cited and trans. in James Nohrnberg, *The Analogy of 'The Faerie Queene'* (Princeton: Princeton University Press, 1976), p. 553. See also Virgil, *Aeneid* VI, 730–1.

24 Michael J. B. Allen comments on the impact of this Platonic concept on medieval theology in 'Marsilio Ficino's Interpretation of Plato's *Timaeus* and its myth of the Demiurge', *Supplementum Festivum: studies in honour of Paul Oskar Kristeller* (New York: SUNY Press, 1987), pp. 399–419. He notes that: 'Accommodating such a universal soul-being into the conceptual system of Christianity was no easy matter. Some accepted it at face value and tried to adjust their metaphysical schemes accordingly; others identified it with the

concept of Nature; others went so far as to see it as an adumbration of the Holy Ghost' (p. 415).

25 Arthur Golding, *Ovid's Metamorphoses Englyshed* (London: 1567), sig. D iii v. In Ovid, *Metamorphoses*, 2 vols, trans. Frank Justus Miller (London: Heinemann, 1916), the passage is rendered as follows:

> And as curved ships, without their proper ballast, roll in the waves, and, unstable because too light, are borne out of their course, so the chariot, without its accustomed burden, gives leaps into the air, is tossed aloft and is like a riderless car

(II, 161–6).

26 Hesiod, 'Works and Days', in *The Homeric Hymns and Homerica*, trans. Hugh G. Evelyn White (London: Heinemann, 1967), ll. 50–2, 565–70. In Plato's *Phaedo* (69C), the giant fennel stalk, or *narthex*, is also described as an attribute of Dionysus; this ritual object was apparently given to initiates into his mysteries.

27 Jonathan Bate, *Shakespeare and Ovid* (Oxford: Clarendon Press, 1993), p. 178.

28 In 'Queen Mab and the Mobled Queen, Madness and the Method', to be published in *The Texture of Renaissance Knowledge* (eds) Philippa Berry and Margaret Tudeau-Clayton (forthcoming), Marie-Dominique Garnier shows how Mab is a suggestively amplified representation of the 'space of the figural' itself; this 'mobled fairy', whom Garnier compares most suggestively to *Hamlet*'s 'mobled queen', does not only personify the lateral 'paronomastic drift' of signifiers within the Shakespearean text, as they collide like the Lucretian atoms; she also reveals how, far from being the site of a lack or fall in meaning, 'Shakespeare's "nothing" sits in an entire crowd of overlapping signifiers'.

29 For a rather different account of the carnivalesque elements in the play, see Ronald Knowles, 'Carnival and Death in *Romeo and Juliet*: a Bakhtinian reading', *Shakespeare Survey*, 49 (1996), pp. 69–85.

30 Lammas opposed Candlemas in the Celtic calendrical system of cross-quarters, and the day after Candlemas, 3 February, was the earliest day possible for Shrovetide. See Laroque, *Shakespeare's Festive World*, p. 48.

31 David Wiles, *Shakespeare's Almanac: 'A Midsummer Night's Dream', marriage and the Elizabethan calendar* (Cambridge: D. S. Brewer: 1993), p. xvi.

32 Eamon Duffy, *The Stripping of the Altars: traditional religion in England 1400–1580* (New Haven: Yale University Press, 1992), p. 47.

33 Ibid., p. 48.

34 Ibid., p. 394. For a detailed account of the uneven process of image elimination in Devon and Cornwall, see Robert Whiting, *The Blind Devotion of the People: popular religion and the English Reformation* (Cambridge: Cambridge University Press, 1989), pp. 48–82.

35 W. R. Trimble, *The Catholic Laity in Elizabethan England, 1558–1603* (Cambridge, Mass.: Harvard University Press, 1964), p. 150. Trimble notes that a strong Catholicism survived in parts of Warwickshire as late as the 1590s (p. 31).

36 David Cressy, *Bonfires and Bells: national memory and the Protestant calendar in Elizabethan and Stuart England* (London: Weidenfeld and Nicholson: 1989).

37 Peter Milward, *Shakespeare's Religious Background* (Bloomington: Indiana University Press, 1973), p. 21. For Shakespeare's plausible links, as a young

man, with the Catholic aristocracy of Lancashire, see Ernst Honigmann, *Shakespeare: the 'lost years'* (Manchester: Manchester University Press, 1985), and Richard Wilson, 'Shakespeare and the Jesuits'.

38 Wilson, ibid., p. 13.

39 *The Second Tome of Homelyes* (London: 1563), 2, 'Agaynste parell of Idolatry and superfluous decking of churches', sigs. Dd4 ff.

40 In his *Prognostication Nouvelle* of 1544, François Rabelais refers to 'les jours caniculaires' as falling between 10 July and 20 August, but in *An Almanack and Prognostication for the Year 1598* (London: 1597) Thomas Buckminster marks the dog days as beginning on 19 July.

41 Claude Gaignebet, *A Plus Hault Sens: l'érotisme spirituel et charnel de Rabelais*, 2 vols (Paris: Maisoneuve et Larose, 1986), I, pp. 237–317. I am grateful to François Laroque for directing me to this encyclopedic work.

42 Aratus, *Phaenomena*, trans. G. R. Mair (London: Heinemann, 1969), 326–36.

43 Manilius, *Astronomica*, trans. G. P. Gould (London: Heinemann, 1977), V, 206–14.

44 Aratus, *Phaenomena*, op. cit.

45 Manilius, *Astronomica*, I, 396–411.

46 Marcel Detienne, *The Gardens of Adonis: spices in Greek mythology*, trans. Janet Lloyd (New Jersey: Humanities Press, 1977), pp. 120–2.

47 Hesiod, 'Works and Days', ll. 586–88, in *The Homeric Hymns and Homerica* (see note 26); in his *Natural History*, Pliny claims that Sirius causes rabies (I, ii, 107).

48 Bernard Capp, *English Almanacs 1500–1800: astrology and the popular press* (Ithaca: Cornell University Press, 1979), pp. 64–5, 120. I am grateful to Jayne Archer for researching this reference.

49 For Shakespeare's very material interest in Time as the ultimate consumer (*tempus edax*), as explored in the many metaphors of cooking and food that appear in another drama of tragic desire, *Troilus and Cressida*, see Ann and John O. Thompson, *Shakespeare, Meaning and Metaphor* (Brighton: Harvester, 1987), pp. 25–8.

50 St Jerome thought that the name Samson was etymologically derived from *shemesh*, the Hebrew word for sun. See Gaignebet, *A Plus Hault Sens*, I, pp. 343–6.

51 François Laroque notes that there is a possible (second meaning) Latin pun in this exchange, on head/*caput*, 'that refers us directly to the name Capulet, so that the word "maidenhead" could already be an indirect allusion to the play's heroine – Juliet Capulet' ('Tradition and Subversion in *Romeo and Juliet*', *Shakespeare's 'Romeo and Juliet': texts, contexts and interpretations* (ed.) Jay L. Halio (Newark: University of Delaware Press, 1995), pp. 18–36).

52 In *A Dictionarie of the French and English Tongues* (London, 1611), Randle Cotgrave comments that *gueule* is 'the mouth, also (and most properly) the throat, gullet, pipe, or passage, whereby meat is sent from the mouth downe to the stomacke; also the stomacke itselfe; or the mouth, or orifice thereof'.

53 *The Hieroglyphics of Horapollo*, trans. George Boas (Princeton: Princeton University Press, 1993), I, 6–7.

54 Pico della Mirandola, *Commentary on a Canzone of Benivieni*, p. 151. Pico proceeds to describe how:

... *binsica*, that is, death from kissing [the *mors osculi*], occurs when the soul, in an intellectual rapture, unites so completely with incorporeal things that it rises above the body and leaves it altogether.... It is this kind of kissing which our divine Solomon desires when he exclaims in his Song of Solomon, "Kiss me with the kisses of thy mouth"

(pp. 150–1).

Another biblical source for this imagery may be *Isaiah* 6, 7, where the prophet relates a dream in which a seraphim brings him a live coal from the heavenly altar: 'And he laid *it* upon my mouth, and said, Lo, this hath touched thy lips; and thine iniquity is taken away, and thy sin purged'. In his late Renaissance appropriation of the *mors osculi* trope, Giordano Bruno accords it a more material significance than it had formerly enjoyed, associating it with a closeness to an immanent, rather than a transcendent God: the hidden creative principle within nature.

3 Echoic language and tragic identity

1 Alice A. Jardine, *Gynesis: configurations of woman and modernity* (Ithaca: Cornell University Press, 1985), p. 59.

2 Jacques Derrida, *Margins of Philosophy*, trans. Alan Bass (Brighton: Harvester Press, 1986), pp. xxviii–xxix.

3 Maurice Blanchot, *L'Espace littéraire* (Paris: Gallimard, 1955), pp. 162–4. This passage is translated and eloquently commented upon by David Farrell Krell in *Lunar Voices: of tragedy, poetry, fiction and thought* (Chicago: University of Chicago Press, 1895), pp. 136–8.

4 For a discussion of Kristeva's concept of *chora*, see Philippa Berry, 'Woman and Space according to Kristeva and Irigaray', in *Shadow of Spirit: postmodernism and religion* (eds) Philippa Berry and Andrew Wernick (London: Routledge, 1992), pp. 250–64.

5 Plato, *Timaeus*, 51A.

6 See Julia Kristeva, 'Jackson Pollock's Milky Way, 1912–1956', in *Journal of Philosophy and the Visual Arts*, I, 1989, pp. 34–9. (In fact, there is no obvious etymological link between *chorus* and *chora*.)

7 Julia Kristeva, *La Révolution du langage poétique* (Paris: Editions du Seuil, 1974), pp. 27–6. Author's translation.

8 For an excellent discussion of the importance of Echo in English Renaissance literature, see Joseph Loewenstein, *Responsive Readings: versions of Echo in pastoral, epic, and the Jonsonian masque* (New Haven: Yale University Press, 1984).

9 Longus, *Daphnis and Chloe*, trans. George Thornley (1657), with introduction by G. Saintsbury (London: Richard Lesley & Co. Ltd, 1947), p. 130.

10 In Ben Jonson's *Masque of Beautie*, the song of Echo represents 'the world's *soule*, true harmony' (*Works of Ben Jonson* (eds) C. H. Herford and P. and E. Simpson, 11 vols (Oxford: Clarendon Press, 1925–52), VII, l. 374).

11 Jonathan Goldberg, *Voice Terminal Echo: postmodernism and English Renaissance texts* (New York: Methuen, 1986), p. 162, n. 41.

12 Abraham Fraunce, *The Third Part of the Countesse of Pembrokes Yvychurche: Entituled, Amintas Dale* (London: 1592), sig. 15r.

13 Jonathan Bate, *Shakespeare and Ovid* (Oxford: Clarendon Press, 1993), pp. 150–1.

14 Joel Fineman, 'Fratricide and cuckoldry: Shakespeare's doubles', in *Representing Shakespeare* (eds) Murry Schwartz and Coppelia Kahn (Baltimore and London: Johns Hopkins University Press, 1980), p. 106.

15 Francesco Piccolomini, 'De virtute heroica', *Universa philosophia de moribus* (Venice: 1594), VI.

16 Jonathan Goldberg, 'Shakespearean inscriptions and the voicing of power', in *Shakespeare and the Question of Theory* (eds) Patricia Parker and Geoffrey Hartman (New York: Methuen, 1985), pp. 116–37 (p. 130).

17 Brian P. Copenhaver and Charles B. Schmitt, *Renaissance Philosophy* (Oxford: Oxford University Press, 1992), pp. 170–1.

18 *La Theologie naturelle de Raymond Sebond*, trans. Michel de Montaigne (1581; Paris: 1611), dedication (to Montaigne's father), sig. aii v; Ben Jonson, *Timber: or Discoveries*, in *Works*, VIII, 330–2, p. 573.

19 Patricia Parker, *Literary Fat Ladies* (London: Methuen, 1987), *passim*.

20 See in particular David Wilbern, 'Shakespeare's Nothing', in *Representing Shakespeare* (eds) Murray Schwartz and Coppelia Kahn.

21 Maurice Charney, *Hamlet's Fictions* (London: Routledge, 1988), p. 9.

22 In *Roman Shakespeare: warriors, wounds and women* (London: Routledge, 1997), Coppelia Kahn explains how the play opposes the maternal womb to that of the daughter:

> To sum up the relationship [in *Titus*] between chaste daughter and whorish mother implied by the burgeoning metaphoricity of the pit: the virginal daughter's fertility is cut off at a womb-like place that associates rape and murder with the maternal. The father's treasure [the daughter] is stolen and destroyed by the mother.
>
> (p. 54)

Kahn's argument is compelling in its elucidation of the subtle structural patterning of the plot; however, both her choice of Bassianus and her saucy address to Tamora associates Lavinia with a quality of sexual knowingness that may compromise her perceived identity as dutiful daughter.

23 See Rebecca W. Bushnell, *Tragedies of Tyrants: political thought and theater in the English Renaissance* (Ithaca: Cornell University Press, 1990), *passim*.

24 There are several examples of this pun in the *Sonnets*, including 58, l.3; 121, l.8; 136, l.10. They are discussed in Stephen Booth (ed.) *Shakespeare's Sonnets* (New Haven: Yale University Press, 1977).

25 Randle Cotgrave, in *A Dictionarie of the French and English Tongues* (London: 1611), notes that 'Noc' is 'Con, Turned backward (as our Tnuc) to be the lesse offensive to chast eares' (sig. Kkk i v). He also equates 'knocking' and 'leacherie, Venerie' as translations for the slang French term 'coignaufond' (sig. S 4v).

26 In an essay which affords some very interesting intersections with my own argument, '*Hamlet* ou le rhétorique du secret', Pierre Iselin associates Hamlet's self-representation as a wind instrument with that 'miraculous organ' through which murder 'will speak' (*Histoire et secret à la Renaissance* (ed.) François Laroque (Paris: Presses de la Sorbonne Nouvelle, 1997), pp. 199–211).

27 In *Shakespeare, Meaning and Metaphor* (Brighton: Harvester, 1987), Ann and

John O. Thompson stress the numerous synecdochic references to ears in *Hamlet*, as they explore another important strand of this ear imagery – its association with different levels of violence: for example, in the poisoned ears both of old Hamlet and of the Danish state, and in various assaults by noise, such as the First Player's supposed ability to 'cleave the general ear with horrid speech' (2.2. 557).

28 Helgë Kökeritz, *Shakespeare's Pronunciation* (New Haven: Yale University Press, 1953), pp. 90–1, 111. Kökeritz observes that air/heir is punned on by Lyly in *Mother Bombie,* and that the words are given as homonyms in Charles Butler, *English Grammar* (1634) and R. Hodges, *A Special Help to Orthographie* (1643). He emphasizes that 'no homonymic pun has been admitted here which has not stood the combined test of phonology and context' (pp. 64–5). See also Margreta de Grazia and Peter Stallybrass, 'The Materiality of the Shakespearian Text', *Shakespeare Quarterly*, 44 (Fall 1993), 3, pp. 255–83, where the wordplay in *Macbeth* on air/hair/heir is discussed.

29 Kökeritz, *Shakespeare's Pronunciation,* p. 111. See also Stephen Booth's comment on 'hearsay' in Sonnet 21, l. 13, in his edition of *Shakespeare's Sonnets* (New Haven: Yale University Press, 1978).

30 Gregory Ulmer, 'The Puncept in Grammatology', in *On Puns* (ed.) Jonathan Culler (Oxford: Basil Blackwell, 1988), pp. 164–90.

31 Henry Peacham, *The Garden of Eloquence* (London: 1577), sig. K ii r; George Puttenham, *The Arte of Englishe Poesie* (London: 1589), pp. 168–9.

32 Pliny, *Natural History*, trans. H. Rackham, 10 vols (London: Loeb, 1938), 3, X, ii, p. 294.

33 Richard Linche, *The Fountaine of Ancient Fiction* (London: 1599), sigs R i r–R i v.

34 Macrobius, *The Saturnalia*, trans. Percival Vaughan Davies (New York: Columbia University Press, 1969), pp. 114–15.

35 Charles Dempsey, *The Portrayal of Love: Botticelli's 'Primavera' and humanist culture at the time of Lorenzo the Magnificent* (Princeton: Princeton University Press, 1992), p. 40.

36 This aspect of Mercury's classical identity has been discussed in Joseph A. Porter, *Shakespeare's Mercutio: his history and drama* (Chapel Hill: University of North Carolina Press, 1988). Porter contends that late Elizabethan representations of Mercury typically carry 'some of the current of homeroticism that swept through the nineties . . . ' (p. 90). In '*Hamlet* ou le rhétorique du secret', Pierre Iselin notes of Hamlet's comparison of himself to a wind-instrument (3.2.333–54): 'L'enchaînment des références corporelle, l'insistance marquée sur les trous ("ventages" "stops") et la necessité de les boucher donnent une sequence ou l'analité est corollaire de la dimension pneumatique' (p. 206).

37 Charles Nicholl, *The Chemical Theatre* (London: Routledge Kegan Paul, 1980), p. 46.

38 Douglas Brooks-Davies, *The Mercurian Monarch: magical politics from Spenser to Pope* (Manchester: Manchester University Press, 1983), *passim.*

4 Disclosing the feminine eye of death

1 Jean-Pierre Vernant, *Mortals and Immortals: collected essays* (ed.) Froma I. Zeitlin (Princeton: Princeton University Press, 1991), p. 95.

2 Somewhat strangely, Terence Cave makes no reference to the significant but complex visual associations of *anagnorisis* in his impressive study of this Aristotelian concept, *Recognitions* (Oxford: Oxford University Press, 1990), although he does list among the synonyms of the term illumination, revelation, insight, unveiling and so on.

3 John Donne, 'Death's Duell' (1631), in *Donne: Sermons* (eds) E. M. Simpson and G. R. Potter, 10 vols (Berkeley: University of California Press, 1962), X, p. 232.

4 Plato, *The Republic*, vii, 537C.

5 Martin Heidegger, 'Science and Reflection', in *The Question Concerning Technology and Other Essays* (ed.) William Lovitt (New York: Harper and Row, 1977), p. 166.

6 See the Orphic *Hymn to Nature*; Apuleius, *The Golden Ass*, IV, 30; and Plutarch's *De Iside et Osiride*, 9. In Proclus' *Commentaire sur le Timée*, trans. A.-J. Festugière, 5 vols (Paris: Vrin, 1966), he allegorizes the *peplon* worn by Athena as the tissue woven by the order of things (I, pp. 181–3). For the relevance of such texts to Spenser's representation both of Truth and Nature, see James Norhnberg, *The Analogy of 'The Faerie Queene'* (Princeton: Princeton University Press, 1976), *passim*.

7 Cited in W. von Loewenich, *Luther's Theology of the Cross*, trans. H. J. A. Bauman (Belfast: Christian Journals Ltd, 1976), p. 83.

8 Michel Foucault, *The Birth of the Clinic* (New York: Random House, 1975), p. 89. See also Christopher Pye, *The Regal Phantasm: Shakespeare and the politics of spectacle* (London: Routledge, 1990) chs. 3 and 4.

9 René Descartes, *Discourse on Method, Optics, Geometry and Meteorology*, trans. Paul J. Olscamp (Indianapolis: Indiana University Press, 1965), p. 65.

10 Heidegger's critique of everyday seeing, already adumbrated in *Being and Time* (1927), is repeated and developed in much of his later work, influencing (among others) Maurice Merleau-Ponty, Jacques Derrida, Michel Foucault, and Luce Irigaray. For more recent explorations of Western 'ocularcentrism', see David Levin, *The Opening of Vision* (London: Routledge, 1987); *Modernity and the Hegemony of Vision* (ed.) Levin (Berkeley: University of California Press, 1993); and Martin Jay, *Downcast Eyes: the denigration of vision in twentieth-century French thought* (Berkeley: University of California Press, 1993).

11 Levin, *The Opening of Vision*, p. 106.

12 Luce Irigaray, *Speculum of the Other Woman*, trans. Gillian C. Gill (Ithaca: Cornell University Press, 1985), p. 55.

13 Ibid., p. 328. I discuss this feminist dilation of vision in Berry, 'The Burning Glass: paradoxes of feminist revelation in *Speculum*', in *Engaging with Irigaray: feminist philosophy and modern European thought* (eds) Margaret Whitford, Naomi Schor and Carolyn Burke (New York: Columbia University Press, 1994), pp. 229–46.

14 Heidegger, 'The Age of the World Picture', in *The Question concerning Technology*, p. 136; Maurice Merleau-Ponty, *Phenomenology of Perception*, trans. Colin Smith (London: Routledge Kegan Paul, 1981), p. 26.

15 The OED notes that 'a well-known property of the juice [of deadly nightshade] is to enlarge the pupil of the eye', and cites an eighteenth-century reference to the cosmetic use of this juice by Italian ladies. In *The Elizabethan Woman: a panorama of English womanhood 1540 to 1640* (London: Cleaver-Hume Press, 1951), Carroll Camden states that Elizabethan women used

belladonna to dilate their pupils, but offers no source to corroborate this. Vives, in his *Instruction of a Christian Woman* (1523), inveighs against those women who 'paint the black of eyes'. I am indebted to Jayne Archer for researching this information.

16 Martin Heidegger, *Der Satz vom Grund* (Pfullingen: Neske, 1958), p. 78, translated in Levin, *The Opening of Vision*, p. 423.

17 Plutarch, *De Iside et Osiride* (ed. and trans.) John Gwyn Griffiths (Cambridge: University of Wales Press, 1970), 33, 364B, pp. 170–1.

18 Francis Bacon, 'Sylva Sylvarum', vii, 693, *Collected Works*, II, ii (London: Routledge, 1996), p. 555.

19 W. Engel, *Mapping Mortality: the persistence of memory and melancholy in early modern England* (Amherst: University of Massachusetts Press, 1995), p. 72.

20 Edgar Wind, *Pagan Mysteries in the Renaissance* (London: Faber and Faber, 1956), p. 135, n. 22.

21 Michael Neill, *Issues of Death: mortality and identity in English Renaissance tragedy* (Oxford: Oxford University Press, 1997), ch. 3.

22 Gail Kern Paster, ' "In the Spirit of Men there is no Blood": blood as trope of gender in *Julius Caesar*', *Shakespeare Quarterly*, 40, iii (Autumn 1989), pp. 284–98; Marie-Dominique Garnier, '"Women's Matters": césures, seizures, dans *Julius Caesar*', *Q/W/E/R/T/Y: arts, littératures et civilisations du monde Anglophone*, 4 (October 1994), pp. 51–6.

23 Janet Adelman, *Suffocating Mothers: fantasies of maternal origin in Shakespeare's plays, from 'Hamlet' to 'The Tempest'* (New York and London: Routledge: 1992), p. 164.

24 Marjorie Garber, *Shakespeare's Ghost Writers: literature as uncanny causality* (London: Methuen, 1987), p. 116.

25 Ruth Padel, *In and Out of the Mind: Greek images of the tragic self* (Princeton: Princeton University Press, 1992), pp. 68–75.

26 Pico della Mirandola, *Conclusiones sive theses DCCCC* (Rome: 1486), ed. Bohdan Kieszkowski (Geneva: Librairie Droz, 1973), p. 66, 6. In *La Nuit et les enfants de la Nuit dans la tradition Grecque* (Paris: Flammarion, 1986), Clemence Ramnoux observes that this pre-Olympian deity encompasses all opposites, including those of black and white, dark and light.

27 For the figurative association of Shakespeare's Lucrece with Night, see Philippa Berry, 'Woman, Language and History in *The Rape of Lucrece*', *Shakespeare Survey*, 44 (1992), pp. 33–40.

28 Plutarch, *De Iside et Osiride*, p. 171; *The Hieroglyphics of Horapollo*, trans. George Boas (Princeton: Princeton University Press, 1993), 21, pp. 57–8.

29 Patricia Parker, 'Fantasies of "Race" and "Gender": Africa, *Othello*, and bringing to light', in *Women, 'Race,' and Writing in the Early Modern Period* (eds) Margot Hendricks and Patricia Parker (London: Routledge, 1994), pp. 84–100.

30 Patricia Parker, 'Shakespeare and Rhetoric: "dilation" and "delation" in *Othello*', in *Shakespeare and the Question of Theory* (eds) Patricia Parker and Geoffrey Hartman (New York: Methuen, 1985), pp. 54–74; 'Fantasies of "Race" and "Gender"'; and *Shakespeare from the Margins*, ch. 7.

31 Neill, *Issues of Death*, p. 143.

32 This quotation provides the title and starting point for an interesting essay by Arthur L. Little Jr, '"An Essence that's not Seen": the primal scene of racism in *Othello*', *Shakespeare Quarterly*, 44, iii (Fall 1993), pp. 304–24.

33 I am indebted here to a very suggestive discussion of Iago's role of ensign in James L. Calderwood, *The Properties of Othello* (Amherst: University of Massachusetts Press, 1989), ch. IV.

34 For a discussion of how the dark materiality of the text intersects with literary meditations upon death in the English Renaissance, notably in Shakespeare's *Sonnets*, see Philippa Berry, 'Authorship Overshadowed: death, darkness and the feminization of authority in late Renaissance writing', in *What is an Author?* (eds) Maurice Biriotti and Nicola Miller (Manchester: Manchester University Press, 1993), pp.155–72.

35 See M. M. Mahood, *Shakespeare's Wordplay* (London: Routledge, 1988), p. 43; and Parker, *Shakespeare from the Margins*, chs 4 and 5.

36 Parker has pointed to these lines from *The Merchant of Venice*: 'In such a night stood Dido with a willow in her hand / Upon the wild sea banks, and waft her love / To come again to Carthage' (5.1. 9–12).

37 OED; John Florio, *Queen Anna's New World of Words* (London: 1611), p. 590; Thomas Campion, *A Book of Ayres* (London: 1601).

38 'Libitina Venus in Latinis existimata fuit, ea quae sepulchris praeesset, ut copiose docuimus in nostris sepulchralibus', Lilio Gregorio Giraldi, *De deis gentium* (Basel: 1548), p. 550.

39 Julia Kristeva, *Powers of Horror*, trans. Leon S. Roudiez (New York: Columbia University Press, 1982).

40 Gail Kern Paster, *The Body Embarrassed* (Ithaca: Cornell University Press, 1992), ch. 1.

41 See *Shakespeare's Sonnets* (ed.) Stephen Booth (New Haven: Yale University Press, 1977), notes to sonnets 116, 136 and 153.

5 Fortune's fools

1 Jacques Derrida, 'Freud and the Scene of Writing', *Writing and Difference*, trans. Alan Bass (London: Routledge and Kegan Paul, 1978), p. 214.

2 On the application of the concept of *epistrophe* to the mythology of Saturn or Time, see Plotinus, *Enneads*, V i 7, and Edgar Wind, *Pagan Mysteries in the Renaissance* (London: Faber and Faber, 1956), p. 135, n. 22.

3 Michel de Montaigne, *Essayes*, trans. John Florio (London: 1603), III x, p. 604. For further discussion of this theme of circular motion in Montaigne, see Jean Starobinski, *Montaigne in Motion*, trans. Arthur Goldhammer (Chicago: University of Chicago Press, 1985), p. 279.

4 Marjorie Garber, ' "What's Past is Prologue": temporality and prophecy in Shakespeare's history plays', in *Renaissance Genres* (ed.) Barbara Lewalski (Cambridge, Mass.: Harvard University Press, 1986), pp. 301–31. See also Patricia Parker, *Literary Fat Ladies: rhetoric, gender, property* (London and New York: Methuen, 1987), pp. 94–5.

5 Garber, ' "What's Past is Prologue"', pp. 322–23.

6 Francis Barker, *The Culture of Violence: tragedy and history* (Manchester: Manchester University Press, 1993), p. 60.

7 See Mircea Eliade, *The Myth of the Eternal Return* (Princeton: Princeton University Press, 1954), ch. 4. Although Christian conceptions of temporality privileged a linear movement towards the ending of history with the Second Coming of Christ, Christianity had inherited an awareness of temporal cycles from Judaism. See for example *Ecclesiastes I*, vv. 9–10.

8 This movement was described by the alchemists as the *opus contra naturam*. See Lyndy Abraham, *Marvell and Alchemy* (Aldershot, Hants: Scolar Press, 1990), pp. 64–5.

9 Giordano Bruno, *De gli eroici furori*, trans. as *The Heroic Frenzies* by Paul Eugene Memmo Jr (Chapel Hill: University of North Carolina Press, 1964), I, 4th Dialogue, p. 142.

10 Ovid, *Fasti*, I, ll. 119–25.

11 Julia Kristeva, 'Women's Time', in *The Kristeva Reader* (ed.) Toril Moi (Oxford: Basil Blackwell, 1986), pp. 187–213.

12 Ned Lukacher, *Time Fetishes: some versions of eternal recurrence* (Durham, North Carolina: Duke University Press, 1998).

13 For a strikingly different account of temporal reversal in *Macbeth*, see Susanna Hamilton, ' "The Charm's Wound Up": reference back in *Macbeth*', *English* XXXV, 152 (Summer 1986), pp. 113–19. Hamilton links the 'indissolubility of end and beginning' in the play with Calvinist concepts of predestination. See also Lukacher, *Time Fetishes*, and Jonathan Baldo, 'The Politics of Aloofness in *Macbeth*', *English Literary Renaissance*, 26, iii (Autumn 1996), pp. 531–60.

14 Among the numerous studies of this concept, see G. W. Trompf, *The Idea of Historical Recurrence in Western Thought from Antiquity to the Reformation* (Berkeley: University of California Press, 1979); Nicholas Campion, *The Great Year: astrology, millenarianism and history in the Western tradition* (Harmondsworth: Penguin, 1994); and S. G. F. Brandon, *History, Time and Deity* (Manchester: Manchester University Press, 1965).

15 Plato, *Timaeus*, trans. R. A. Archer-Hind (London: Macmillan, 1888), 36B–C, pp. 110–13.

16 Ibid., 38B–C, pp. 122–3.

17 Ibid., 39D pp. 80–1.

18 Aristotle, *Physics*, trans. Philip H. Wickstead and Francis M. Cornford, 2 vols (London: Heinemann, 1929) I, pp. 422–5, 223B.

19 *Virgil*, trans. H. R. Fairclough, 2 vols (London: Heinemann, 1986), 'Aeneid', VI, ll. 745–51.

20 See Victor Goldschmidt, *Le système Stoicien et l'idée de temps* (Paris: Vrin, 1977).

21 Macrobius, *Saturnalia*, trans. Percival Vaughan Davies (New York: Columbia University Press, 1969), p. 65.

22 The changing status of Fortune in the Renaissance has not yet been adequately explored; Frederick Kiefer, in *Fortune and Elizabethan Tragedy* (Los Angeles: Huntington Library, 1983), presents a fairly limited view of her highly complex significance within English Renaissance culture. For excellent studies of the figure's importance to two Renaissance authors, see Thomas Flanagan, 'The Concept of Fortuna in Machiavelli', in *The Political Calculus: essays on Machiavelli's philosophy* (ed.) Antony Pavel (Toronto: University of Toronto Press, 1972), pp. 127–56, and Daniel Martin, *Montaigne et la fortune: essai sur le hasard et le langage* (Geneva: Librairie Slatkine, 1977). There is also a very useful discussion of the Renaissance Fortuna in Peggy Munoz Simonds, ' "To the very heart of loss": Renaissance iconography in Shakespeare's *Antony and Cleopatra*', *Shakespeare Studies*, xxii (1994), pp. 220–76.

23 'Of Clemencie', in *The Workes of Lucius Annaeus Seneca, both Morrall and Naturall*, trans. Thomas Lodge (London: 1614), f. 589.

24 Montaigne, *Essayes*, III, ix, p. 560. For the classical sources of Montaigne's concept of fortune, and the difficulties which its frequent usage caused him with the Roman Curia, see Martin, *Montaigne et la fortune*, chs 1 and 2.

25 Richard Linche, *The Fountaine of Ancient Fiction* (London: 1599), sigs Ciiv-Ciiir. Linche translates Claudian's verse as follows:

> She [Eternity] sends fourth Times, and cals them backe againe,
> For Times and Ages aye with her remaine.
>
> Upon her lap a greene-scal'd Serpent lies,
>   Whose hugenesse fils her wide rotunditye,
> Darting forth fierie sparckles from her eyes,
>   And what she finds, devoures most hungrilie,
> Her wrinckled taile fast twixt her teeth she ties,
>   Even when she seemes to gnaw most greedilie,
> All in a circle thus she sitts involved,
> Whose firme tenacitie is neere dissolved.

26 'Asclepius', in the *Hermetica*, trans. Brian P. Copenhaver (Cambridge: Cambridge University Press, 1992), 30, p. 85.

27 Edgar Wind, *Pagan Mysteries in the Renaissance* (London: Faber and Faber, 1966), p. 126, n. 45. See also *The Hieroglyphics of Horapollo*, trans. with introduction by George Boas (Princeton: Princeton University Press, 1993), I, ii.

28 Jean Bodin, *Methodus ad facilem historiarum cognitionem* (Paris: 1566); Louis Le Roy, *Of the Interchangeable Course, or Variety of Things in the Whole World . . . from the beginning of civility, and memory of man, to this present*, trans. Robert Ashley (London: 1594).

29 Pietro Pomponazzi, *Libri quinque de fato, de libero arbitrio, et de praedestinatione*, written around 1520, cited and trans. in Eugenio Garin, *Astrology in the Renaissance: the zodiac of life*, trans. Carolyn Jackson and June Allen (London: Routledge and Kegan Paul, 1976), p. 98.

30 Niccolo Machiavelli, Letter 116, in *Machiavelli: the chief works and others* (ed.) A. Gilbert (Durham, North Carolina: Duke University Press, 1965), II, pp. 896–7.

31 See Cecil C. Seronsy, 'The Doctrine of Cyclical Recurrence and some related Ideas in the Works of Samuel Daniel', *Studies in Philology*, liv, 3 (July 1957), pp. 387–407.

32 François Laroque, *Shakespeare's Festive World*, trans. Janet Lloyd (Cambridge: Cambridge University Press, 1991), p. 207.

33 Valeriano, *Hieroglyphica* (Venice: 1595), p. 477. For the association of Isis with Fortuna, see Achille Bocchi, *Symbolicarum quaestionum, de universo genere quas serio ludebat, libri quinque* (Bologna: 1574), 3, cxxxvi.

34 *Hermetica*, VIII, 2, p. 26.

35 Charles Nicholl, *The Chemicall Theatre* (London: Routledge and Kegan Paul, 1980), chs 6 and 7.

36 Valeriano, *Hieroglyphica*, p. 115.

37 Lambspringk, *De lapide philosophico* (ed.) Nicolas Barnaud (Prague, 1599), cited in Nicholl, *The Chemicall Theatre*, p. 95.

38 Thomas Moffett, *The Silkwormes and their Flies* (London: 1599), pp. 6–8. See also Frankie Rubinstein, *A Dictionary of Shakespeare's Sexual Puns and their*

Significations (London: Macmillan, 1992), on silk as an attribute of whores. She further notes that silkworms 'were believed to engender backward, tail to tail' (pp. 241–2).

39 In 'The Sound of *O* in *Othello*', in Joel Fineman's *The Subjectivity Effect in Western Literary Tradition: essays towards the release of Shakespeare's will* (Cambridge, Mass.: MIT Press, 1991), pp. 143–64, he interprets *deisidaimon* as 'the unfortunate', but this is slightly inaccurate; it means fearing the gods, which can be interpreted as piety or superstition.

40 The OED lists 'weyard' as an attribute of the Fates or Parcae. But the 'weyard sisters' who appear to Macbeth and Banquo were variously described in accounts of Scottish history. In Holinshed, they appear as 'three women in strange and wild apparell, resembling creatures of elder world'. In Buchanan's *History of Scotland*, Macbeth has a dream in which 'he seemed to see Three Women, whose Beauty was more August and Surprizing than bare womens useth to be . . . ' (I, p. 210). In the 1605 pageant devised by Matthew Gwinne, performed before James and Queen Anna at the gates of St John's College during their visit to the University of Oxford, the royal couple were greeted by three boys dressed 'like nymphs or sybils', who reminded them of the three sisters' greeting to Banquo.

41 See Lilian Winstanley, *Macbeth, King Lear and Contemporary History* (1922; New York: Octagon Books, 1970). Just as suggestive in this connection are Duncan's and Banquo's references to the delicate 'air' of the castle: with an equally tragic irony, Darnley had removed to the Edinburgh house in which he was later murdered because its 'good air' was expected to help his convalescence from an illness attributed to poison.

42 1.6.25–28, 2.3.1–20. For the sexual pun in accounting, see Stephen Booth, (ed.) *Shakespeare's Sonnets* (New Haven: Yale University Press, 1977) on Sonnet 58, line 3, p. 234.

43 Orson Welles' film of *Macbeth* ends with a shot which pans out from the dead tyrant's castle, where Macduff has just 'hailed' Malcolm as King, to the witches, observing events on a distant hilltop. The first sister declares: 'Peace! – the charm's wound up'.

44 John Bale, *The First Two Partes of the Actes, or Unchast Examples of the Englysh Votaryes* (London: 1551) f. 40v.

45 York Minster Library MS XVI.L.6, p. 259. See Jason Scott-Warren, 'Sir John Harington as a Giver of Books', Ph.D. dissertation (University of Cambridge, 1997), ch.4.

46 Hector Boece was the first chronicler to incorporate Banquo into the Stuart genealogy, in *The Chronicles of Scotland*, trans. into Scots by John Bellenden in 1531.

47 George Marcelline, *The Triumphes of King James the First* (London: 1610), p. 65.

48 From 'Phoenix' by James VI, cited in Caroline Bingham, *James VI of Scotland* (London: Weidenfeld and Nicolson, 1979), ch. 3.

49 John Nichols, *The Progresses . . . of King James the First*, 4 vols (London: J. B. Nichols, 1828), I, p. 355.

50 For a discussion of 'close' in relation to the 'secret place' of woman, see Patricia Parker, '*Othello* and *Hamlet*: spying, discovery and secret faults', in *Shakespeare from the Margins: language, culture, context* (Chicago: Chicago University Press, 1996), pp. 229–72. Rubinstein, op. cit., stresses the punning association of 'closing' with copulation (pp. 50–1).

51 Rubinstein, op. cit., notes that while one Latin word for ditch, *scrobis*, evoked the vulva, another, *fossa*, had a homonymic relation to *fesses*, the French for buttocks (xvi, pp. 78–9). See also the use of *fosso*, Italian for ditch, as slang for the anus by Aretino, noted in David O. Frantz, *Festum Voluptatis: a study of Renaissance erotica* (Columbus: Ohio University Press, 1989), p. 72.

52 The 'bolt in the door' was a common colloquialism for copulation: Cotgrave, op. cit., comments of *beluter* that 'A bon bleuteur may propice. *Prov.* A wooer speeds (oft times) the better for his weapon'.

53 In *Shakespeare's Pronunciation* (New Haven: Yale University Press, 1953), Helgë Kökeritz notes the homonymic relationship between hair/whore as well as hair/heir/here/hare. For a slightly different perspective on the hair/heir/air homonym in *Macbeth*, see Margreta de Grazia and Peter Stallybrass, 'The Materiality of the Shakespearean Text', *Shakespeare Quarterly*, 44, iii (Fall 1993), pp. 255–83.

54 Parker discusses the duplicate which 'cousins', but also 'cozens' in *Shakespeare from the Margins*, op. cit., pp. 127–33. For extended discussions of the trope of the 'preposterous' or *hysteron proteron*, see *Shakespeare from the Margins*, ch. 1, and *Literary Fat Ladies: rhetoric, gender, property* (London and New York, Methuen, 1987), ch. 5.

55 Jonson described the hags' dance in the *Masque of Queenes* as 'a *magicall Daunce* full of praeposterous change and gesticulation . . . dauncing, back to back, hip to hip, theyr handes joyn'd, and making theyr *circles* backwards to the left hand, with strange, phantastique motions of theyr heads and bodyes' *Works of Ben Jonson* (eds) C. H. Herford and E. and P. Simpson, 11 vols (Oxford: Clarendon Press, 1925–52), VII, 301. The epithet 'praeposterous' further emphasizes the association of witches' dances with that disturbing reversal of chronology and order discussed by Parker. See n. 46 above.

56 '[H]e gave many remarkable Items of his Disposition, before we had any relation to him . . . amongst which may be reckoned his not inquiring into, at least not revenging the murther of his own Father . . . ' (Michael Sparke, *Truth brought to Light: or the history of the first 14 years of King James I* (London: 1692), sig. A3v). For contemporary Scottish reference to Darnley as 'the King', see George Buchanan, *Ane Detectioun of the Duinges of Marie Quene of Scottes touchand the Murder of hir Husband, and hir Conspiracie, Adulterie, and Pretensed Mariage with the Erle Bothwell* (London: 1571).

57 *Geneva Bible*, 1560 edn; *Genesis* 25, vv. 23–6.

58 Parker, *Shakespeare from the Margins*, pp. 62–5.

59 Marcelline, *The Triumphs*, p. 19.

60 *The Historie of Jacob and Esau* (London: 1568), I i 10.

61 The OED derives this usage of 'fell' from Teutonic Old English, and explicates it as the skin or hide of animal with its hair or wool; a covering of hair or wool, especially when thick and matted.

62 John Thornborough, *The Joieful and Blessed Reuniting the Two Mighty and Famous Kingdomes, England and Scotland* (London: 1604), sig. A3.

63 Cited in Donna B. Hamilton, '*The Winter's Tale* and the Language of Union, 1604–1610', *Shakespeare Studies*, xxi (1993), pp. 228–50.

64 I am indebted here to Willy Maley's observation that English Renaissance representations of Ireland often refer obliquely to the Scots. See Maley, 'The British Problem in three Irish tracts by Spenser, Bacon and Milton', in *British Identity and British Consciousness in the Making of the United Kingdom*,

1533–1707 (eds) Brendan Bradshaw and Peter Roberts (Cambridge: Cambridge University Press, 1998), pp. 159–84.

65 John Derricke, *The Image of Ireland with the Discoveries of Wood Karne* (London: 1581), sig. Di v; Barnaby Rich, *A Short Survey* (London: 1609), sig. B2.

66 Richard Stanyhurst, *A Plain and Perfect Description of Ireland*, cited in Sheila T. Cavanagh, 'The Fatal Destiny of that land: Elizabethan Views of Ireland', *Representing Ireland: literature and the origins of conflict, 1534–1660* (eds) Brendan Bradshaw, Andrew Hadfield and Willy Maley (Cambridge: Cambridge University Press, 1993), pp. 116–31; Edmund Spenser, *A View of the State of Ireland* (1633), (eds) Andrew Hadfield and Willy Maley (Oxford: Blackwell, 1997), p. 57.

67 George Buchanan, *Rerum Scoticarum historia* (1582), trans. into English (London, 1690), p. 51.

68 William Camden, *Britannia*, trans. Philemon Holland (London: 1610), p. 31.

69 Henry N. Paul, *The Royal Play of Macbeth* (New York: Octagon Books, 1971), *passim*.

6 Cordelia's bond

1 Michel de Montaigne, *Essais*, 3 vols, (ed.) Alexandre Micha (Paris: Gallimard-Flammarion, 1979), III, ix, 'De la vanité', p. 186. In his recent translation of the *Essays*, M. A. Screech renders the passage as follows: 'Nature brought us forth free and unbound: we imprison ouselves in particular confines' (Harmondsworth: Penguin, 1987), p. 1101.

2 Elizabeth Bronfen, *Over her Dead Body: death, femininity and the aesthetic* (Manchester: Manchester University Press, 1992), p. 264

3 See David Bevington's introduction to his edition of *Antony and Cleopatra* (Cambridge: Cambridge University Press, 1990), pp. 1–2; Stanley Wells and Gary Taylor, *William Shakespeare: a textual companion* (Oxford: Clarendon Press, 1987), pp. 129–30; and J. Leeds Barroll, *Politics, Plague, and Shakespeare's Theater: the Stuart years* (Ithaca: Cornell University Press, 1991), ch. 4. As a result of his research into opportunities for court performances in this period of plague, Leeds Barroll concurs with the general view that *Macbeth* was first performed sometime in 1606; he also makes a cogent argument, based on similar evidence, for the first performances of both *King Lear* and *Antony and Cleopatra* in 'the same plague-delayed 1606 Christmas season' (p. 151).

4 See for example Anthony Munday, *The Triumphes of Re-united Britannia*, the Lord Mayor's pageant of 1605.

5 Noted in Patricia Parker, *Shakespeare from the Margins* (Chicago: University of Chicago Press, 1996), p. 89. I am much indebted to Parker's exploration of this concept.

6 See William C. Carroll, 'The Virgin Knot: language and sexuality in Shakespeare', *Shakespeare Survey*, 46 (1994), pp. 107–20.

7 Peter Stallybrass, 'Patriarchal Territories: the body enclosed', in *Rewriting the Renaissance: the discourses of sexual difference in early modern Europe* (eds) Margaret W. Ferguson, Maureen Quilligan, and Nancy Vickers (Chicago: University of Chicago Press, 1986), pp. 123–42. The relationship between boundaries and sexuality is also discussed in the introduction to *Enclosure Acts: sexuality, property and culture in early modern England* (eds) Richard Burt and John Michael Archer (Ithaca: Cornell University Press, 1994).

8   Plato, *Timaeus*, trans. R. D. Archer Hind (London: Macmillan, 1888), 35A.
9   'Hymenaei', in *Works of Ben Jonson* (eds) C. H. Herford and P. and E. Simpson, 11 vols (Oxford: Clarendon Press, 1925–52), VII, pp. 203–42, ll. 141–2.
10 Parker, *Shakespeare from the Margins*, pp. 83–115.
11 A notable example of the elision of soul and ass occurs in the first edition of François Rabelais's *'Le Tiers Livre'*, 1552 edn in *Les cinq livres* (eds) Jean Céard *et al.* (Paris: Librairie Générale Française, 1994), xxii, l. 21, where Rabelais writes *asne* for *âme*. The medicinal properties of dung are set out in detail in *The Greek Herbal of Dioscorides*, trans. John Goodyer (London: 1655), II, 98. I am indebted to Jayne Archer for this information.
12 The figurative prominence of beasts of burden in this play, notably the horse and the ass, is discussed in Ann and John O. Thompson, *Shakespeare, Meaning and Metaphor* (Brighton: Harvester, 1987), pp. 60–68.
13 Claire McEachern, *The Poetics of English Nationhood, 1590–1612* (Cambridge: Cambridge University Press, 1996), p. 29; see also Philippa Berry, *Of Chastity and Power: Elizabethan literature and the unmarried queen* (London: Routledge, 1989), ch. 3. English Renaissance interest in the paronomastic associations between 'state', 'throne', 'land' and two bodily orifices – the anus and the female genitalia – is explored in Frankie Rubinstein, *A Dictionary of Shakespeare's Sexual Puns and their Significance*, 2nd edn (London: Macmillan, 1989), *passim*.
14 George Peele, *The Arraignment of Paris* (1584). For details of this classical conception of Britain, see Josephine Waters Bennett, 'Britain among the Fortunate Isles', *Studies in Philology*, 53, (1956), pp. 114–40. Jeffrey Knapp discusses the association between Eliza and Elysium in *An Empire Nowhere: England, America and Literature from 'Utopia' to 'The Tempest'* (Berkeley: University of California Press, 1992), ch. 2.
15 Rabelais, 'Le Tiers Livre', xxii, 85–90.
16 I am indebted here to Ann Lecercle's discussion of this homonymic relationship, which she terms a *rebus*, in 'Reflections on the Feminist approach to Shakespeare and Lacanian Psychoanalysis', *Shakespeare Jahrbuch: Shakespeare and France* (eds) Holger Klein and J.-M. Maguin, (1994), V, pp. 181–90.
17 Richard Helgerson, *Forms of Nationhood: the Elizabethan writing of England* (Chicago: University of Chicago Press, 1992), p. 141.
18 Brian P. Levack, *The Formation of the British State: England, Scotland and the union, 1603–1707* (Oxford: Clarendon Press, 1987).
19 C. H. McIlwain, *The Political Works of James I* (Cambridge: Harvard University Press, 1918), p. xiii.
20 'Basilikon Doron' (1599), II, in *The Political Works of James I*, p. 18. See also Jonathan Goldberg, *James I and the Politics of Literature* (Baltimore: Johns Hopkins University Press, 1983).
21 'The Trew Law of Free Monarchies', in *The Political Works of James I*, pp. 62–3.
22 See J. G. A. Pocock, *The Ancient Constitution and the Feudal Law: a study of English historical thought in the seventeenth century* (Cambridge: Cambridge University Press, 1957). In *The Trophies of Time: English antiquarianism of the seventeenth century* (Oxford: Oxford University Press, 1995), Graham Parry discusses the growing interest of the Society of Antiquarians in parliamentary history and privilege, and suggests that this may well have prompted the king's decision, around 1607, to discontinue the Society's meetings.

23 Sandra Billington, *Mock Kings in Medieval Society and Renaissance Drama* (Oxford: Clarendon Press, 1991), p. 113.

24 Humphrey Lhuyd, *The Breviary of Britaine*, trans. Thomas Twyne (1573), sig. 7v.

25 William Camden, *Britannia*, trans. Philemon Holland (London: 1610), p. 3.

26 ibid., p. 24.

27 ibid., p. 368.

28 ibid., p. 388.

29 'The King's Entertainment in passing to his Coronation', *Works of Ben Jonson*, VII, pp. 65–110, ll. 27–30.

30 See Thomas Dekker, 'The Magnificent Entertainment: given to King *James* ... upon the day of his Maiesties triumphant passage (from the Tower) through his honourable citie (and chamber) of *London*', in Dekker, *Dramatic Works* (ed.) F. Bowers, 4 vols (Cambridge: Cambridge University Press, 1961), I, p. 297.

31 See Lynda Levy Peck, *Court Patronage and Corruption in Early Stuart England* (Boston: Unwin Hyman, 1990), 'Women as Court Brokers: Queen Anne's household' pp. 68–74; J. Leeds Barroll, 'The Court of the First Stuart Queen', in *The Mental World of the Jacobean Court* (ed.) Lynda Levy Peck (Cambridge: Cambridge University Press, 1991), pp. 191–208, and 'Inventing the Stuart Masque', in *The Politics of the Stuart Court Masque* (eds) David Bevington and Peter Holbrook (Cambridge: Cambridge University Press, 1999), pp. 121–43; Barbara Lewalski, *Writing Women in Jacobean England* (Cambridge, Mass.: Harvard University Press, 1993), ch. 1.

32 'The Masque of Beautie', *Works of Ben Jonson*, VII, pp. 181–94, l. 374; 'The Masque of Queenes', *Works of Ben Jonson*, VII, pp. 277–317, l. 148.

33 *Britannia*, p. 31; see Pliny, *Natural History*, trans. W. H. S. Jones, 10 vols (London: Heinemann, 1966), vol. 7, XXII, ii.

34 H. Neville Davies, 'Jacobean *Antony and Cleopatra*', *Shakespeare Studies*, 17 (1985), pp.123–58.

35 Nigel Llewellyn, 'The Royal Body: monuments to the dead, for the living', in *Renaissance Bodies: the human figure in English culture c.1540–1660* (eds) Lucy Gent and Nigel Llewellyn (London: Reaktion, 1990), pp. 218–40.

36 Julia M. Walker, 'Reading the Tombs of Elizabeth I', *English Literary Renaissance*, 26, iii (Autumn 1996), pp. 510–30.

37 Sir Anthony Weldon, *The Court and Character of King James* (London: 1651), p. 168.

38 Camden, *Britannia*, p. 1.

39 For a detailed discussion of the play's location, see F. T. Flahiff, 'Lear's Map', *Cahiers Elisabéthains*, 30 (1986) pp. 17–33.

40 *Diodorus Siculus*, trans. C. H. Oldfather, 12 vols (London: Heinemann, 1961), III, v, 31, 1.

41 Anne-Marie LeCoq, *François premier imaginaire: symbolique et politique à l'aube de la Renaissance française* (Paris: editions Macula, 1987), pp. 416–21.

42 'Sileni Alcibiades', in *Collected Works of Erasmus, 34: Adages*, trans. and annotated by R. A. B. Mynors (Toronto: University of Toronto Press, 1992), pp. 262–82. The alchemical imagery in *King Lear* is examined in detail by Charles Nicholl, *The Chemicall Theatre* (London: Routledge and Kegan Paul, 1980), chs 6 and 7.

43 Jean Bodin, *De Republica Libri Sex*, 3rd edn (Frankfurt: 1594), p. 132.

44 Camden, *Britannia*, p. 97.

45 *Diodorus Siculus*, III, v, 21, 5; *Tacitus*, trans. M. Hutton (London: Heinemann, 1970), 15.

46 See William C. Carroll, *Fat King, Lean Beggar: representations of poverty in the age of Shakespeare* (Ithaca: Cornell University Press, 1996).

47 *Diodorus Siculus*, III, v, 28, 2.

48 Herodian, *History*, trans. C. R. Whittaker (London: Heinemann, 1969), iii, 14.

49 Flahiff, 'Lear's Map'.

50 My interpretation of *Lear*'s equivocal end differs in substance and detail from that proposed by Stephen Booth in *'King Lear', 'Macbeth', Indefinition and Tragedy* (New Haven: Yale University Press, 1983). But Booth's very different argument reinforces my own to a surprising extent. Arguing that 'the impossibility of finality permeates the play', and that 'the characters constantly and vainly strive to establish the limits of things', he also observes that 'Shakespeare represents the culminating events of his *story* after the *play* is over' (pp. 11–13).

51 Henry Lyte, *A New Herball* (London: 1595), pp. 78, 665. Pliny, *Natural History*, 7, XXI, xciii.

52 *A New Herball, passim*. Some critics have also commented on the relevance of several of these herbs to female fertility: thus dock helps excessive menstrual flow, and marjoram is beneficial for irregular menstruation, as is cuckoo flower, which 'cures maidens of the green sickness and bringeth down their terms' (John Gerard, *The Herball* (London: 1597), p. 201).

53 Pliny, *Natural History*, vol. 7, XXI, xxii, iv–vii.

54 Camden, *Britannia*, sig. B i r–v.

55 Deborah Baker Wyrick, 'The Ass-Motif in *The Comedy of Errors* and *A Midsummer Night's Dream*', *Shakespeare Quarterly*, 33, iv (Winter 1982), pp. 431–48. See also Nuccio Ordine, *Giordano Bruno and the Philosophy of the Ass*, trans. Henryk Baranski (New Haven: Yale University Press, 1997).

INDEX